DEMYSTIFYING THAI CUISINE WITH
AUTHENTIC RECIPES TO MAKE AT HOME

HOT THAI KITCHEN

PAILIN CHONGCHITNANT

appetite
by RANDOM HOUSE

Appetite by Random House® and colophon are registered trademarks of Penguin Random House Canada LLC.

Library and Archives of Canada Cataloguing in Publication is available upon request.

ISBN: 978-0-449-01705-0
eBook ISBN: 978-0-147-52992-3

Cover photo of the author by Janis Nicolay
Recipe photos and portraits of the author by David Tam
Thailand photos by Art Chongchitnant
Photo on page 53 by Stephen Fortner
Printed and bound in China

Published in Canada by Appetite by Random House®
a division of Penguin Random House Canada Limited

www.penguinrandomhouse.ca

10 9 8 7 6 5 4 3 2

appetite
by RANDOM HOUSE

Penguin
Random
House

To my family

Contents

Introduction

It's hard for me to believe, as I am sitting here writing a Thai cookbook, that less than 10 years ago, I had a "been there, done that" attitude towards Thai food and was completely engrossed in the exotic world of Western cuisine. But there's something about the food you grow up with: no matter how far away you go from it, it always tracks you down.

Growing up in Southern Thailand, I spent a lot of time in the kitchen with our live-in nanny, who was also the family cook, and my grandmothers, who visited from time to time. We didn't have many pre-made ingredients or time-saving appliances, so cooking involved laborious tasks like squeezing fresh coconut milk, mincing ground pork with a cleaver, and removing peanut skins. When you spend that much time working intimately with raw ingredients and witnessing their transformation into a meal, a bond is inevitable.

I've always had an affinity for food and cooking, but the first time I left Thailand, affinity turned into right-out obsession. I was twelve years old, and my parents sent me to New Zealand so that I could learn English. I remember being thoroughly mesmerized by the variety of new foods I encountered: mashed potatoes, lamingtons, schnitzel, and fish and chips. Things that seem mundane to New Zealanders were fascinating culinary discoveries to me.

My home-stay mom noticed and fostered my passion for food; she first asked me to show her a Thai dish, so I made a Thai omelette, the first thing that almost every Thai person learns how to make. She then coached me through scones, a pineapple meringue pie, and chocolate soufflés. After one whirlwind year, I went back to Thailand with a realization that there was so much more to food than I had imagined, and that I loved every bit of it.

In high school, we moved to the big city: Bangkok. With that move came cable TV, and with cable TV came cooking shows imported from abroad. I found myself glued to these shows with a paper and pen in hand, ready to write down the recipes (there were no online recipes back then!). I idolized the chefs, who looked like they were having the time of their lives, and I dreamed of one day having my own cooking show.

I left for Canada to attend university, and I was once again in a wonderland of Western food. After graduation I started cooking professionally. Convinced that cooking was what I want to dedicate my life to, I moved to San Francisco for culinary school. Why San Francisco? Someone had told me it was a great city for food, and so off I went.

Life in culinary school was a dream come true. I revelled in all the new knowledge and experience I was gaining daily—even culinary math was so much fun to me! Being surrounded by hundreds of other passionate people energized me like nothing else had before. I admired all of my chef instructors who not only educated me, but also influenced and inspired me. That was the beginning of my desire to be a culinary educator myself.

As much fun as I was having learning about Western cuisine, I was missing Thai food. I frequented many Thai restaurants, and while there were many good places, more often than not, I left disappointed. In fact, I was angry. I was angry because I felt that Thai food was being misrepresented, and I was frustrated by the thought that people would have to visit Thailand in order to understand how delicious Thai food can really be.

Around that same time, I had a conversation with my older brother, Eddie, which would change my life. I mused to him about having a cooking show of my own, to which he said, "Why don't you make your own show on YouTube?" Until that moment, I thought

YouTube was just a place for funny cat videos. This sparked a fire. I was so excited by the idea of having my own cooking show that I talked Eddie into being my camera man, and Hot Thai Kitchen was born in my small San Francisco apartment. While we did brainstorm different show concepts, it was clear to me that the show had to be about Thai food. It was the perfect combination of all my dreams. It would be my way of showing people how to make incredible Thai food at home. I would get my own cooking show. And I could finally become a culinary educator—it was the answer to everything I wanted to accomplish.

They say that the best way to learn a skill is to teach it to someone else, and this couldn't be truer for me. Producing Hot Thai Kitchen pushed me to study my own cuisine from the perspective of an outsider. It forced me to look at Thai food and question every element. Why do we do what we do? What is the purpose of these ingredients? How do these flavours work together to create the balance we're aiming for? All these questions made me realize that I hadn't actually "been there, done that" with Thai cuisine. There was so much more that I didn't know, that my nanny and my grandmothers never taught me. My passion and excitement for Thai food came back at full speed, and the support from Hot Thai Kitchen fans all over the world became the fuel for my endeavour.

I wrote this book to present the knowledge that is foundational to understanding Thai cuisine in one complete package. I wanted to emphasize my philosophy: that in order to cook great food with confidence, we need to understand the dish. Certain concepts, once understood, apply across cuisines. For example, a chicken breast will always react to heat in the same way, whether the dish is Thai or Swedish. But if we're trying to gain confidence in cooking an unfamiliar cuisine, then we also need to understand

what makes that cuisine distinct. I want to show you the things that make Thai cuisine, well, Thai.

So what does it take to understand a cuisine that is foreign to you? There are three dimensions of any cuisine that are essential to your ability to cook it like a native: culture, ingredients, and the structure of dishes. This book will explore these three dimensions.

In order to be "in control" of what we're cooking, we need to know what's happening to it every step of the way. Once we understand 1) what the food is doing at any given point and 2) how each ingredient adds to the final product, we can adjust the recipe to our liking, fix problems when they occur, and most exciting of all, CREATE our own dishes! It's the reason why a restaurant chef can constantly come up with new items, while my grandmother, as wonderful as her cooking is, makes mostly dishes that already exist.

This book is also in some ways a memoir. Most of the recipes I've chosen have played a memorable role in my life, and I've shared many personal stories with you throughout these pages. I hope that this book will help you become more confident in your Thai cooking, and most of all, inspired. When you have created that wonderful Thai meal, please remember to share your success story with me.

Pailin

How to Use This Book

In *Part 1: Understanding Thai Cuisine*, you'll learn about the three dimensions that are the core building blocks of Thai cuisine: Thai food culture, ingredients, and the structure of Thai dishes. You may be tempted to skip this part and go straight to the recipes, but I strongly recommend that you give it a chance before you begin—after all, it's the main reason why I wrote this book!

After reading *Part 1*, you will be able to approach the recipes with a whole new level of insight. It could mean the difference between simply making Thai food according to instructions and understanding Thai cuisine, which is the key to becoming proficient in Thai cooking.

Part 2 of the book contains recipes. I intend for these recipes to be used as "case studies" to demonstrate how the concepts you will learn in *Part 1* actually play out. So, to help you bridge the gap between theory and practice, you'll find references back to terms and ideas that I have previously discussed. It's like first learning the rules of football and the role of each player, and then stepping onto the field and playing. For each recipe, I will include side notes that further explain points that I think are important for your success, just like I usually do in my Hot Thai Kitchen videos online.

At the suggestion of a few Hot Thai Kitchen fans, throughout the book I have provided QR codes for my videos that are related to the recipes or the concepts being discussed. I am excited about this feature because it adds an interactive element to your learning that is very helpful for visual learners like me!

> *"After reading Part 1, you will be able to approach the recipes with a whole new level of insight."*

Most importantly, embrace the learning curve. There will be a few forehead-slapping moments and not-so-awesome dishes, but don't be discouraged by them. It's a natural part of learning for everyone, myself included. Every single recipe in this book was preceded by iterations that weren't quite right, and on occasion, flat out failed. In fact, my best learning always happens when things don't work, because only then am I forced to retrace my steps and ask the most important question: why?

So, get ready to enjoy the adventure, and let's dive in!

About the Recipes

Many cookbooks on the market can be thought of as "recipe books"—collections of recipes rather than books that teach you how to cook. My intention for this book is not simply to provide recipes; after all, I post video recipes online on a regular basis. So, my goal for this book is to use recipes to *reinforce and model* the concepts and principles that I show you in *Part 1*.

"Once you are familiar with several Thai recipes, you'll start recognizing patterns . . . that's when you'll feel confident enough to improvise and be creative with Thai cooking."

In my view, this book is a true "cookbook," in that it aims to provide you with the knowledge and skills to cook Thai food confidently and eventually without recipes—basically like a native Thai! So, treat these recipes as "case studies." For example, we discuss five types of Thai salads in *Part 1*; in *Part 2*, you will find recipes representing all of the five types, so that once you've made them, you will have a concrete understanding of those concepts.

Here's the exciting part: once you are familiar with several Thai recipes, you'll start recognizing patterns. And once you are familiar with these patterns, that's when you'll feel confident enough to improvise and be creative with Thai cooking. Learning a foreign cuisine is like navigating a new city; in the beginning you follow the GPS everywhere, but once you're familiar with the roads, you'll confidently try new routes and explore shortcuts like a local!

Lastly, remember that practice alone won't transform your Thai cooking, but mindful practice, in which you seek to understand the hows and whys of your cooking, will certainly get you there.

Tasting Your Own Cooking

Tasting your food sounds logical, but you'd be surprised by how many people forget to do it because they're too busy trying to get everything done. This is why I've included "taste and adjust the seasoning" as a friendly reminder in the instructions.

Even though all my recipes have been tested with the exact measurements provided, there are so many other factors that affect the final product: not all tablespoons are the same size, all limes are not equally sour, and not all brands of fish sauce are equally salty. There is also moisture loss during cooking, which varies depending on the heat of your stove, the size of your pan, and the cooking time.

The most important factor, of course, is your unique palate. If there's anything I've learned through my professional culinary career, it's that people have different preferences for saltiness, acidity, and sweetness. So, it is critical that you TASTE your food and adjust accordingly, and remember that you can always add, but you can't take away!

After You Taste . . .

We've all tasted our cooking and felt that it "needed something," but were not sure what that "something" was. It takes experience, even for a professional chef, to identify the changes that will transform a dish from good to great. Often though, when a dish "needs something," it's just under-seasoned and can be fixed with a little salt or acid. Other times, the issue can be more subtle, such as a poor-quality ingredient.

Beware of over-tasting. Our senses can become desensitized after prolonged exposure to a particular input. So, tasting the same thing too many times can "numb" your taste buds. If you feel like the dish tastes the same no matter what you do to it, just give yourself a few minutes, drink plenty of water or eat something bland, and come back with a fresh palate.

Measuring Ingredients

Though I encourage you to cook intuitively eventually, without needing to measure every ingredient, measurements are very helpful in the beginning. For clarity, here is how I measure some potentially ambiguous ingredients.

Palm sugar: When measuring palm sugar by volume, chop it finely, and then pack it tightly into the measuring cup or spoon.

Vegetables, herbs, and fruits: Measure the item after it has been prepared according to the description. For example:

> 3 Tbsp   Shallots, finely chopped

Chop the shallots and then measure them. I realize that the technically correct way is to write "3 Tbsp finely chopped shallots," but I purposely put the name of the ingredient first so that you can quickly scan the list for that item when you need to refer to it while cooking.

Leafy herbs: Measurements of herbs do not have to be exact, and you can add more or less if you wish. Having said that, consider "1 cup of Thai basil" to be a loosely packed cup.

Powders and grains: For salt and granulated sugar, level off the measuring cup or spoon with a straight edge. When measuring flour, spoon the flour into the measuring cup, then level it off without shaking or tapping it.

Liquid seasoning: When measuring soy sauce, oyster sauce, and fish sauce, make sure the product is level with the rim and not bulging over due to surface tension. It doesn't take too much more of these potent seasonings to render your dish too salty.

Meat and vegetables by weight: Only weigh the edible portion of the ingredient. This means that any skin, fat, core, root, seeds, or any part of the ingredient that will not be going into the dish must be removed before weighing. If the recipe calls for shrimp, for example, peel and devein them before weighing. When you shop for ingredients, make sure you allow for the weight of whatever parts need to be discarded.

Cooking Time vs Prep Time

I have provided a cooking time for each recipe so you can quickly get an idea of how far in advance you need to plan the dish. However, cooking time *does not* include prep time. I define "prep time" as the time it takes you to chop vegetables, cut meat, measure out ingredients, etc., which varies significantly from person to person. "Cooking time" counts only the time it takes you to do the things described in the instructions. So, for a stir-fry, this could be 10 minutes, but for a slow-braised curry, it might be 2 hours.

If you see a recipe with a long cooking time, check to see if it includes idle time, like 2 hours of simmering. Use this idle time to prep other ingredients.

Number of Servings

The number of servings per recipe is based on the assumption that the dish is served with rice, as is traditional for a Thai meal. The only exception is for fried rice and noodle dishes, in which case they are one-dish meals (see p.10). The number also assumes that it is the only dish you are serving for that meal.

Abbreviations and Equivalents

To avoid any confusion, here are the abbreviations I use for measurements in the recipes. In recipes, some measurement conversions are rounded off to a number that's easier to measure.

Abbreviations

Imperial	Abbreviation
Teaspoon	tsp
Tablespoon	Tbsp
Cup	cup
Pound	lb
Ounce (weight)	oz

Metric	Abbreviation
Millilitre	ml
Litre	L
Gram	g
Kilogram	kg

Equivalents

Imperial	Metric
½ tsp	2.5 ml
1 tsp	5 ml
1 Tbsp	15 ml
¼ cup	60 ml
⅓ cup	80 ml
½ cup	120 ml
1 cup	240 ml
1 fl oz	30 ml
1 oz (weight)	28.35 g
1 lb	454 g
1 inch	2.54 centimetres

Tips for Making Curry Pastes in a Mortar & Pestle

If you're making a large amount of curry paste, using a blender or food processor might be a good solution. If you're making a small amount, however, a mortar and pestle will yield a much finer texture. For all curry pastes in this book, the amount provided is just enough for that one recipe, so you won't end up with extra that might go to waste. This means that if you make just one recipe, it'll be a small amount that is much better suited for manual pounding.

Having made many, many batches of curry pastes in a mortar and pestle, here are some tricks I have found that help make the grinding a little easier. Scan the QR code for my yellow curry paste video which uses these techniques.

You need a heavy-duty stone mortar and pestle. The dainty little marble set or even the clay or wood set are not going to cut it for this job. I recommend a 7–8-inch heavy-duty stone mortar and pestle like the one I use often in my videos.

Use a spice/coffee grinder to grind dry chilies. This trick is the biggest time-saver of all. While coffee grinders don't grind moist curry pastes as well as I'd like, they do a fantastic job of pulverizing dry food. So, I use it to grind dry chilies separately, then add the powdered chilies to the mortar after the other herbs are pounded. This saves a lot of time, as the chilies' stubborn skins take a long time to break down. I have an old coffee grinder that I promoted to be my official chili grinder, so I don't end up with spicy coffee!

Chop herbs finely. You may be tempted to roughly chop the herbs since they will be pounded anyway, but if you take the time to finely slice them beforehand, you will spend less time pounding big pieces of herbs.

Use dry spices as a moisture absorber. If you have ground dry spices and chilies, add them in when the mixture in the mortar feels too wet and splashes and slips.

Yellow curry paste

Other Kitchen Tips & Tricks

- If you've found a curry paste you like, make extra and freeze it in individual portions or flattened in a freezer bag so you can easily break off a portion. Don't forget to label the bags!

- Before measuring oyster sauce, black soy sauce, or anything viscous, coat the measuring spoon in some vegetable oil and the sauce will slide out easily. This also works well with honey.

- If you use oyster sauce often, transfer it to a squeeze bottle. It's so much easier to get out!

- Chop solid pucks of palm sugar in advance and store them in an airtight container so they are easy to use. Pounding them in a mortar and pestle also works well.

- For your favourite stir-fries that you want to make often, make extra sauce in advance by combining all the liquid seasonings. Measure and note the total volume of sauce needed per recipe, and tape it onto the container; so, your label might say, "Basil Fried Rice Sauce—30 ml per recipe." Do not add dry ingredients, such as sugar and salt, as they don't dissolve well in thick sauces and may settle at the bottom.

- If you have a lot of peanuts and cashews that you can't use up quickly, store them in the freezer to prevent rancidity.

- When cooking with store-bought curry pastes, always taste before adding the salting agents; some brands can be very salty.

Always Here to Help

One of the things that I do almost every day is answer online viewers' cooking questions. Even though this book is "offline," I am still here to help you in your Thai cooking adventures. If you are unclear about certain instructions, need help modifying a recipe, or want to tell me how a recipe turned out, please don't hesitate to contact me, either through social media or my website's contact form!

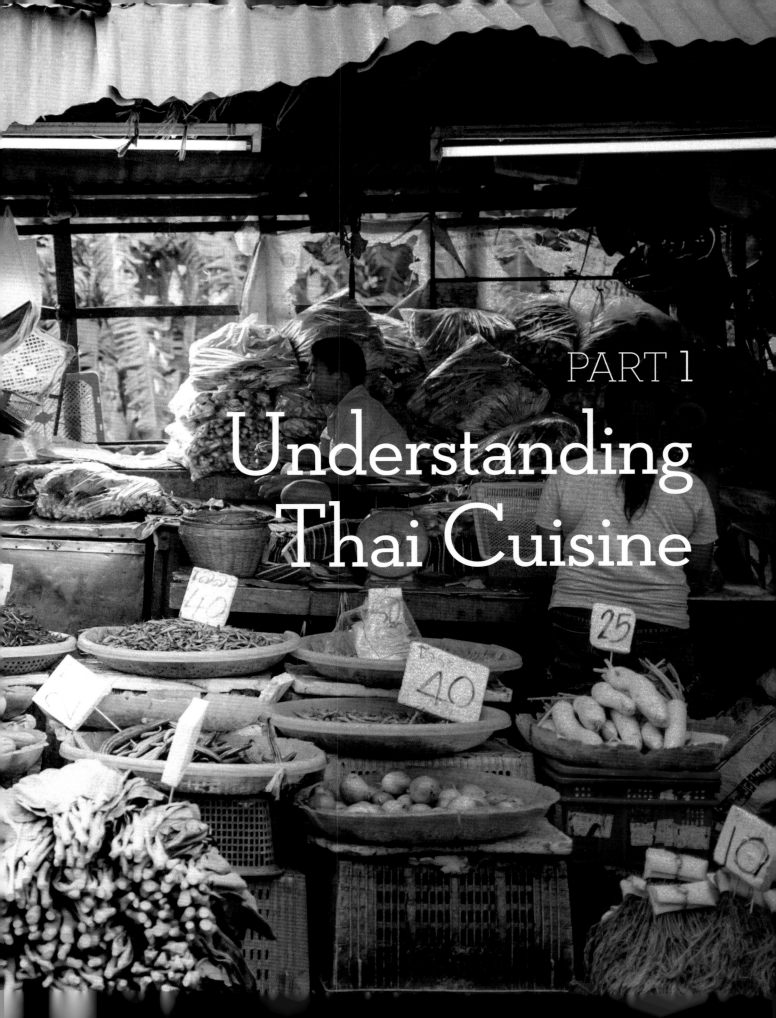

PART 1

Understanding Thai Cuisine

1. The Culture of Eating

What Is Cuisine?

We use the word "cuisine" often, but rarely do we think concretely about everything that it encompasses. When we say "Thai cuisine" or "French cuisine," are we referring to the dishes of that specific culture? Of course, but a cuisine is more than the mere sum of its dishes. To look at it from a different angle, what are the things that make Thai cuisine . . . Thai?

Ingredients, cooking techniques, and dishes—old and new—are integral to any cuisine, but there is one other indispensable component: culture.

By culture, I'm essentially referring to the many facets of how Thai people eat, whether in general or specific to each dish: How is dinner served in Thailand? Is this dish eaten on its own or with something else? What do Thai people drink with their meal? Is this for a special occasion or is it an everyday dish? How do flavours differ across regions?

How Does Understanding Thai Food Culture Impact Your Cooking?

Learning a new cuisine is like navigating a map of a foreign country—context makes a BIG difference in how confident you feel about where you're going. You could use Google Maps, complete with landmarks, your current location, and everything to scale. Or you could ask someone to draw up a map on a bar napkin, with only the streets you need to take, your destination X'ed into a box, and nothing else.

You certainly don't have to practise the Thai way of eating, so please feel free to read this chapter simply to feed your interest. However, I believe you will find that your knowledge of Thai food culture will increase your confidence in the kitchen, because in your mind, you will see where your food fits into the bigger picture, and you will feel like you know what you're doing!

How Thais Eat

Dining Etiquette

As with many cultures, eating is a social and communal activity for us. Dinners are served family-style, with dishes placed in the middle of the table for everyone to share.

Not all family-styles are identical. In Western culture, some families also eat "family-style," especially on special occasions, but it's not quite the same. At the typical North American Christmas dinner, for example, the food starts out in the middle of the table and diners fill up their plate with everything they think they want for the meal before they start eating. If there is enough food and tummy space, people can go back for seconds.

> *"Your knowledge of Thai food culture will increase your confidence in the kitchen, because in your mind, you will see where your food fits into the bigger picture."*

In Thailand, however, "family-style" works differently: everyone starts by putting a little bit of rice on their plate (because everything is eaten with rice). Instead of selecting all of their food at the beginning of the meal, each person takes a small amount of food from the centre at a time, going back for more once the first helping is finished. Throughout the meal, there is a constant flow of people taking a bit and eating a bit, then taking a bit more and eating a bit more.

The idea behind this etiquette is that, by taking just a couple of bites of each dish at a time, there will always be enough for everyone. This way, diners also get to sample everything first before deciding if they want more of it.

At a large table, where people cannot reach all the dishes, food is rearranged on the table a few times during the course of the meal to ensure that everyone has had a chance to try everything. If you can reach a dish on the table, but the person next to you cannot, it's also good etiquette to ask if they would like to be served.

It's also common for a person to take food from the middle and serve it to someone else as a gesture of kindness and a display of respect. There is no rule as to who should serve whom, and by no means is it rude not to serve others, but in general it's appropriate to serve the elderly and guests.

The Fork & Spoon

Shortly after I left Thailand, I went to stay with my brother in Virginia for the summer and took a job as a waitress in a Thai restaurant. I noticed that the restaurant's table setting consisted of only a fork and a napkin, so I asked a senior employee why they didn't put out any spoons. "We used to, but most customers don't use them," she replied. I remember thinking how difficult it must be to eat rice with just a fork.

We eat with a spoon and a fork. Incredible though it may seem, using a spoon can make your meal taste better! Since Thais eat everything with rice, including soups, curries, and dips, the spoon is essential for holding in all the delicious liquids. With only a fork, half the flavour would be left on the plate.

> "ความเข้าใจในวิถีการกินของคนไทย
> จะทำให้คุณมีความมั่นใจในการ
> ทำอาหารไทยมากขึ้น"

What about knives and chopsticks? Many people have asked me to clarify if it's "culturally incorrect" to ask for chopsticks in a Thai restaurant. Let me settle it here: we use chopsticks, but only for noodles. Most people use chopsticks for noodle soups, and some also use them for pan-fried noodles. The only other exception is when we're eating food from other cuisines that use chopsticks, such as Chinese and Japanese food. Dinner knives, on the other hand, are non-existent. They are of no use because everything is already cut up into bite-sized pieces, and anything that isn't pre-cut is soft enough to be cut with a fork and a spoon, such as a whole fish.

How to use a fork and a spoon like a Thai

If you're right-handed, the spoon is held in your right hand and the fork in your left. Hold them like you would loosely hold a pen. The back of the fork pushes the food onto the spoon, and it's the spoon that goes into your mouth.

Note: When sticky rice is served with the meal, it is usually eaten by hand. You can use the sticky rice to soak up sauces.

The Rice Nightmare

What happens at the end of the meal when someone eats rice with only a fork? The last 21 grains of rice on the plate are now slippery from all the sauce. You try to get them onto the fork, but to no avail—they keep sliding, escaping the tines, taunting you. Your patience runs thin, so you decide to use your fingers to push the rice, but wait . . . you remember that this is a business dinner and the finger thing just isn't classy. You consider leaving them, but that would leave you unsatisfied for the night. Finally, you resort to extreme measures and squish! You mash the rice with the back of your fork so the grains are stuck to the tines, defeated. It's not graceful, but you were desperate. Of course, the spoon fixes that problem.

How to Construct a Thai Meal

"When dishes complement each other well, it can really mean the difference between a good meal and a great meal."

....

" ถ้ากับข้าวแต่ละอย่างเข้ากันดี อาหารมื้อนั้นก็จะยิ่งอร่อย "

Most Thai dishes are designed to be eaten with rice and with other dishes. So, when you are cooking the traditional multi-dish meal, it's important that the items complement each other well. To help you get started, I created a guideline for how to put together a well-balanced Thai meal. The first version of this guideline was an article I wrote for the *San Francisco Chronicle* as a guide for ordering food at a Thai restaurant, and it was very well received. I've provided an expanded version of it for you on the next page.

By "a well-balanced meal," I am referring to a balance of sensory input. Eating is a sensory experience with many interacting variables: flavour, aroma, texture, mouthfeel, and temperature, among others. A little attention to what characteristics each dish contributes to the meal can greatly elevate the diner's enjoyment.

In the end, of course, you can eat whatever you want, but I do think that when dishes complement each other well, it can really mean the difference between a good meal and a great meal.

Deep-fried fish with a green mango salad

A Guideline for Constructing a Thai Meal

1. Something Wet

Always have something with a lot of liquid, such as soups and curries. If you're serving two wet dishes, it's best if one is richer, like a coconut-milk-based curry, and the other lighter, such as a brothy soup. These dishes make the meal luscious and juicy.

2. Something Dry

"Dry" in this case means non-soupy dishes, as opposed to the wet category above, even though they may still be saucy. Basically this is anything that comes on a plate, such as a stir-fry, a deep-fried item, or something grilled.

3. Something Fresh

I'm using the word "fresh" to refer to dishes with a lot of raw vegetables or herbs. In the context of Thai cuisine, this includes salads and dips. I will talk more about the characteristics of Thai salads and dips in Chapter 4, but essentially, they are the light and refreshing elements of the meal. Thai salads always have plenty of acid from fresh lime juice, an abundance of fresh herbs, and a light dressing, making them the perfect palate cleanser between bites. Dips contribute freshness because they are always served with a lot of of raw or steamed vegetables.

4. Something Spicy

Thais like to make sure that at least one dish is spicy. It doesn't have to be anything tear-jerking, just whatever feels good for your tolerance level. Spice isn't a flavour, but a sensation that adds another dimension to the eating experience, much like an adrenaline rush. Food feels more "fun" when it's spicy! Make sure, however, that not all the dishes are spicy. A good range of spice levels in a meal will prevent flavours from getting lost in the heat.

5. Rice

Thais eat everything with rice, unless we're having noodles. This is an important factor to keep in mind when you're cooking and tasting food, because something that tastes a bit strong may mellow out perfectly with rice. We love to eat jasmine rice, which actually has a beautiful jasmine-like fragrance. People in the north and the northeast of Thailand eat a lot of sticky rice, so if you're serving food from those regions, it would be appropriate to serve sticky rice, either instead of or along with jasmine rice.

6. Balance the Main Ingredients

Have an assortment of fish, meat, shellfish, poultry, vegetables, eggs, etc. Having repeats is fine when you have several dishes, but when there are only three or four, the meal is better balanced if all the dishes feature a different main ingredient.

Note: It may look like you need to have five or six dishes in order to follow this guideline, but remember that one dish can contribute more than one element. For example, a green curry would double as a wet and a spicy dish, and a salad would be both "fresh" and "dry." This guideline is meant for a meal with at least three dishes.

OVERVIEW: A well-balanced Thai meal of at least three dishes should have . . .

Attribute	Description	Examples
Something Wet	• Dishes with a lot of liquid • Keeps the meal moist and juicy • If serving two wet dishes, balance their richness	• Soups • Curries
Something Dry	• Dishes with little or no liquid	• Stir-fries • Deep-fried items • Grilled items • Salads
Something Fresh	• Dishes with plenty of raw vegetables and/or herbs • Light, crisp, and refreshing • Acts as a palate cleanser	• Salads • Dips served with vegetables
Something Spicy	• Provides another dimension to the eating experience • Only as spicy as you can enjoy • Don't make every dish spicy; have a mix of spicy and non-spicy dishes	• All types of dishes can be spicy
Rice	• Provides a canvas for all dishes • Mellows out strong flavours	• Jasmine rice • Sticky rice
Varied Main Ingredients	• Each dish should feature a different main ingredient, i.e., fish, poultry, meat, eggs, or vegetables.	

One-Dish Meals

In Thailand we have a category of food called *ahaan jaan diew* which can be translated as "one-dish meal." It's the antithesis of family-style dining: a complete meal on one plate, not served with anything, and not shared with anyone.

Consider these the sandwiches of Thai cuisine, and in the same way that you wouldn't serve sandwiches for your family dinner, we don't normally include *ahaan jaan diew* in ours. These are eaten as quick lunches, takeaways, and solo meals, which is why they are most commonly found on the street and in food courts.

Almost all noodle dishes fall into this category, such as pan-fried noodles and noodle soups. *Ahaan jaan diew* can also be a rice-based dish, such as fried rices and rice-meat combinations, such as *kao ka moo*, a stew of pork leg served over rice.

อาหารจานเดียว	one-dish meal
เครื่องปรุง	condiments
พริกน้ำปลา	prik nam pla
พริกน้ำส้ม	prik nam som

Table-Side Condiments

The West has salt and pepper, we have . . . well, many options depending on what you're eating! Here are the common ones that are versatile and used often.

Prik nam pla: *Prik* means chilies and *nam pla* is fish sauce. And that's essentially what this is—fish sauce spiked with chopped bird's eye chilies. It is our closest equivalent to salt and pepper, in the sense that if something tastes a little bland, we would go for *prik nam pla*. Some people like to dress it up with a squeeze of lime, which is what I do, while others also add chopped garlic and/or shallots.

Standard Noodle Condiments: Noodles are always served with a posse of condiments on the side. You can see these neatly set up on the tables of noodle restaurants all over Thailand. The set always contains the following flavours: salty, sour, sweet, and spicy.

Salty: *Prik nam pla* or just straight-up fish sauce.

Sour: Spur chilies pickled in white vinegar, which is sometimes blended into a thin pesto-like consistency. This is called *prik nam som*.

Sweet: Granulated sugar.

Spicy: Dry chili flakes or chili flakes fried in oil. There can sometimes be more than one spicy option.

Table-side condiments at a noodle restaurant in Bangkok

A Note about Spiciness

I want to address this issue because I've come across people who don't like spicy food and so assume that they won't like Thai food. This is kind of like saying, "Since I don't like sushi, I don't like Japanese food." Yes, a large number of Thai dishes are spicy, but equally many aren't, and of those that are spicy, the majority of them can be made milder. This is why the measurement for chilies in my recipes is usually a big range. Rest assured that even with toned-down heat, the flavours of Thai food are complex and bold enough that they will hold their own, so don't feel like you're not making "real" Thai food if it doesn't make your nose run!

Do All Thai People Like Spicy Food? Contrary to popular belief, no. Sure, many of us love things to be painfully spicy, but just as many like it very mild, which is why you can easily find Thai dishes in Thailand that are not spicy at all. Spice preference is also region-dependent: people of the South and the Northeast can cook up things that make Thais from other regions cry.

When you construct a Thai meal, I believe that involving spiciness to your comfort level in a dish or two creates a more well-rounded meal. Eating is a sensory experience, and the sensation of "heat" fills a little gap that the "flavours" (i.e., salty, sweet, sour, and bitter) cannot fill.

Various chilies at the market

On Beverage Pairing

When I say "Thailand," what images come to your mind? Beaches. Street food. Smoggy Bangkok. Crowded outdoor markets. Rice paddies in the glaring sun . . . What do these images make you want to drink? A robust glass of red wine? No! Beer, of course! Or perhaps a very large cocktail, but certainly something ice cold and maybe even fizzy.

Although wine drinking is becoming trendy in Bangkok within Thai "high society,"* the hot climate just makes you want to gulp, not sip. And when we do sip, it's usually hard liquor with a lot of ice. However, all hope is not lost with wine and not all beers will pair well with all dishes, so here are some points to consider when it comes to choosing your beer or wine.

"High Society" or "Hi-So" for short, is the English-turned-Thai word for people of the upper socioeconomic class.

Wine Pairing

When people ask me, "What kind of wine pairs well with Thai food?" I semi-facetiously reply, "Beer." Drinking wine is not a part of Thai food culture, and for good reason. The fact that we eat multiple dishes in a family-style meal presents an obvious issue: with which dish are we pairing the wine?

To make matters worse, a well-constructed meal will have dishes with different leading flavours, so trying to find a wine that pairs well with every dish is pretty much impossible. Having said that, if you are only cooking one dish, then we've got something to work with.

Consider Sweetness & Acidity. Wine should not be less sweet than the food it is served with or it will taste sour. This makes Thai food a difficult match due to the notes of sweetness in many of our dishes. Sweeter

wines, such as Gewürztraminer, Reisling, or Viognier, generally hold up better than others. Sweetness also helps counteract spiciness, making these wines particularly great with Thai food.

> *"When people ask me, 'What kind of wine pairs well with Thai food?' I semi-facetiously reply, 'Beer.'"*

> "ถ้ากินอาหารไทย ดื่มเบียร์นี่แหละ อร่อยที่สุด"

A large number of Thai dishes are also high in acid, which is the enemy of tannin. Tannin is the stuff in red wine that feels astringent and dry on your tongue, and the effects of tannin are magnified, in a bad way, by acid. In general, stay away from red wine, particularly the full-bodied, tannic ones such as Cabernet Sauvignon, Syrah, or Petite Syrah. If you must have red wine, ask the people at the wine store to help you pick out a high-acid, low-tannin bottle.

Remember that a bad food-wine pairing will ruin the wine more than the food, so think twice before you pull your 1961 Lafite Rothschild from the cellar!

Beer Pairing

When I was living in San Francisco, a friend from Thailand came for a visit, and we went out for dinner and drinks. When my drink arrived, my friend looked at it and asked, "What is that?" I had ordered a Chimay Red, a deep copper-coloured beer. "It's beer," I said. "That doesn't look like beer," he protested.

I gave him a taste, and he gave back a look that said, "and it doesn't taste like beer either."

Years ago, I would have had the same reaction. If you've been to Thailand, you may have noticed that golden lagers and not much else dominate the market, so when Thai people think beer, we think lager.

Think Summer Beer. Singha, Chang, and Leo are the three biggest Thai beer brands, and Heineken is our most popular import: they are all lagers, and it's not a coincidence. Here in the West, dark porters and stouts are associated with winter, while light wheat beers and lagers are associated with summer. Well, it's summer nearly every day in Thailand, hence the lagers!

But what if you're eating Thai food in the cold winter of Ireland? You almost have a point there, but the nature of Thai food also encourages lighter beers. Like wine, the body of beer should match the food, so while a rich, creamy Guinness will complement a beef stew, it will overpower and diminish the brightness of many Thai dishes—it's kind of like drinking a mocha with fresh oysters. It also helps that light beers just feel better after a spicy bite of food.

So while you need not drink a lager with Thai food, choose a beer with high carbonation, a light body, and refreshing flavours. I very much love wheat beers, such as a Hefeweizen or a Witbier, with my Thai meal, or an ice cold Blonde Ale . . . mmm.

Regional Thai Food

Just like people, foods from different regions have their own personality, which I think is part of the charm of Thai food! "Thai food," as most people around the world know it, is really food from the Central region because it's the most influential when it comes to the spread of Thai culture.

> *"Just like people, foods from different regions have their own personality . . ."*

....

"อาหารก็เหมือนคน แต่ละภาคก็มี เอกลักษณ์เป็นของตัวเอง"

Culinarily speaking, there are four regions in Thailand: North, Northeast, Central, and South. The regional differences in Thai cuisine could be an entire book in themselves, but I will touch upon as much as is relevant to getting you started with Thai food. I will discuss later why it's important for someone learning to cook Thai food to be aware of these regional differences; but first, here are the general characteristics and the iconic dishes of each of the four regions.

The Northeast ภาคอีสาน

The Northeast has a special place in my heart because it is where my mother comes from, and my grandmother still lives there today. The town she lives in, See Kiw, had a charming simplicity to it that I have yet to find in other places. I remember wandering through the market and not being sure if I was in someone's living room or a store—no doors were closed.

The official term for the Northeast is *paak tawan awk chiang neua*, which is quite a mouthful, so most people call this region by its other name, "*isaan.*" From this region come some of the most internationally popular dishes, namely green papaya salad and *laab*.

Because the Northeast borders Laos, the dialect, culture, and food are similar to those of Laos, and it is no longer clear what comes from where.

Much of the Northeast is rural, and people live simple agricultural lifestyles, growing and gathering much of their own food. The climate here can be harsh with a long drought season, making food hard to grow, which pushes people to become creative with their food.

Edible Critters: The Northeast is where unusual critters, like insects, lizards, frogs, and even red ant eggs, are given culinary treatment. Because the main ingredients could be, well . . . anything, Northeastern dishes are rooted in bold flavours from generous amounts of seasoning, an abundance of fresh herbs, and a painful amount of chilies! Saltiness and spiciness are the two leading characteristics of Northeastern cuisine, closely followed by acidity, but sweetness is a rarity in their savoury food.

Light & Lean: Food here is leaner than in other regions, with most of the soups and curries brothy and coconut-free. Oil is used for deep-frying, but it's minimally used as an ingredient in a dish. *Isaan* people make many types of salads, all of which use no added fats. This is a great cuisine to indulge in if you're trying to eat healthy!

Fermentation of Protein: *Isaan* typically has very hot summers, causing meat to spoil quickly, especially without refrigeration, so people in the olden days got creative with the art of fermentation. Fermented pork and rice sausage *(sai grok isaan)* is uniquely sour and satisfying, and fermented fish paste *(pla ra)* gives many Northeastern dishes a pungent, savoury boost.

Herbs: Fresh herbs are treasured here, as they can mask gaminess, fishiness, and other odd flavours that today's proteins might bring. In addition to the basic repertoire of Thai herbs, there are many others that are unique to Northeastern cuisine, such as mint, sawtooth coriander, dill, and Mexican oregano.

Sticky Rice: Sticky rice is the primary kind of rice consumed here. It's perfect to pack for lunch out on the farm, because it has high caloric density and can be eaten without utensils. Sticky rice is traditionally steamed using a woven bamboo cone-shaped steamer called a *huad* which, in my opinion, is the best tool for this job! Sticky rice is also used to make *kao kua*, or toasted rice powder, which is used often in dishes with a lot of lime juice, including salads, soups, and dipping sauces. Since sugar is not used much here, the nuttiness of *kao kua* is what helps balance the acidity in these dishes.

Iconic Dishes:

- *Som tum*—Green papaya salad (recipe p.150)
- *Laab*—Salad of ground meat (recipe p.144)
- *Nam tok*—Salad of grilled meat (recipe p.147)
- *Sai grok isaan*—Fermented pork & rice sausage

Toasted rice powder in the making. See recipe p. 230

The North ภาคเหนือ

Many people who have been to Thailand have made it to the North because of its famous province Chiang Mai. The people of the North are known for their gentle-sounding dialect and polite manners, and this is reflected in their food.

Well-Balanced Flavours: Unlike the fierce flavours of Northeastern cuisine, Northern food has well-rounded and balanced flavours. Chilies are used in moderation and acidity is mild. Because food is richer here, the fat coats the tongue, softening the sharpness of salt.

Rich & Hearty: The North and the Northeast both share a border with Laos, and as a result, share many culinary similarities. However, there is one very clear distinction: Northern food is much fattier! Because the North is the coldest part of Thailand (yes, Thailand can be cold sometimes), the food is naturally richer and heartier than in other regions. Pork belly is used often in soups and curries, like in the iconic *gaeng hung lay*. *Kao soi*, a popular curry noodle soup, is the only noodle soup in Thailand I know of that is enriched with coconut milk. The North is also known for its spiced fatty sausage called *sai ua*.

Unique Spices: Today's natives of northern Thailand are made up of various cultural groups that have immigrated there over time, including those from Myanmar and the Yunnan region of China. For this reason, there are some spices used here that are nonexistent anywhere else in Thailand. *Laab neua*, or "northern *laab*," is a great example of this, because it uses a few of these spices, such as Indian long pepper, and others for which there are no equivalent English names.

Fermented Soybeans: While the Northeast is known for fermented fish, the North is known for fermented soybeans, or *tua nao*. The idea of *tua nao* is similar to that of Japanese natto, but it comes in a few different forms, including a dried, cracker-like version. *Tua nao* is salty and pungent, and it is added to enhance the flavours of various dips, sauces, and curries.

Kantoke: *Kantoke* is a unique Northern dining tradition for special occasions. Several dishes are elegantly presented together on an elevated wooden tray, like colours on a paint palette. Sticky rice, crispy fried pork rind, and Northern-style dips are standard fixtures for a *kantoke*. In touristy cities in the North, there are restaurants that offer a "dinner and show" featuring *kantoke* and Thai dancing, but because it's a set menu for all guests, the food at these establishments tends to be modified to ensure that guests from any cultural background will find the meal acceptable. When I attended one of these dinners, there was fried chicken and what looked like french fries made with kabocha squash on the platter . . . Not exactly the cultural experience I was hoping for!

Iconic Dishes:

- *Gaeng hung lay*—Slow-braised pork curry
- *Kao soi*—Northern curry noodle soup
- *Laab neua*—Salad of ground meat with Northern spice blend
- *Sai ua*—Pork sausage spiced with curry paste
- *Nam prik ong*—Pork and tomato dip (recipe p.200)

Kao soi

Gaeng hung lay, *a rich and hearty pork curry of the North*

The Central Region ภาคกลาง

The rich and the powerful, the scandalous and the beautiful . . . they are all here. The parliament, the palace, the economy, and showbiz all operate out of this one city—Bangkok, the capital and the city visited by virtually every foreigner who has ever been to Thailand. So, naturally, it exerts the most influence when it comes to the spread of Thai food culture to other countries. This is why Thai food, as most of the world knows it, resembles food from the Central Region.

The Royal Fare: The royal palace has been located in the Central Region for hundreds of years, and needless to say, the best of chefs are here, creating the most elaborate meals. Over time, these culinary creations have spread beyond the palace walls, making Central Region food seem more sophisticated and elegant than others. The flavours are more gentle but well balanced, and the aesthetics are of importance. While people in other regions are concerned with finding food to fill their stomachs, the royal chefs are concerned with making food to please the eyes.

Desserts Central: In most cultures, desserts are a luxury, not a necessity. It's no wonder, then, that most Thai desserts come from here—the country's most affluent region. Other regions have sweets, too, of course, but they tend to be simpler. Desserts of the Central Region are more intricately crafted, and many of them are time-consuming. Perhaps this is why Central folks tend to like their food sweeter than others, and this will be apparent if you get a chance to compare the same dish from Bangkok with one from another region.

Internationalism: For hundreds of years, foreign affairs and trade have been conducted through the Central Region, so culinary influences from other countries have the biggest impact here. The Chinese gave us noodles for our *pad thai*, the Indians gave us coconut milk for our curries, and the Portuguese brought to us many ingredients from their world explorations, including chilies.

This is still true today. Bangkok is bustling with people from all over the world, and Thai-fusion and ethnic restaurants have never flourished so rapidly. Bangkok is also the centre for regional Thai food—if you're in Bangkok, you can sample food from any region, but if you're in the South, Northern food will be harder to come by!

Jasmine Rice: People of the Central Region eat predominantly jasmine rice. Sticky rice is also consumed, but only when it is the standard accompaniment for the dish, such as barbecued pork skewers *(moo ping)* or fried chicken.

Iconic Dishes:

- *Tom yum*—Spicy & sour lemongrass soup (recipe p.121)
- *Gaeng ped bped yang*—Red curry with barbecued duck (recipe p.99)
- *Pad thai*—Pan-fried rice noodles with beansprouts and garlic chives (recipe p.170)
- *Lohn goong*—Coconut shrimp dip (recipe p.204)

Pad thai

The Central Region is known for its intricately crafted sweets such as kanom beuang, *crispy crepes with various fillings.*

The South ภาคใต้

I am particularly fond of the South, because it's where I was born and raised for 12 years before my family moved to Bangkok. Southern people are known for their speedy dialect, which is spoken so fast that dialogue sounds like a heated argument. Their food is not much different, as it's arguably the fieriest food of all the regions!

Malay Influence: The South borders Malaysia, and therefore has a large number of people of Malay ancestry who are primarily Muslim and speak a different language. Southern food is influenced by Malaysian cuisine, which is in turn influenced by southern Indian cuisine, and it's probably where the spiciness comes from. Turmeric, an Indian spice, is used more in the South than in any other region.

Seafood: Thailand is shaped like an axe, and the South makes up the entire handle that points into the ocean, giving it a long coastline and an abundance of seafood. Naturally, there are many seafood-based dishes and ingredients here. One of the South's iconic seasonings is *gapi*, which is often called "shrimp paste" in English, even though it is made from fermented krill. It's salty, pungent, and full of umami, much like the fermented fish of the Northeast and fermented soybeans of the North!

Stinky Stuff: Southern food is full of ingredients considered stinky by most standards, such as the shrimp paste mentioned above. Other Southern funky-smelling ingredients include *tai pla*, or fermented fish guts, found in curries; *sataw*, or stinky beans, often used in stir-fries; and *boodoo*, which is a thicker version of fish sauce, commonly used in dips and salads.

Iconic Dishes:

- *Kua gling*—A stir-fry of ground meat and Southern-style curry paste
- *Gaeng leuang*—Spicy and sour turmeric curry
- *Kao yum*—Rice salad with fresh vegetables and *boodoo* dressing

Turmeric-marinated fried fish, a popular Southern dish

Friendly crispy cricket vendor. These critters are more commonly enjoyed in the Northeast.

Regions Differ . . . So What?

Many of you may find the subject of regional Thai cuisine to be an interesting read, but some may wonder how it is relevant to someone who is just beginning to learn about Thai food.

The truth is, I don't expect anyone to remember everything I just wrote. In fact, not all Thai people are even aware of these regional nuances. What I hope you take away from this is that there is no such thing as the universally correct flavour. As you have seen, each region emphasizes different ingredients and flavour notes, and the same dish can have very different flavours depending on which region, or even which province, you're in!

So, when you cook Thai food, relax. Your food doesn't need to taste a certain way in order to be "correct" or "authentic," so if you want to cook a Southern dish with a Central Region flavour-style, then go for it! Or if you want to incorporate a Northern ingredient into your Northeastern dish, then go ahead and take that leap. Thai people make these crossovers constantly when we cook at home.

What's most important when it comes to cooking any cuisine is that you, the eater, like it. If you make a traditional Northern Thai dish following an ancient recipe to a tee but you don't like the flavour, it's no fun in the end, is it?

Getting Over the
Fear of Ethnic Cuisine

Consider this scenario: Jane wants to cook a Thai dinner tonight. Her last vacation was in Thailand, and she fell in love with Thai food. She has been wanting to cook Thai food at home, but hesitates because she doesn't quite know where to begin. Today is the day. So, Jane goes online and searches for a recipe that looks "legit." After hours on the Internet, she prints out the recipe and takes it to the Asian grocer to look for the ingredients. She can't find them all . . . darn it. Back to the Internet, searching for the right substitutions, visiting countless forums, and wondering if any of the information is reliable . . .

Somsri, too, wants to cook a Thai dinner tonight. She's a native Thai living in Thailand. She looks in the fridge and then the pantry. She pulls out a handful of ingredients and starts cooking. Dinner is done.

These are two very real scenarios, and you may even have been in Jane's situation yourself. One must then ask, what is it that Thai people know that allows them to create delicious Thai food on a whim, without ever needing recipes? Because THAT is what you need to know to start cooking Thai food with confidence, and THAT is what I will talk about in Part 1.

Why People Don't Cook Ethnic Food More Often

Having read hundreds of emails from Hot Thai Kitchen fans, I've discovered that there are two main reasons why people are reluctant, or even scared, to cook Thai or any ethnic cuisine. The first is that they don't know where to start. This is an issue of knowledge, which is easily fixed. Reading this book is a great start.

Mangosteens (left) and rambutans (right).

The second, and most important, reason is the fear of making it "wrong." This isn't as simple a fix, as it's not a technical issue but rather a matter of mindset. People are afraid that, after all their efforts, they're not making "real Thai food." So, they postpone it until they feel "confident enough," or they decide to "leave it to the experts."

I get it. I remember feeling the same way when I started cooking Western food. I wanted to make the most authentic Bolognese sauce, so I searched for recipes written in Italian because, after all, they MUST be more authentic!

Maybe it's out of respect for the culture or from a belief that the "right" way tastes better, but whatever the reason, it's holding us back from taking that leap into the exciting world of an ethnic cuisine.

How Do People Cook at Home?
Authentic vs Traditional Thai Food

As our friend Somsri demonstrated earlier, our pantries and fridges determine our dinner. But this is nothing extraordinary; it's probably how you cook dinner most of the time, too. When we cook within our "comfort cuisine" we're relaxed about it. We don't have to have all the ingredients, because we will improvise and figure out something to make.

This means then that Thai people are constantly creating new dishes, adding new twists to old classics, or simply throwing random stuff together . . . but can you call that "real Thai food" or even "authentic Thai food"?

Of course you can. If what Thai people regularly eat at home isn't authentic Thai food, then I don't know what is. The thing is, most of what we eat isn't what you find in restaurants, isn't half as complicated, and may not even have a name.

Thai restaurants, too, are always creating new dishes. I often get emails from fans who ask "I love this dish called X at our local Thai restaurant. Do you have a recipe for it?" On many occasions, I have never even heard of it! Many of the dishes you find on Thai restaurant menus are the chef's own creations or perhaps are unique family recipes. The point is, Thai people create new dishes all the time, and once you learn the basics of Thai cooking, you can create your own as well.

"The word 'authentic' encompasses an infinite variety of dishes, and it continues to evolve day after day."

The Meaning of "Authentic"

So what does this mean? This means that the word "authentic" encompasses an infinite variety of dishes, and it continues to evolve day after day. The common thread that runs through all these dishes is the use of Thai ingredients—ingredients are the only constants in this equation. (I use the word "constant" loosely because even commonly used ingredients evolve over time.)

So, as long as you are using ingredients that the average Thai cook uses, your food is authentic as far as I'm concerned. There are more Thai ingredients than you or even I can ever learn, but the ones you need to worry about most of the time are listed and explained in the next chapter.

The Meaning of "Traditional"

I like to say that all traditional dishes are authentic, but not all authentic dishes are traditional. "Tradition," in the context of food, refers to the way a dish has been prepared over a long period of time, and is generally accepted as the "standard version." For example, the traditional *pad thai* uses rice noodles, but in my lifetime I have seen versions with glass noodles, crispy wontons, or even strings of green papaya! If you browse Thai food blogs, you will see hundreds more of these creative ideas.

These dishes are born out of innovation and are authentic because they're made with Thai ingredients. Over the years, however, some of them may become considered "traditional," because, after all, today's traditional dishes were once new and different!

So, if your goal is to make a traditional dish, you might want to do some research. But even then, within the realm of "traditional," there are inevitably variations between recipes, so really, don't get hung up on it!

Don't Wait to Do It Right

I am a firm believer that traditional Thai food has invaluable cultural importance and that it should always be preserved and passed on to new generations. This is one of the main reasons why, at the time of this writing, most of my Hot Thai Kitchen recipes would be considered traditional.

Having said that, I don't believe that you should let tradition limit your creativity in the kitchen. So, don't wait until you have it all figured out; don't stop because you don't have every ingredient on the list—the best food is created in non-ideal circumstances. Food history is being written right now, in your kitchen and mine!

"Don't wait until you have it all figured out; don't stop because you don't have every ingredient on the list—the best food is created in non-ideal circumstances."

Recipes Are Guidelines, not Rules

Okay, so it sounds like I just said to go do whatever you want with Thai ingredients and you'll be fine, which I'm sure isn't what you were hoping for! You're reading this book because you want to recreate the wonderful flavours that you fell in love with when you first encountered Thai food, so you will need some more directions.

That's what recipes are great for. Having said that, the only way to develop independence and confidence in cooking any cuisine is to stop treating recipes like the gold standard, and start treating them as guidelines or starting points. Make the dish by following the recipe once to get an idea of the flavour profile, how the ingredients come together, and how the methods get them there. Then, the next time, try it free-form using the concepts and principles you learned from the previous round.

Note: This doesn't always apply to dessert recipes, where ratios of some ingredients can make or break the result.

If you do this enough times with a wide variety of recipes that use different ingredients and cooking techniques, you will soon develop a deeper understanding of Thai cooking, and you will start to cook like a Thai!

2. Understanding Thai Ingredients

The Six Categories of Thai Ingredients

As I explained in Chapter 1, ingredients are really what make Thai food Thai. Becoming familiar with the flavours of staple Thai ingredients and how to use them is not only key to your ability to cook Thai food, but more importantly, it will also give you the confidence to modify existing recipes and create your own dishes.

> *"Cooking without knowing how ingredients taste and behave is like trying to paint a picture in the dark."*

Cooking, at its very basic level, is the art and science of combining ingredients into a hopefully delicious end product. So, cooking without knowing how ingredients taste and behave is like trying to paint a picture in the dark.

To help you mentally organize all of these new ingredients, I have divided them into categories based on their function. I've included substantial details about ingredients that I consider to be integral to Thai cuisine. There are some lesser-used ingredients that you do not need to worry about in most situations, so I just briefly discuss them.

Category by Function	Ingredient
Sturdy Herbs	Lemongrass
	Galangal
	Kaffir lime
	Chilies
	Garlic
	Shallot
	Cilantro root
	Fingerroot
	Ginger
	Turmeric
Finishing Herbs	Thai basil
	Holy basil
	Cilantro/coriander
	Green onion
	Mint
	Sawtooth coriander/culantro
Spices	White and black pepper
	Coriander seeds
	Cumin seeds
	Five-spice
	Young peppercorns

Category by Function	Ingredient
Sweeteners	Palm sugar
	Granulated sugar
	Brown sugar
	Sugar cane
Acids	Lime juice
	Tamarind juice
	White vinegar
Salting Agents	Fish sauce
	Regular soy sauce
	Black soy sauce
	Seasoning sauce
	Fermented soybean paste (tao jiew)
	Oyster sauce
Others	Coconut milk
	Curry pastes
	Dried shrimp
	Chili paste (nam prik pao)
	Shrimp paste (gapi)
	Noodles
	Rice
	Stock

"การทำอาหารโดยที่ไม่
เข้าใจวัตถุดิบก็เหมือนการ
วาดภาพในความมืด"

Sturdy Herbs

Sturdy herbs are just what their name implies: herbs that are sturdy and tough, and can handle rigorous cooking without wilting.

LEMONGRASS : *Takrai* ตะไคร้

Lemongrass is one of the most commonly used herbs in Thai cuisine. It has a beautiful citrusy aroma, but yields no acidity, as the name might suggest.

How to Buy: When buying fresh lemongrass, squeeze the bottom part near the root end, and choose stalks that feel firm. Old lemongrass will have lost moisture and feels squishy. If you cannot buy fresh stalks, lemongrass also comes in frozen, dried, and powdered forms. Frozen is the next best option, followed by dry, and use powdered form only if you absolutely have to.

How to Store: If you're going to use lemongrass within a week, you can keep the whole stalk in the fridge in plastic wrap to retain its moisture. For long-term storage, you can cut the stalks into 2-inch pieces and freeze them according to the instructions under *How to Freeze Sturdy Herbs*, p.35.

How to Use: Cut off the dry green top—you should remove about 1/2 of the stalk; save the top for making stock or tea. Cut off about 1/2 inch of the root end, which is holding all of the layers together, then peel off one or two of the outer layers, which are usually dry and dirty. What you're left with now is the part with the most concentrated flavour, and it's ready to be used. There are three common ways you can use lemongrass:

1. Infusion—Smash the lemongrass with the back of your knife repeatedly until the stalk splits to help release the fragrance. Then cut it into 2-inch pieces and let it infuse in hot liquids. Lemongrass is not meant to be eaten in this form, because it's very tough and chewy, so make sure you inform your guests or remove it before serving!

2. Finely sliced—You can eat lemongrass comfortably if it's small enough. Slice the lemongrass crosswise into rounds, as thinly as you can. You can mince the rounds further if you feel they're not quite thin enough. In this form, you can toss lemongrass into salads, stir-fries, or dips.

3. Paste—Lemongrass can be pounded into a paste as part of a curry paste or a dip.

Lemongrass

GALANGAL : *Ka* ข่า

It may look like the sister of ginger, and you may be tempted to use the two interchangeably, but trust me, the flavours are as different as yin and yang. The part used for cooking is the rhizome of the galangal plant. Galangal flourishes in my family's home garden in Bangkok, and last I saw, the plants were over 8 feet tall because we just can't use them fast enough! It has a cooling, woodsy fragrance that reminds me of a lush pine forest after the rain. It's a very calming, zen-inducing aroma.

How to Buy: Most people don't have much of a choice when it comes to buying fresh galangal—some are lucky if they can even find it at all. Fresh galangal should look plump and feel firm. Galangal also comes frozen, dried, and powdered. Frozen is the best alternative, and though I've had decent results using dried galangal in soups, you would need to use more than the recipe calls for. Use the powdered version only if necessary.

How to Store: Unless you're going to use it within a week, I recommend freezing galangal to retain its quality. Wash, dry, and then slice it into thin rounds, about ⅛-inch thick. Lay the rounds flat on a plate or a tray and put it in the freezer just until the rounds freeze; this is to prevent the pieces from sticking together. When frozen, store them following the instructions under *How to Freeze Sturdy Herbs*, p.35. You can use galangal directly from frozen. Do not freeze a big chunk of galangal, because it will be very hard to cut.

How to Use: Galangal does not need to be peeled, but make sure you wash it well before using or freezing. Use only the yellowish-white part and discard the pinkish part, which is the base of the stalk that is sometimes left on. Slice the galangal into rounds about ⅛-inch thick. It can be used in ways similar to lemongrass:

1. **Infusion**—Place the sliced rounds in hot liquids to infuse. It is not meant to be eaten in this form, so make sure you inform your guests or remove it before serving.

2. **Finely chopped**—First, slice it into thin rounds. Then, slice the rounds into thin juliennes that can be added to your stir-fries. To toss into salads, chop the juliennes into even smaller pieces.

3. **Paste**—Like lemongrass, galangal can be ground down into a paste to be used as part of a curry paste or a dip.

KAFFIR LIME†: *Magrood* มะกรูด

In most recipes, you will only need to worry about the leaves of the kaffir lime. The zest is sometimes added to curry pastes, but the juice is rarely called for. So, I will focus on the leaves in the following discussion. These leaves are tough, much like a bay leaf, and have a powerful fragrance similar to, yet clearly distinct from, lime zest. The leaves are used more often than the fruit.

How to Buy: Look for leaves that seem full of life, as though they are still on the trees. Since they are sturdy, the leaves remain fresh for a long time after they have been picked. If they are sold with the stems on, watch out for the thorns! Dried and frozen ones are also available, but use a little more dried leaves than what is called for in the recipes.

How to Store: Kaffir lime leaves will last several days in the fridge, but freezing is the best option for long-term storage. These leaves have a low moisture content and, therefore, handle freezing well. Follow the instructions under *How to Freeze Sturdy Herbs*, p.35. You can use them directly from the freezer without thawing.

How to Use: The leaves can be used in ways similar to lemongrass, except we don't grind them into a paste. This is because the leaves are fibrous and hard to grind; so, for pastes, we use the zest instead.

1. Infusion—Tear the lime leaves into chunks and let them infuse in a hot liquid. They are not meant to be eaten in large pieces, so make sure your guests are aware, or remove them before serving.

2. Thin juliennes—To eat kaffir lime leaves comfortably, you want to julienne them as thinly as you possibly can. You can also remove the central rib of the leaf, which can be tough. You can add these juliennes into salads, dips, forcemeats, stir-fries, or anything you wish!

† *There is a movement to change the name "kaffir lime" to "makrut lime" due to the controversial connotation of the former; however, at the time of publication, the majority of vendors still use the term "kaffir lime."*

GARLIC: *Gratiem* กระเทียม

Garlic isn't exotic, but it's important to Thai cooking simply because of how much it is used. Thai garlic, or *gratiem thai*, has tiny cloves about the size of the smallest inner cloves of Chinese or American garlic. This makes them a pain to peel, so we often don't, and it's fine because the peel is very thin. They have a more concentrated flavour than larger garlic, though, so a little goes a long way. Using garlic is pretty straightforward and generally common knowledge, so I will just give you some tips for buying and storing it.

How to Buy: Because garlic is so common and inexpensive, many people overlook the importance of choosing good garlic, which is also why there's so much bad garlic for sale. (If we had to spend $50/lb for garlic, I'm sure people would pay more attention to quality!)

The older the garlic, the less flavourful it becomes, but lucky for us, it's not hard to tell old garlic from fresh. The papery skin on fresh garlic should be tight and intact—it should not be breaking or falling apart. The cloves should be tightly bound together and feel very hard when squeezed. Most importantly, they should not be sprouting!

How to Store: Garlic is still alive, so if you give it what it needs to grow, it will start sprouting and losing flavour. Keep it away from the two things plants need to grow: sunlight and moisture. Somewhere dark, dry, and cool is ideal. Finally, buy only as much as you need until your next grocery trip so you always have fresh garlic on hand.

SHALLOTS : *Hua Hom Dang* หัวหอมแดง

Again, these are nothing exotic, but they are important nonetheless. Shallots are a staple item in any Thai kitchen, just as onions are in a Western kitchen. In fact, they are the most frequently used type of onion in Thai cuisine. Thai shallots are small, about the size of a marble, and are more round in shape, rather than long and tapered, but North American shallots can be used in any Thai recipe.

How to Buy: The most important feature to look for and avoid is mold. Mold on shallots looks like black dust that is usually in between the first couple of layers. This mold is toxic, so I recommend throwing out the shallot to be safe. Choose shallots that look clean, feel firm when squeezed, have undamaged skin, and aren't sprouting.

How to Use: Shallots are more pungent than onions, so when using raw shallots, slice them very thinly. Shallots are sometimes charred to develop a smoky flavour and added to soups. They are also a major ingredient in most Thai curry pastes.

How to Store: Like garlic, shallots are alive and you want to prevent them from growing, so the mantra is dry, dark, and cool.

Thai garlic (left) and Chinese garlic (right)

CHILIES : *Prik* พริก

As unlikely as it may sound, chilies are not actually native to Thailand! They were originally brought to Thailand from the Americas by Portuguese explorers in the 1500s, but despite their foreign origin, they have become an integral part of Thai cuisine. There are several types of chilies, but for the most part, you only need to worry about three:

Bird's Eye Chilies, Bird Chilies, Thai Chilies: I'm not sure why these are associated with birds in English, because in Thai, they are known as *prik kee nu* or "rat's poop chilies". . . perhaps they're the same size. I refer to these in all my recipes as "Thai chilies," because this is how they are often labelled in grocery stores. These small but violent chilies are our most common source of heat. They come in both red and green; the red ones are simply the ripe version of the green. You can use either one for most recipes, though they impart slightly different flavours.

Spur Chilies: Known in Thai as *prik chee fa*, these chilies are about 6–8 inches long and are very mildly spiced, if at all, making them a wonderful source of chili flavour without adding much heat. In Thailand, spur chilies can be red, green, or orange, so they are used often as garnish or to add bright colours to many dishes.

Dried Chilies: *Prik hang*, or dried chilies, come in two major forms: small and large; both are red. The small ones are spicy, while the large ones are milder. When dried, chilies go from fruity to smoky, turning them into an entirely different ingredient. They can be pounded into curry pastes, crushed to make chili flakes, or fried to obtain crispiness and even more distinct smokiness.

How to Buy: For fresh chilies, look for ones that seem plump and full of life. The rule of thumb is: the smaller the chilies, the spicier they tend to be. For dried chilies, be careful of mold, which is unfortunately quite common. It is often hard to see in a bag, but mold on dried chilies looks like dark grey dust. If you find mold on the inside of the chilies, discard them. After buying dried chilies, I always rinse them quickly in cold water to get rid of any mold dust. After rinsing,

Bird's eye chilies (left) and spur chilies (right)

I dry them with a tea towel and then let them dry off completely on a tray (in the sun or in front of a fan) before storing. Do not rinse them for more than a few seconds or they will absorb too much water and take a long time to dry off.

> *"I'm not sure why these are associated with birds in English, because in Thai, they are known as ... 'rat's poop chilies.'"*

How to Store: Fresh chilies freeze very well, so you can freeze them following the tips described under *How to Freeze Sturdy Herbs*, p.35. However, be sure to use them directly from frozen, as they turn mushy once thawed. Store dried chilies in a cool, dry place in a sealed container.

How to Use: When cooking with spicy chilies, they should either be made very fine by mincing or pounding into a paste, or they should be in large, visible pieces. What you want to avoid is inconspicuous little pieces that are too small to be detected, but large enough that they are a painful surprise. This is particularly important when using green chilies, since they blend in with green vegetables, as I learned the hard way . . .

How Spicy Are Your Chilies? Every batch of chilies you buy, even from the same store, can have different levels of spiciness. If you are concerned about this, you should find out how spicy your chilies are before using them. How? Taste them! Yes, I said taste them. One day I'm sure someone will come up with a spice meter, but for now, all you've got is your tongue. This may sound scary, but all you have to do is bite into one, and without needing to chew, you should be able to tell how spicy it is just from what's on your teeth. Keep a glass of milk with you if you need to. Remember: you can always add heat afterwards, but it's much harder to fix a dish that is too spicy.

CILANTRO ROOTS : *Raag Pakchee* รากผักชี

Cilantro roots are just what the name describes: the roots of the cilantro plant (or coriander roots for those using British English). It is probably the most under-appreciated herb outside of Thailand, making it one of the hardest ingredients to find in the marketplace. This always frustrates me because the leaves are available just about everywhere! The roots are even more fragrant than the leaves, and most importantly, unlike the leaves, they can withstand cooking.

How to Use: The most prominent use of cilantro roots in Thai cuisine is in our version of the French mirepoix called *raag pakchee gratiem prik thai*. This is a paste made by pounding cilantro roots, garlic, and white peppercorns using a mortar and pestle. It is used as a flavour base for a lot of different dishes, such as meat marinades, stir-fries, and sauces. You can also crush the roots slightly and add them whole to infuse soups, stews, and stocks. Cilantro stems make a decent substitute, and I usually use about three stems per root.

How to Buy: Once in a blue moon, I'll see cilantro sold with the roots still attached, but most of the time, I buy the roots from specialty Thai grocery stores, either fresh or frozen. The only other way is to grow cilantro yourself!

How to Store: Once you've obtained the roots, freeze them according to the instructions under *How to Freeze Sturdy Herbs*, p.35. You can use them directly from frozen. Some people like to use a thin paring knife to scrape the skin and the small hairs off the roots before using, but I don't usually bother as long as I clean them well.

> *I once saw a farmer selling fresh herbs at a farmers' market in Vancouver. I noticed his rootless cilantro, so I asked him what he did with the roots. "We just leave them in the ground," he replied, looking slightly confused as to why I wanted to know. So I proceeded to spend the next few minutes telling him about the culinary usefulness of cilantro roots!*

Other Sturdy Herbs

These are herbs that are used less often, so you don't need to worry too much about them. I will discuss them briefly as a reference.

FINGERROOT : *Grachai* กระชาย

Grachai is also known as "lesser galangal," "Chinese keys," or "Chinese ginger." Its culinary use is in the rhizome of the plant, just like galangal and ginger. Each rhizome is about the size of a finger (hence the name). They can be thinly julienned and added to stir-fries, soups, and curries. They can also be pounded into curry pastes. They are available fresh or brined in a glass jar, and surprisingly, the brined form works very well in most dishes. Fingerroots pair wonderfully with red meat and fish because the fragrance helps soften gaminess and fishiness.

GINGER : *King* ขิง

Ginger is a Chinese influence on Thai cuisine, so it shows up mostly in dishes of Chinese origin. It can be sliced into rounds and infused in hot liquid, or finely julienned and added to stir-fries or steamed dishes. Ginger also works wonders in masking strong fishy flavours.

TURMERIC : *Kamin* ขมิ้น

This is yet another edible rhizome that is used a lot in the South. It is used primarily for its bright yellow colour, and you can be pretty certain that any dish that appears yellow gets its colour from turmeric. Subtle turmeric flavour is beautiful in combination with other herbs and spices, but too much turmeric gives an unpleasant, medicinal taste to food. There is a related, but very different, herb called "white turmeric," which we often eat raw. It has a crunchy texture with an interesting nutty flavour that goes very well with Thai dips or *nam prik*.

Fingerroot (grachai)

How to Freeze Sturdy Herbs

I used to just put sturdy herbs into a zip-top bag and throw them in the freezer, but I found that they quickly develop ice crystals, get freezer burn, and absorb that awful "freezer smell." Air is the enemy of frozen food, so the idea is to minimize air exposure. Here is how you can prolong the quality of your frozen Thai herbs:

1. Wash your herbs and dry them well before freezing. Excess moisture will cause them to stick together and create more ice crystals.

2. Wrap the herbs in plastic wrap or put them into a small plastic bag, such as a sandwich bag, squeezing out as much air as possible. (I prefer using a bag for this as I find re-wrapping plastic wrap rather annoying!) If you have a lot of herbs, divide them up so that you're making a few small packages so as to minimize the number of times you expose them to air.

3. Wrap the plastic packet in a layer of aluminum foil, pressing out as much air as possible. Unlike plastic, aluminum foil is impermeable to air and therefore offers better protection. Label the packet since you can no longer see what's inside.

4. Put the foil packets into a freezer bag and close, squeezing out as much air as possible. You can consolidate all the foil packets into one big freezer bag, but since I freeze many different types of herbs, I have a separate freezer bag for each type. Your herbs are now well protected and ready for the freezer!

Finishing Herbs

I named these herbs "finishing herbs" because they are added at the end to "finish off" a dish. In contrast to sturdy herbs, these are delicate, leafy herbs that cannot withstand prolonged exposure to heat. I am not including a section about how to buy finishing herbs, because it's the same as buying any leafy greens: choose ones that look healthy and fresh!

GREEN ONIONS & CILANTRO/CORIANDER :
Tonhom & Pakchee ต้นหอม ผักชี

I like to talk about these two herbs together because they're often used together. The duo of chopped green onion and cilantro (or coriander in British English) is the chopped parsley of Thai cuisine—the go-to garnish for any dish that needs a touch of green. You'll find them sprinkled over your fried rice, dips, and soups, and tossed into most salads. The stems of cilantro are even more fragrant than the leaves, so don't throw them out! I use stems instead of leaves in a few dishes, such as my Dipping Sauce for Seafood (p.207) and Beef "Ceviche" (p.140). Unlike the leaves, the stems can withstand bruising and heat without turning an unappetizing colour. Cilantro stems are also the best substitute for cilantro roots.

THAI BASIL : *Horapa* โหระพา

Thai basil has become quite widely available in North America. Some varieties have purple stems, while others have green stems, but the fragrance of these two varieties is very much the same. Thai basil has a distinct sweet fragrance that pairs well with coconut-milk-based curries. It is also used often in stir-fries.

Holy basil

HOLY BASIL : *Gaprao* กะเพรา

Gaprao is often mispronounced by Thai people as *grapao*, and you'll find it written in English a few different ways. Holy basil is not widely available, as it is harder to grow outside of the tropics (in my garden in Thailand it grows like weeds!). The leaves are more delicate than Thai basil's and have wavy edges. The fragrance is slightly peppery, so it is most often used in spicy dishes, including stir-fries, curries and soups.

The fragrance of holy basil isn't as strong or enduring as Thai basil, so it's a good idea to smell it to make sure it is still potent before buying. I have bought "weak" holy basil a few times, which was rather frustrating! In my experience, Italian basil is actually a better substitute for holy basil than Thai basil is.

MINT : *Saranae* สะระแหน่

Mint is used primarily in spicy dishes from the Northeast, but not much else. Mint does not withstand cooking well at all, so it is only used in cold applications, such as salads and dips.

SAWTOOTH CORIANDER : *Pakchee Farang* ผักชีฝรั่ง

Sawtooth coriander has long leaves with serrated edges. Like mint, it's often used in Northeastern salads and soups such as *laab* (p.144), *nam tok* (p.147) and *tom sap* (p.127). The fragrance of sawtooth coriander is somewhere between mint and cilantro, which I find very refreshing!

Left to right: *Cilantro, green onions, Chinese celery, sawtooth coriander*

How to Use Finishing Herbs

The important rule for cooking with finishing herbs is: don't cook them. Prolonged exposure to heat will turn them black and mushy. When using them in hot dishes, mix in the herbs at the end, using the residual heat to wilt and distribute the flavours. Cilantro leaves and mint are the two herbs used in Thai cooking that should not be tossed into hot dishes at all. However, they will be fine in a warm salad or as a last-minute garnish on top of hot dishes. In cold applications, add them in at the very end so they don't wilt from the moisture of your dish.

How to Store Finishing Herbs

To make them last longer, I store my delicate herbs like fresh-cut flowers. Wash the herbs in cold water and trim the stems to create a fresh opening (do not trim the roots of green onions). Put the stems in a glass of water and then cover them loosely with plastic bags. For cilantro, green onion, mint, and sawtooth coriander, I set this up in the refrigerator. For basils, I leave them on the counter in a cool place. Change out the water every few days.

Mint

How to Freeze Whole Basil Leaves

People often ask me if they can freeze Thai and holy basils, since these varieties can be hard to come by. While you can preserve the flavour of basil by freezing it in a pesto-like form, chopped up and in oil, Thai cuisine usually uses whole leaves. I've discovered a way to freeze whole basil leaves with acceptable results. The fragrance won't be as strong after freezing, so I would only use this method if your supply of fresh basil is highly unpredictable, and remember to use more than called for in a recipe.

1. Blanch the leaves in boiling water for a few seconds, just long enough to wilt them. This process will destroy the enzymes that are responsible for browning the leaves. Remove them from the water using a perforated or mesh skimmer, and immediately shock them in ice water to stop the cooking.

2. Remove the leaves from the ice water and spread them out on a towel to absorb excess water. Gather the leaves into loose clusters, arrange the clusters on a plate or tray, and freeze them.

3. Place the frozen clusters in an airtight container and keep them in the freezer. Do not put them in a freezer bag, as they may get crushed by other things. You can also wrap the container in aluminum foil to prevent air penetration.

4. To use, put the frozen clusters in cold water to thaw. Drain and add to dishes as usual.

Pakchee farang? Or pakchee farang?

Sawtooth coriander has many names in Thai, and strangely, its most common name is pakchee farang, *which is best translated to "Western cilantro," even though it isn't used in Western cooking. More logically, parsley, which is not used at all in Thai cooking, is also called* pakchee farang. *This can get quite confusing!*

Spices

Unlike Indian cuisine, Thai cuisine doesn't use a plethora of dry spices. But much of our spice usage is because of an Indian influence! Here are a few that you will probably run into as you start cooking Thai food.

WHITE PEPPER : *Prik Thai Kao* พริกไทยขาว

When Thai people simply say "pepper," or *prik thai,* we mean white pepper, because it is the most commonly used type. When black pepper is needed, it will be specified as *prik thai dum.* In simple terms, white pepper is black pepper without the black skin. It is hotter and has different flavour notes.

White pepper is not used as a universal table-side seasoning the way black pepper is in Western food culture. Instead, white pepper is often integrated into a dish as an ingredient. A handful of dishes call for white pepper as a standard condiment (like ketchup is to french fries) such as *pad see ew* (recipe p.158) and our breakfast rice porridge.

How to Use: You can find white pepper sold as whole peppercorns or in powdered form. I keep a small bottle of powdered white pepper for a quick, last-minute sprinkle, but for cooking I grind whole peppercorns in my mortar and pestle as the flavour and pungency are stronger when it's freshly ground.

CUMIN SEEDS : *Yeera* ยี่หร่า

People don't usually associate the flavour of cumin with Thai cuisine, because it is never used as the prominent spice. In fact, cumin is used almost exclusively in coconut-based curry pastes, where it plays a small, but important, part in the symphony of herbs and spices.

How to Use: Always buy cumin seeds whole for the highest flavour potency. Toast the seeds before using to enhance their flavours by adding them to a dry sauté pan over medium heat. Keep them moving until they start to darken slightly. I have found that some cumin seeds are contaminated with sand and dirt, which can be removed by sifting them with a mesh strainer.

CORIANDER SEEDS : *Look Pakchee* ลูกผักชี

We've talked about the leaves, the stems, the roots, and now for the seeds! These are simply the seeds of the coriander or cilantro plant. Interestingly, the flavour of the seeds is entirely different from the flavour of the leaves, stems, and roots. Its aroma reminds me of orange peel, and it has a warming, comforting effect that really blooms when toasted. It is most often used in coconut-based curry pastes and is sometimes added to meat marinades.

How to Use: I always buy whole coriander seeds, rather than ground, to prolong their flavour potency. Always toast the seeds before using to enhance the fragrance. Simply add them to a dry sauté pan over medium heat and keep them moving until they darken slightly.

FIVE-SPICE : *Kreuang Palo* เครื่องพะโล้

Originally a Chinese flavour combination, *kreuang palo* has become a household term in Thai cuisine. Different combinations of spices can be used, but cinnamon and star anise are always in the mix. The other three can be any combination of coriander seeds, cloves, cardamom, white peppercorns, Sichuan peppercorns, fennel seeds, and cumin. Sometimes, people use more than five spices, which is perfectly fine, so treat "five" as just a guideline!

How to Use: Pre-mixed five-spice powder can be added directly into dishes or used in a marinade or a spice rub. For soups, I prefer whole spices so I can toast them before using. You can wrap the spices in a piece of cheesecloth, let them infuse into a simmering soup, and remove the spice bag before serving. If you want to use whole spices but don't want to buy each one separately, look for pre-packaged whole five-spice blends at Chinese grocery stores.

YOUNG PEPPERCORNS : *Prik Thai On* พริกไทยอ่อน

At your Asian grocer, you may have come across something that looks like tiny green balls tightly arranged along a stem. These are simply peppercorns, the same ones used to make black and white pepper, in their fresh and unprocessed state.

They are spicy, but not in the same way that chilies are spicy—it's the kind of heat that makes you feel warm, like your mouth's temperature is rising. Apart from heat, we add young peppercorns for their distinct flavour, which cannot be found in their mature dried forms.

How to Use: You can buy them fresh or brined in a glass jar. When frozen, the peppercorns turn black, but the flavours are still intact. You can add whole stems into stir-fries and soups, and the flavours will subtly infuse into the dish. Diners can then decide whether or not they want to pick the peppercorns off the stem and eat them. If you know you want to eat them, go ahead and pick the peppercorns off the stems before adding, and whenever you bite into one it'll be a burst of heat in your mouth!

How to Store Dry Spices:

Cool, dark, and dry is, again, the mantra. Many people keep spices near the stove for convenience, which is fine, as long as the heat from the stove doesn't get to them. Heat activates the release of fragrance from the spices, and you want to make sure that this only happens when the spices are in your food, not in the cupboard! Keep them in a tightly closed container, and if you haven't used a spice for a while, smell it before using to make sure it's still potent.

Sweeteners

PALM SUGAR : *Namtaan Bpeeb* น้ำตาลปี๊บ

Palm sugar is so tasty I sometimes eat it like candy! It's made by reducing and caramelizing the nectar collected from either coconut trees or sugar palm trees. We also drink the unreduced nectar of the sugar palm tree as a refreshing, sweet beverage. Unlike granulated sugar, which provides only sweetness, palm sugar also offers a deep, butterscotch-like flavour.

How to Buy: Palm sugar comes in two major forms: hard and soft. The soft kind is sticky and can be messy to use but it dissolves more readily, so I prefer it in cold applications. Unfortunately, I haven't had much luck finding it outside of Thailand. The hard type comes in little pucks, large pucks, or tubs. It doesn't matter which type you get, but look for one with a deep tan colour rather than yellow as this is a sign of good caramelization and fuller flavour. Some poor-quality palm sugar has granulated sugar mixed in, resulting in a coarser texture and a weaker flavour.

How to Use: You can shave solid pucks with a big chef's knife like you would shave a block of chocolate. Then, I usually run my knife through the shavings to get rid of big chunks. You can also grate the pucks using graters of various sizes, depending on how quickly you need it to dissolve. I try to avoid the solid mass that comes in a tub or a jar, but if that's what you have, heat it in the microwave briefly to soften and spoon out what you need. It will solidify again as it cools down, so work quickly!

How to Substitute: The best substitute for palm sugar really depends on the dish. Thai people usually use granulated sugar as a substitute, and while it won't replace the flavour, it also won't introduce any new flavours that might clash with the dish. However, if palm sugar is a major component of the dish and you want to retain the richness of flavour, try playing around with brown sugar, maple syrup, agave syrup, golden syrup, or honey, and see what works best for that particular dish. If the substitute has a strong, distinct flavour, such as maple syrup or honey, you can mellow it out by combining it with white sugar. I've recently seen granulated "coconut sugar" on the market, which is technically made from the same nectar as palm sugar, but the flavour may differ due to differences in processing.

GRANULATED SUGAR : *Namtaan Sai* น้ำตาลทราย

Thai people didn't always use as much granulated sugar as we do now, but since it is much easier to use than palm sugar, it has quickly worked its way into every Thai household. We sometimes use white sugar when we want to maintain the white colour of a dish, especially in desserts. My rule of thumb is that if sweetness plays a major role in that dish, using palm sugar will make a difference in flavour. But for a small, supporting role, granulated sugar will be just fine.

BROWN SUGAR : *Namtaan Sai Dang* น้ำตาลทรายแดง

Brown sugar plays a very small role in Thai cooking, but deserves a mention nonetheless. It is used in some soups or desserts when a dark colour and/or a subtle molasses flavour is desired.

SUGAR CANE : *Oy* อ้อย

Though not a common source of sweetness, fresh sugar cane is sometimes added to soups in chunks to slowly infuse its sweetness. Fresh sugar cane juice is also enjoyed as a refreshing beverage. As a kid, I used to love chewing on cubes of sugar cane to extract the juice and then spit out the fibres like chewing gum.

Top to bottom: *Soft palm sugar, hard palm sugar, granulated sugar, brown sugar*

Acids

We use sour fruits to provide acidity in our food, and the two most commonly used fruits are lime and tamarind. Vinegar is rarely used as an ingredient in a dish, but is used often in condiments and dipping sauces.

LIME : *Manao* มะนาว

Limes are probably the most commonly used acid in Thai cuisine, and thankfully they are quite widely available. The citrusy freshness of lime juice stands out best in cold and light dishes, such as salads, dips, and light, brothy soups. You can add lime juice to hot dishes, but it should go in at the very end because cooking lime juice deteriorates its flavour. Interestingly, we do not use lime zest in our cooking, possibly because Thai limes are very small and have thin skins that can't be easily zested like the big limes in North America.

Always, always, always use freshly squeezed lime juice in Thai cooking. When lime juice is used in Thai dishes it's usually a major flavour component, and you will compromise the dish greatly if you use that yukky, bottled, shelf-stable stuff! If you cannot find fresh limes, use freshly squeezed lemon juice instead.

TAMARIND JUICE : *Nam Makaam Piak* น้ำมะขามเปียก

Tamarind fruit comes in a hard pod with a dark brown, sticky flesh, much like dates. There are many varieties of tamarind, ranging from very sour to very sweet. We eat the sweet ones whole and cook with the juice of the sour ones. The acidity of tamarind juice is not as sharp as lime juice and has a hint of sweetness. It holds up well in heavier dishes, such as curries, and it can be cooked for an extended period. Sometimes tamarind is used in combination with lime juice to produce a more complex acidity; this is commonly done in green papaya salad.

You can find ready-to-use tamarind juice on the market, which is usually labelled "tamarind concentrate." Unlike lime juice, the flavour of tamarind juice is more stable, making the commercially sold juice a very good option in most dishes. However, the level of acidity varies significantly between brands, and even batches, so always treat the amount indicated in a recipe as a rough guideline only. You can also buy tamarind pulp compacted into a block. You have to soak it in hot water to soften, then squeeze out the juice and strain off any fibres or seeds.

It's important to note that there is a product from India that is also labelled "tamarind concentrate." This is not the same kind we use, so when you shop, check that it is a product of Thailand or Vietnam.

Store-bought tamarind juice lasts several weeks in the fridge once opened, and it can be frozen indefinitely. If you make the juice from the pulp, it won't last as long because it has not been heat-treated, so it's best to keep the extra juice in the freezer. If you have a lot to freeze, making tamarind ice cubes, or freezing it into a flat disc, makes it easy for you to take only as much as you need.

WHITE VINEGAR : *Nam Som Sai Choo* น้ำส้มสายชู

Unlike Western cuisine, we don't have a variety of fancy vinegars to choose from. We have one: the humble white vinegar. It's rarely added to food during the cooking process, but it's used often in condiments and dipping sauces, such as our dipping sauce for chicken and fried foods (recipe p.211).

Salting Agents

Thai cuisine has several salting agents for you to choose from, each with its own unique character, so here is where you get to have some fun!

FISH SAUCE : *Nam Pla* น้ำปลา

This is my favourite sauce in the kitchen and the primary salting agent in Thai cuisine. Fish sauce may not taste good on its own to many people, but it blends well with other seasonings and boosts the umami quality of a dish. It also has a sharper flavour than soy sauce. Good-quality fish sauce should be reddish-brown and transparent enough that you can see through the bottle. If it is opaque and dark brown, it's a sign that the fish sauce is old, and what is supposed to be "good fish smell" will turn into "bad fish smell." Unless you use fish sauce on a regular basis, I recommend storing it in the fridge, tightly closed, to slow down the aging process.

SOY SAUCE : *See Ew* ซีอิ๊ว

Not all soy sauces are created equal, and soy sauces used in Thailand are quite different from those used in other Asian countries. We use several types of soy sauce, but the following are the most common. Also check out my video on Thai salty sauces (QR code below) where I go through each of them in detail!

Salty sauces

Regular Soy Sauce: I'm using "regular" as a qualifier because it's the closest thing to most people's idea of "soy sauce," even though Thai soy sauce has a unique flavour. In Thai it is called *see ew kao*, or "white soy sauce," even though it's not white. It's termed white to highlight the fact that its colour and consistency are much lighter than our "black soy sauce."

Left to right: *oyster sauce, fermented soybean paste, mushroom soy sauce, seasoning sauce, sweet soy sauce, fish sauce, black soy sauce, regular soy sauce*

In my recipes I refer to this simply as "soy sauce," and you may use other types of regular or light soy sauce as a substitute. If you're using a non-Thai soy sauce in my recipes, I recommend not adding all of it at once, reserving some for final adjustment, just in case it is saltier.

Mushroom Soy Sauce: We call this *see ew kao hed hom*, and it is simply regular soy sauce infused with shiitake mushrooms. You can use this interchangeably with regular soy sauce, and which one to choose is a matter of personal preference. You may have noticed in many of my videos that this is what I use as my regular soy sauce. I should note that mushroom soy sauces from other countries are not necessarily the same as ours, so do not assume that you can use non-Thai mushroom soy sauce as your regular soy sauce.

Black Soy Sauce: *See ew dum* is named after its main purpose: to add "black" colour to food, which is actually closer to dark brown, such as in *pad see ew* (recipe p.158). It is mildly salty and slightly sweet, with a molasses flavour and a thicker consistency than regular soy sauce. It can be unpleasantly bitter if used excessively, so a little goes a long way. Do not confuse this with the similar-looking sweet soy sauce described below.

Sweet Soy Sauce: Known in Thai as *see ew waan*, this isn't an essential part of your Thai pantry as it's used mostly in dipping sauces rather than as an ingredient in a dish. Nonetheless, it's worth mentioning because it's often confused with the black soy sauce described above. The two sauces are both black and thick, but sweet soy sauce is much sweeter and is more viscous. It also doesn't darken the food as intensely as black soy sauce, so it cannot be used as a substitute.

SEASONING SAUCE : *Sauce Proongrot*
ซอสปรุงรส

This type of soy sauce doesn't have an English name, so I've translated it literally to "seasoning sauce" from its Thai name. It's essentially a type of soy sauce with a different flavour and a slightly more intense colour and aroma. It's usually used in combination

Clockwise from top left: Seasoning sauce, black soy sauce, regular soy sauce, fermented soy paste

with regular soy sauce and/or oyster sauce to achieve a more complex result. There are many brands but the most commonly known outside of Thailand are Golden Mountain Sauce and Maggi Seasoning. Note, however, that these two do not have the same flavour, so what you choose will be a matter of preference. If you cannot find it, simply use regular soy sauce as a substitute. As a side note, we love to drizzle Maggi Seasoning over our boiled or fried eggs!

> *"When we use flavoured salting agents such as soy sauce . . . we are introducing more flavour to the dish. Adding salt, on the other hand, merely brings out the flavours that are already there."*

SALT : *Gleua* เกลือ

In savoury food, Thai cuisine rarely uses salt as the primary salting agent; it is more often used in combination with other seasonings. I often use salt to boost the seasoning power of fish sauce in certain dishes where too much fish sauce could be overpowering, such as in a milder flavoured soup like *tom ka gai* (recipe p.118). I also find salt to be handy in the final, taste-and-adjust stage of cooking when I am happy with the overall flavours but need them to pop out more distinctly.

It's important to understand that when we use flavoured salting agents such as soy sauce or fish sauce, we are introducing more flavour to the dish. Adding salt, on the other hand, merely brings out the flavours that are already there. My chef instructor in culinary school put it this way: "When you properly salt a potato, the potato doesn't taste like salt—it just tastes more like a potato." This is why salt is used in essentially every Thai dessert—it accentuates the existing flavours of the ingredients without introducing any new, unwanted taste. No one would want to eat desserts salted by fish sauce!

Another unique quality of salt is that, unlike other salting agents, it's dry and white. So when you need to boost the seasoning of a dish without any added liquid or colour, such as in marinades or in food preservation, salt is your friend.

Straight-up, I prefer sea salt to table salt, because it has a more pleasant, ocean-like flavour. However, in most cases, this difference is negligible when met with the many complex flavours of Thai dishes, so whatever salt you have on hand will be fine.

OYSTER SAUCE : *Nam Man Hoi* น้ำมันหอย

Oyster sauce is used most often in stir-fries and in combination with other salting agents. It was originally a Chinese ingredient, and stir-frying is a Chinese cooking technique, which explains why these two often go together. Oyster sauce is widely available and you need not look for ones that come from Thailand. However, look for brands that list "oysters" or "oyster extracts" as the first ingredient because poor-quality brands use few oysters and a lot of artificial flavourings.

FERMENTED SOYBEAN PASTE : *Tao Jiew* เต้าเจี้ยว

Tao jiew has a deep tan colour and a thick, chunky consistency (photo on facing page), as it contains whole or crushed soy beans. It's not used as often as the other salty sauces, but the best substitute for it is Chinese salted black beans or diluted Japanese miso paste. You can watch how I use *tao jiew* in my *rad na* and *kao mun gai* episodes (QR codes below).

Rad na

Kao mun gai

Various curry pastes at the market

Other Important Ingredients

CURRY PASTE : *Prik Gaeng* พริกแกง

Most people think of curry pastes as being the base for curries, but we use it in so many other wonderful ways: stir-fries, marinades, sausages, dips, fish cakes, and even custards. So, think of curry pastes simply as a mix of herbs and spices that you can use to flavour your food. There are no limits to what you can do, so don't let the word "curry" hold back your imagination!

What are curry pastes made from? Different pastes vary significantly, and while there are some traditional mixes, there really are no rules. Having said that, there are some common ingredients. Most curry pastes contain shallot, garlic, chilies (dried or fresh), galangal, lemongrass, and shrimp paste (*gapi*). We also often use cilantro roots, kaffir lime zest, white peppercorns, fingerroot, turmeric, ginger, cumin, and coriander seeds.

To make? Or to buy? Some people feel like they're cheating by using store-bought curry pastes . . . like making pancakes from a box mix. Let me tell you what my family in Thailand does, it's simple and logical: if we have the time and the ingredients, we make it. If we don't, we buy it. Some curries have relatively simple pastes, such as *gaeng som* (recipe p.111), so we tend to make them. Others have a long list of herbs and spices, such as *massaman*, so we buy those pastes more often.

I enjoy making curry pastes because I think it is fascinating to witness how separate ingredients blend and transform into a delicious paste. More importantly, it will help you understand where the complex flavours come from. So, I encourage you to try it as part of learning about Thai cuisine. That said, there is no shame in keeping a few packets of pre-made pastes in the cupboard for a quick weeknight dinner—that's what I do!

"Making curry paste will help you understand where the complex flavours come from . . . [but] there is no shame in keeping a few packets of pre-made pastes for a weeknight dinner."

Caution! When cooking with store-bought curry pastes, be prepared to adjust for spiciness and saltiness because they differ greatly between brands. If you are spice-sensitive, it's a good idea to start with less or have extra liquids around so you can dilute the dish if it turns out to be too spicy.

COCONUT MILK : *Gati* กะทิ

When I was a kid, making coconut milk was a regular kitchen task. My nanny would crack a mature coconut into two halves, and I would then grate the meat into tiny shreds to "milk" it. Sometimes we would get lazy and buy pre-grated coconut meat from the market, since the milking is the easy part. Nowadays, a modernized, hurried lifestyle has led many city-dwelling Thai people to buy pre-made coconut milk.

In North America, pre-made coconut milk comes in several forms: canned, in UHT cartons, frozen, creamed, powdered . . . and I'm sure there are others I have yet to discover. Conversely, in Thailand, there are only two types: UHT cartons and pasteurized bags (like those old-school milk bags). The sad fact is that none of these are as good as the freshly made variety. Having said that, I've had the best experience with 100% UHT coconut milk that comes in shelf-stable cartons—the same kind we use in Thailand. Not all UHT cartons are 100% coconut milk, though, so make sure you check the label.

Canned coconut milk usually contains additives, such as preservatives, stabilizers, emulsifiers, or thickeners, resulting in a thicker consistency and altered flavour. Different brands vary significantly because of these variables.

Separation of Coconut Milk

Coconut milk is made up of fat-based and water-based portions that exist in an unstable emulsion. If you let coconut milk sit for a while, you will notice a creamy, fatty layer that floats on top of a thin, watery layer, just like salad dressing. If you cook coconut milk for a long time, the emulsion becomes more unstable, and eventually the coconut oil completely separates from the coconut milk (i.e., the emulsion is broken). In Thai curry making, this is desirable because the oil becomes a beautiful, colourful sheen on the surface of the curry. Once the oil separates, the curry paste is added and sautéed in the "broken" coconut milk, so traditionally, there is no added oil in a coconut-milk-based curry.

Homemade coconut milk separates easily, but commercially produced ones are more stable. I usually have to reduce my UHT coconut milk until very thick before the oil separates, and some brands have been processed to prevent separation altogether. So, if the separation doesn't happen, you can still proceed with the recipe and sauté the curry paste in the reduced coconut milk. I have seen products labelled as "coconut cream" that advertise their easy-separation quality on the label (though this is written in Thai) because they are made specifically for Thai curries. Unfortunately, they seem to be quite elusive, so stock up if you find them!

Reduced and separated coconut milk

THAI CHILI PASTE : *Nam Prik Pao* น้ำพริกเผา

Thai chili paste is mildly spiced and tends to be on the sweet side. We use it in soups, stir-fries, and salads, and even as a spread for snacks. If you've tried the famous soup *tom yum goong*, then you've probably tasted *nam prik pao*! Its major ingredients are dried chilies, shallots, garlic, and dried shrimp, which are pounded together and cooked in oil. I have seen many English names for this product, including "Chili Paste" and "Chili Paste with Soya Bean Oil." To make sure you have the right one, ensure it is dark red in colour with a layer of red oil on top. Most importantly, make sure it's a product of Thailand.

SHRIMP PASTE : *Gapi* กะปิ

This funky-smelling, purplish-brown paste is a specialty of the south of Thailand. The term "shrimp paste" is a slight misnomer, because it's made from fermented krill, not shrimp. It's used in curry pastes, dips, and stir-fries. A little shrimp paste is usually all you'll need as it's very salty, but it adds a punch of umami and a unique aroma that many Thais just adore. It's not a must-have ingredient in your pantry, except when you're ready to start making your own Thai curry pastes. To see shrimp paste in action, check out *nam prik gapi* (recipe p.199) or my shrimp paste fried rice video (QR code below).

PRESERVED RADISH : *Chai Po* ไชโป้

This isn't an ingredient that is used often, but I'd like to mention it because it is used in our most famous dish, *pad thai. Chai po* is daikon radish that has been preserved in salt and sugar. There are two varieties that unfortunately look the same: salty (*chai po kem*) and sweet (*chai po waan*). The sweet kind is what goes into *pad thai*, and the salty one is often eaten with plain rice porridge. *Chai po* has a tan colour and usually comes in plastic bags either whole or chopped into various shapes.

Shrimp paste fried rice

Thai chili paste

Different types of shrimp paste at the seafood market in Mahachai

PANDAN LEAF : *Bai Toey* ใบเตย

Pandan leaves are to us what vanilla is to Western desserts. It's the most widely used flavour in Thai desserts, and its unique floral aroma pairs especially well with coconut, our main dessert ingredient. The leaves are dark green, thin, and long. There are two main ways to use pandan leaves: 1) infuse the leaves by simmering them in liquid, and 2) blend the leaves with some water until fine and then strain; the resulting juice provides both a fantastic fragrance and a beautiful green colour (this method is used in *Tako*, recipe p.218). Frozen pandan leaves are available at many Asian grocery stores, and they are the best alternative to fresh leaves. Canned pandan leaf juice and artificial pandan flavouring are also available, but use them only if necessary.

Pandan leaves

RICE : *Kao* ข้าว

I've already touched upon the importance of rice in Thai meals in Chapter 1, but here I want to discuss the choice of rice. You can have Thai food with any kind of rice you wish, but if you want to "go all out," I recommend Thai jasmine rice, which is what we most commonly eat with our meals. You should be able to smell the floral aroma of good-quality jasmine rice as soon as you open the bag, and the fragrance should persist if the rice is stored in a well-sealed container.

If you like the idea of brown rice for its healthfulness but prefer the softness of white rice, give brown jasmine rice a try. It tends to be less chewy and fibrous than short-grain brown rice, and the jasmine fragrance helps soften the flavour of the bran. A good way to start is to mix white and brown jasmine rice; since they take about the same amount of water, they cook up beautifully together. See also, *Cooking the Perfect Rice*, p.233.

Old-Crop Rice vs New-Crop Rice: You may have heard about "old-crop" and "new-crop" rice. "New-crop" simply means that the rice is harvested and sold within the same season; in other words, it's fresher. Old-crop rice must be stored for at least one season before selling, during which time the rice continues to dry. In Thailand, we even have "mid-year rice," which is somewhere in between.

New-crop rice requires less water to cook, and the result is more fragrant, softer, and stickier. Because old-crop rice has been dried longer, it is firmer and not as fragrant, and requires more water.

I prefer new-crop rice for plain rice because of its aroma and softness, but old-crop rice is better for fried rice because 1) it's more mush-resistant, and 2) the grains separate more easily in the pan.

New-crop rice is often labelled as such, so if there is no label, assume it is old-crop or somewhere in between.

What about Fruits and Vegetables?

I like to say that authentic dishes come from authentic ingredients, but what if you're living in a place where you're lucky if they have any papaya at all let alone green papaya?

Fresh exotic produce is hard to find in many parts of the world, and if it exists, freshness is often compromised, because the goods have been transported from far away. There is also a great movement supporting local agriculture. In light of this, I say to be easy on yourself and use whatever is available in your area. It's a chance for you to exercise your cook's brain and think about what other vegetables might work in a particular dish. Should a need to substitute arise, I highly recommend you read *How to Make an "Educated Substitution,"* p.60.

For example, I use the inside stalks and leaves of regular celery in place of Chinese celery. Broccoli or kale also work well where Chinese broccoli is traditional. I love Swiss chard and have used it successfully in many Thai dishes. So, here is where you can have some fun!

The recipes in this book call for whatever vegetables are commonly used for that dish in Thailand. For hard-to-find produce, I will make recommendations for substitutions or make them optional.

Thai cucumber (top), Thai eggplant (left), and long beans (right)

Top to bottom:
*Sen yai, bamee,
woon sen, sen lek,
sen mee*

NOODLES : *Sen Guay Tiew* เส้นก๋วยเตี๋ยว

Noodles came to Thailand with Chinese immigrants and have since become an integral part of Thai cuisine. The following are the major types of noodles used in Thai cuisine. You can learn more about them by watching my *Top 5 Noodle Soup* video (QR code below).

Sen Yai: These are the flat, wide rice noodles known as *ho fun* in Chinese, prized for their satisfying chewiness. They are available in fresh as well as dry forms, but the fresh ones tend to be chewier, which I prefer. They are relatively easy to make, and I have a video tutorial showing how this is done (scan QR code below). *Sen yai* used for stir-frying tend to be thicker and wider than the ones used for noodle soups, because they need to hold up to aggressive tossing.

Sen Lek: These are the skinny rice noodles that you get in Vietnamese *pho*, and indeed, they really shine when used in noodle soups. We don't make many stir-fries with *sen lek*, but it's certainly an option for you.

Sen Pad Thai/Sen Jan: The name says it all! They're what we use for *pad thai* and similar stir-fried noodle dishes such as *pad mee korat*. These are rice noodles, slightly larger than *sen lek*. They absorb flavours well and have a great chew when cooked properly.

Sen Mee: These thread-thin rice noodles are the smallest of all types, great for noodle soups, stir-fries, and even salads. I love the texture of *sen mee*, because they are so small, you get more noodles in every bite, and it just feels like there's a lot more going in your mouth!

Bamee: These are different from the types discussed above in that they are egg noodles made from wheat flour. Being made from wheat, *bamee* have a unique flavour and are also more resistent to being overcooked.

Woon Sen: *Woon sen*, also known as glass noodles, cellophane noodles, or bean threads. They are made from mung bean starch and are white when raw but turn clear when cooked. Their neutral flavour makes them incredibly versatile—we make soups, salads, and stir-fries with them, and there's even a dessert made from a similar type of noodles called *sarim*!

Kanom Jeen: These round, tender rice noodles are unique in that they are served in a very particular way: they're not used in soups or stir-fries, but are most often served drenched in a variety of spicy sauces made specifically for them. They are essentially the same as the Vietnamese *bun* noodles. In Thailand, *kanom jeen* are always sold fresh, but in North America, dry ones are available, usually labelled "rice vermicelli" or "rice sticks."

Sen Mama: I debated whether I should include these in the book, but concluded that they deserve a spot because they have real cultural significance. *Mama* is Thailand's best-known brand of instant noodles, and the name "*mama*" has become a generic term for any instant noodles. *Sen mama* refers to just the noodles, sans seasoning, which we use in soups, stir-fries, and even salads! The flavour of these crispy fried wheat noodles is deliciously distinct from other types, and oh, did I mention we also eat them dry as a snack?

Top 5 noodle soups

How to make fresh rice noodles

THE IMPORTANCE OF STOCK

My chef instructor in culinary school said, "Use stock. There's no love in water." He was speaking in the context of French cuisine, but I believe this to be true in any cuisine. A good stock enhances the flavour of a dish, and it does this in the most subtle of ways.

I've tested this out with *rad na*, a noodle dish with a light gravy-like sauce. I made it three times with different liquids for the sauce: water, store-bought Western-style stock, and homemade Thai-style stock. The results were startling. The store-bought stock had a distinct, overwhelming flavour that didn't match the dish. Water yielded a dish that tasted "weak," even though it was sufficiently seasoned. Finally, the homemade stock created a well-balanced, bold-flavoured sauce that somehow filled the mysterious flavour void of the water-based sauce.

A Note on Store-Bought Stock or Broth: Liquid, paste, powder, or cubes, whatever form it comes in, store-bought stock is usually pre-seasoned with salt, sugar, and/or MSG, and this robs your ability to have complete control over the seasoning of your dish. Even the ones labelled "no salt added" may still have other seasoning added. Secondly, unless they're made for Asian cuisine, store-bought stocks are made with classic French or Western flavours, using aromatics that may result in a flavour mismatch with Asian food.

I understand that making stock from scratch isn't always practical for busy people with a modern lifestyle. One solution is to make a lot of stock in one batch and freeze it for future use (see recipe, p.232). If you don't have ample freezer space, however, this might still pose a problem. So, my rule of thumb is this: it's perfectly fine to have store-bought stock on hand for a quick weeknight dinner, but if you are cooking a special meal in which you have invested time, effort, and money, a little extra time spent on making a good stock will be well worth it. It isn't as much of a hassle as you might think—you're more or less just boiling bones!

The Role of Stock: A good stock should be devoid of salt, sugar, or any other seasoning. It should taste bland on its own because its role isn't to be the star of the dish. A stock's role is to add body, complexity, richness, and a subtle, almost unidentifiable "flavour boost." In a movie analogy, the stock is the camera work, sound, and lighting that help create a level of production quality that the good acting and story alone can't achieve.

Thai people are not generally strict about what vegetables and aromatics to use in making stock; in fact, my stock changes depending on the ingredients I have on hand! I've included my version of basic Thai-style chicken and pork stocks in this book, but truthfully, if your stock has nothing in it but bones and water, you're already far, far ahead of the game.

Where to Buy Thai Ingredients

This is the question almost everyone asks when they start cooking Thai food. Ideally, you want to look for a store that caters primarily to Thai people, but few of us are blessed with such a store. Your next best chance will be Southeast Asian grocery stores—particularly those that are Cambodian, Lao, and Vietnamese—because these cuisines share many ingredients we use.

Chinese grocery stores are your next bet, as many of our ingredients are of Chinese origin. I haven't had much luck at Korean and Japanese stores, but they're still worth a look if all else fails. Remember that many non-Thai stores will carry some Thai ingredients because they want to include multiple ethnic groups in their customer base.

Of course, there is always online shopping. If you're willing to pay for shipping, you can get just about every Thai ingredient, equipment, and, depending on where you live, even exotic fresh produce from online retailers. You can find several online Thai grocers, based in various parts of the world, just with a quick search on the Internet. You can also buy many items through more general e-commerce sites such as Amazon and eBay.

My Best Tip for Looking for Thai Ingredients: The most effective way, by far, is to ask your local Thai restaurants. Chat with a few friendly Thai employees or the owner and ask them where THEY go to shop for Thai ingredients. Many Thai grocery stores are small, family-run places with little or no online presence, but they thrive because they are well known within the Thai community.

How to Make an "Educated Substitution"

I could give you a list of substitutions for all Thai ingredients, but beyond the fact that it would be impractically lengthy, it's out of alignment with my philosophy. Instead of giving you a proverbial fish, I'd rather teach you how to fish so you will always have the ability to figure it out on your own.

Consider the Function: Every ingredient is added for a reason, and once you know what that is, you can figure out how it can best be substituted. I understand that trying to substitute an ingredient you've never tried is a bit like trying to draw something you've never seen, but reading about the ingredients in this chapter should give you an idea of their major characteristics. Be thorough in your consideration, because one ingredient often has multiple functions. Think about:

Significance: Does it play a major role? Is it the major flavour? Or just one of many? How obvious or subtle would it be if it were missing? I recommend considering this first to determine if it can simply be left out, or how critical it is that the substitute be very similar.

Flavour: Is it salty, sweet, sour, spicy, bitter, umami?

Aroma: Think about the unique, identifying fragrance of the ingredient. Is it minty, citrusy, refreshing, pungent, fishy, earthy? Finding the right word to describe it will help you find a substitute.

Texture: Is it a crisp or a soft vegetable? Are they chewy or tender noodles? Is it providing a necessary textural variety? You'll be surprised how much texture contributes to the overall quality of the dish.

Consistency: Is it thick, creamy, watery, or dry? This concerns the sauce or the dressing of the dish.

Colour: What colour does it add, and will the dish look as appetizing without it?

Volume: Does it contribute to the bulk of the end product? If so, make sure you replace it with something with similar volume.

Different Dish, Different Sub: Because an ingredient may have different roles depending on how it's used in that dish, what you use as a substitute isn't constant. For example, say I wanted to make a salad vegan and I needed to replace the fish sauce. In a salad, fish sauce adds saltiness and umami flavour, and also makes up the volume of the dressing. If I replace it with salt, I will lose half the dressing, resulting in a drier salad, and I will be missing the fish sauce flavour, which plays a major role in a Thai salad. Soy sauce would be a better substitute in this case, because it is also a liquid and has substantial umami flavour.

In a green curry, on the other hand, fish sauce contributes saltiness, but doesn't add much volume. Green curry also has very strong flavours from all of its herbs, so the missing flavour in the few teaspoons of fish sauce won't have a big effect. In this case, either salt or soy sauce would be a fine substitute.

Leaving It Out Might Be an Option: Remember that not all ingredients are necessary. After considering the function of the ingredient, you might realize that the dish would probably still be good without it. The iconic Thai dessert mango and sticky rice, for example, is traditionally served with crispy mung beans. The dessert will still be delicious without them, and in fact, some Thai people don't even bother with them.

In another example, most curry pastes contain shrimp paste, but sometimes it's only a small amount. Other ingredients in the paste also have highly potent flavours, so leaving out the one teaspoon of shrimp paste will still yield a delicious curry paste, and you can always adjust the saltiness later when you're making the curry.

Some ingredients are so unique that they simply cannot be substituted with similar results. Galangal is a good example. I have not come across another herb with an aroma similar to galangal, so in this case, you should first look for alternative forms—dry, frozen, powdered—and then look online. Alas, there may come a time when you will have to leave it out or use another ingredient and accept that the dish will taste different, which isn't always a bad thing!

Thai Food for People with Dietary Restrictions

Thai food can be a boon or a booby trap, depending on what your dietary requirements are. So, here is a quick run-down of tips for working around some common allergies, intolerances, and restrictions.

Nut Allergies

If you're allergic to tree nuts, no worries except for the rare instances of cashews. A peanut allergy, however, can be a concern. While Thai cuisine has been associated with peanuts, the majority of Thai dishes are actually peanut-free. If you have a severe peanut allergy, when you eat in Thailand or at Thai restaurants, the real cause for concern is cross-contamination. Very few Thai people have food allergies, which means that cooks are not generally concerned about cross-contamination of allergens. Yet another reason to learn to cook Thai food yourself!

If a recipe calls for peanuts, it's usually fine to leave them out or substitute another kind of nut you can eat. Soy nuts, sunflower seeds, and pumpkin seeds are also great non-nut substitutes.

Vegetarians & Vegans

Unfortunately, Thai food is full of hidden animal products. Fish sauce is in almost everything we make, and if not, then there is oyster sauce to watch out for. Shrimp paste is a standard ingredient in almost all curry pastes, but some brands of pre-made curry pastes do omit it, so you should always read the label before purchasing. Note also that Thai chili paste (*nam prik pao*) contains dried shrimp.

Some Thai restaurants may call certain dishes "vegetarian" even though they contain these ingredients (fortunately, this is becoming less common

Peanuts and cashews are the two most common nuts in Thai cuisine.

with increased awareness). Be suspicious when a meat dish on the menu can be made vegetarian; some restaurants will merely swap out meat for tofu and vegetables, keeping the same non-veg sauce. This is why learning to cook Thai food is particularly helpful for vegetarians and vegans—you can have control over every ingredient.

Vegan Fest! If you are vegetarian or vegan, the best time to go to Thailand is during the Nine Emperor Gods Festival, when millions of people follow a strict vegan diet for nine days. In Thailand, this festival is called *tesagaan gin jay*. I use the word "vegan" loosely, because the dietary restrictions for eating *jay* are stricter than the Western concept of vegan. In addition to all animal products, eating *jay* also prohibits pungent foods such as garlic, garlic chives, and onions, as well as foods that are highly salty, acidic, sweet, or spicy. So, remember that truly *jay* dishes are mildly flavoured—but mild flavour doesn't mean that they weren't well prepared!

Vendors selling *jay* food can be identified by the display of a yellow flag with red writing. The dates for the festival change every year according to the lunar calendar, but they usually fall within September and October.

Gluten Intolerance

Celiacs rejoice, Thai food is your friend! Well, most of it. Wheat is not a tropical crop, so it's not commonly used in our cuisine. Gluten in Thai food usually comes hidden in soy-based seasoning, such as soy sauce and some brands of oyster sauce. This means that many stir-fries are off-limits. When cooking your own Thai food, all these soy-based seasonings can be substituted with gluten-free soy sauce. Curries, salads, and dips are usually safe, as well as most traditional

Thai desserts. However, as wheat flour has become more widely available in Thailand today, some newer desserts are not gluten-free. Also, watch out for deep-fried foods—the batter may contain wheat flour, and even unbattered items may be dredged in wheat flour.

Lactose Intolerance

Again, I have good news! There is zero dairy in all Thai food in its traditional form, and none of my recipes in this book contain dairy. A large percentage of Southeast Asians are lactose intolerant, so you may notice that there is little to no dairy in our cuisines. Anything that appears creamy in Thai cuisine will most likely be made of coconut milk.

But of course, even dairy didn't escape modernization. Milk is now a promoted beverage for children in Thailand, and milk products such as sweetened condensed milk and evaporated milk have become widely used in drinks and, to a lesser extent, desserts. A few savoury dishes have modern variations that contain evaporated milk, such as *tom yum* soup and *moo ping* (barbecued pork skewers).

Fish and Shellfish Allergies

This may or may not be an issue depending on the severity of the allergy. There are many hidden seafood ingredients in Thai food, particularly fish sauce, oyster sauce, shrimp paste, and dried shrimp. The actual content of fish and shellfish that end up in the end product is usually very small, so it may be tolerable for some people. But if even the tiniest trace will trigger a reaction, then cooking your own Thai food is the best solution, as you always know exactly what you put in it. Note that shrimp paste or *gapi* is actually made from krill, so if you are allergic to shrimp, you may be fine eating *gapi*.

3. Equipment & Tools

Tools for Thai Cooking

There are a few nonstandard pieces of equipment used in Thai cuisine; however, after years of cooking I have discovered that if all you owned was a knife, a pot, and a frying pan, you could still pull off most Thai recipes. For years I tried to keep my equipment inventory to a minimum since I was living a nomadic lifestyle, and I still managed to cook most of my favourite Thai dishes.

So, if you don't have any of these items, I am by no means suggesting that you need to go out and buy them. But if you have the desire, the funds, and the storage space, most of the listed tools are also useful for non-Thai cooking and can be fun to play around with. I will talk about the nonstandard cookware in detail, but here's the bird's eye view of Thai cooking tools.

Need	Nice to Have
• Sharp chef's knife* • Paring knife • Cutting board • Large and small good-quality sauté pans* • Small and medium heavy-bottomed pot • Large stock pot • Peeler • Strainer • Tongs • Spatula (for stir-frying) • Rubber spatula (for scraping) • A large spoon or ladle • Some type of steamer* • A device for grinding, such as a mortar and pestle, food processor, or coffee grinder	• Heavy-duty stone mortar and pestle* • Clay/wood mortar and pestle* • Wok* • Large (14-inch) steamer* • Julienne peeler*

See detailed descriptions

MORTAR & PESTLE

Or is it pestle and mortar? Whatever it is, I can quite confidently say that I grew up using our mortar and pestle almost every day. In Thailand, the sound of the granite pestle pounding against the mortar resonates from almost every kitchen, and indeed the sound takes me right back to my childhood, when my main task in the kitchen was to pound whatever needed to be pounded (mostly because I was too young to be entrusted with a knife!).

We use our mortar and pestle often because Thai cooking involves a lot of pastes, which we use for just about anything: curries, stir-fries, marinades, dips, etc. In my Bangkok home, we have a whole family of mortars and pestles ranging from little baby ones for small tasks to a large "granddaddy" size one.

The Two Major Mortar & Pestle Types

The first, and arguably the more useful, type is the heavy-duty stone version, usually made from granite. It's incredibly heavy for its size and is therefore great for things that need to be ground up into a fine paste or powder.

The lighter, less versatile type is the clay or wood mortar that comes with a light wooden pestle. The bowl of the mortar is usually larger and deeper than its stone counterpart, because its main purpose is to make *som tum*, or papaya salad, so it needs to be able to hold more volume. It is also ideal for light crushing; for example, I often use it to roughly crush peanuts or to roughly pound garlic and chilies for stir-fries.

My family's collection of mortars and pestles

Do I need both? Need? No. You don't even need one if you don't plan on cooking Thai food on a regular basis. If you want only one type, I recommend the heavy-duty stone one, purely for its versatility. Not to mention, you can still make papaya salad without the clay mortar, which I did for my very first papaya salad video on Hot Thai Kitchen!

Where do I buy them? Mortars and pestles are becoming more popular in non-Asian kitchenware stores, but they are often the smaller, light-duty types. For Thai-style mortars and pestles, try looking wherever you buy your Thai groceries, as many of these stores also carry tools and equipment. Asian kitchen supply stores are also a good place to start.

> *"In Thailand, the sound of the granite pestle pounding against the mortar resonates from almost every kitchen."*

Can I use a blender or a food processor instead? There are hundreds of electric grinding devices to choose from, and they will work for certain tasks. The major caveat for these is that a minimum volume is required in order for it to grind properly, which is great if you want to make a large batch of curry paste to freeze. They also work better with either completely dry or fairly fluid products; the in-between thick, moist pastes, such as curry pastes, tend to stick to the sides of the bowl, so you may need to add extra liquid.

I usually make small amounts of pastes at a time, so the mortar and pestle are ideal for me. They allow me to grind anything of any amount and thickness, plus I think they are easier to clean. However, I do use a coffee grinder regularly for grinding dry ingredients, such as dry chilies.

WOKS & PANS

For the first several years of my life I only knew of pots and woks. Only in my teenage years did I discover flat sauté pans, and that was when we started experimenting with Western food. When we say "pan" (*gata*) in Thai, it's assumed to mean wok.

So, woks always seemed an indispensable kitchen tool to me, but when I left Thailand and no longer had a wok-friendly gas stove, I had to learn to work with sauté pans. That was when I discovered that nearly everything I could do in a wok, I could also manage in a good, large sauté pan. So, don't be discouraged if you don't have the space (woks are huge!) or the right stove; you can make delicious Thai food without one. I even started Hot Thai Kitchen without a wok, and continued to be without one for years.

Benefits of Woks

Although they are not necessary, if circumstances allow, woks are awesome to have for a few reasons.

Large Bowl: Their large size makes woks perfect for stir-frying. Because you never have to worry about spilling food, you can stir and toss as vigorously as your heart desires, allowing food to cook more evenly.

Direction of Heat: Wok-specific burners are curved to conform to the rounded bottom of a wok. This allows the flame to come up the sides and surround the food rather than coming only from below as when cooking with flat-bottomed pans. This is also why modern flat-bottomed woks designed to work with Western-style flat stoves don't quite replicate traditional wok cooking.

Less Oil for Frying: Woks are the perfect deep-fryer because the rounded bottom means less oil is needed to achieve the required depth than in a flat-bottomed pan. The wok's wide mouth also makes it easier to fry large amounts of food, making it the deep-fryer of choice for most street vendors.

Steamer: My family uses a wok to steam some dishes by putting a round perforated rack into the wok, which serves as a steamer rack. Then all you need is a lid and you're good to go!

One Size Fits All: Finally, the bowl shape allows you to cook a small amount of food, such as sauces, without quickening moisture loss through too much surface area. This is why most Thai homes have only one wok, which we use for nearly everything, large and small, but Western kitchens usually have a few sauté pans of different sizes.

Choosing a Sauté Pan for Thai Cooking

If you're sticking with flat-bottomed sauté pans, not a problem! Here are some points to keep in mind:

Large, Slope-Sided: Most of the time in Thai cooking, you'll be using your pan for stir-frying, so you will need one large enough to be able to toss the food around comfortably. A 12-inch pan is sufficiently large without being overly heavy. You may also want to have

smaller ones of about 8 and 10 inches for small jobs, like toasting rice. I prefer a slope-sided pan, rather than straight-sided, because it allows you to toss and flip ingredients easily without using utensils. (And learning how to toss and flip can be very useful.)

"When we say 'pan' (gata) in Thai, it's assumed to mean wok."

Heavy & Sturdy: In the world of sauté pans, better quality usually means heavier, because thicker materials distribute heat more evenly. I'm not partial to any particular material, so I will leave that to you to decide. You may want to keep in mind that a well-seasoned wok is virtually nonstick, which is important for cooking stick-prone foods, like eggs or fresh rice noodles. So, a pan with a nonstick material (which could even be a well-seasoned cast-iron skillet) is useful for these tasks.

Most street vendors choose woks for deep-frying.

STEAMER

Steaming is an important part of Thai cuisine, particularly for making desserts. In my family, we steam something at least once a week and we prefer it to the microwave for reheating certain foods, because it yields a moist product that is evenly heated throughout.

Most Thai homes have a multi-tiered aluminum or stainless steel steamer that is at least 14 inches in diameter, mostly because we often steam whole fish. The ability to add multiple tiers is also great for steaming a few dishes at the same time.

"In my family, we steam something at least once a week and we prefer it to the microwave for reheating certain foods."

If you don't plan on steaming large amounts of food, the other option is to use a steamer rack and place it in a large pot with a lid. These racks are available, in various sizes and heights, at many Chinese grocery stores. As I mentioned previously, a wok with a lid can also be transformed into a steamer by placing a rack inside it.

In Thailand, particularly in the North and Northeast, we use a bamboo cone steamer made specifically for steaming sticky rice. It makes the best-tasting sticky rice, because it infuses a subtle bamboo aroma into the rice and yields the best chewy texture, in my experience. But it is a single-function piece of equipment that takes up a lot of room, so unless you cook sticky rice on a regular basis, I consider it a nice-to-have-if-convenient tool.

THAI-STYLE JULIENNE PEELER

This is a fun tool that is admittedly unnecessary, but because it's inexpensive and small, there isn't much of a cost or storage barrier. This julienne peeler makes rounded strings, perfect for *som tum* or papaya salad. In fact, that's what this tool is made for. You can also use it to julienne carrots for any salad. I often use it to peel vegetables such as kabocha squash, cucumber, and potatoes to create decorative wavy edges. They are a little harder to find, but you can look for them at Asian grocers or Asian kitchen supply stores.

Note: This is not the same as the Western-style julienne peeler, which yields much thinner juliennes and is usually twice the price!

WHAT ABOUT AN OVEN?

Oven? What oven? Baking and roasting are not part of Thai cooking techniques, especially not for home cooking, and you may have noticed this from my Hot Thai Kitchen videos. In fact, most homes in Thailand don't have ovens or any space designated for them.

There are a handful of desserts that require baking in the oven, but those were originally baked in coal-fired chambers that were owned only by people who made these desserts en masse, usually for sale.

A NOTE ABOUT KNIVES

Having a sharp knife can make a huge difference in your cooking experience. With a sharp knife you will cook faster, you will work more safely, and your food will look better. I'd take a cheap, sharp knife over an expensive dull knife any day, so your knife does not need to be fancy as long as you keep it sharp. Having said that, high-quality knives will stay sharper for longer and are more durable.

4. The Structure of Thai Dishes

WHAT IS THE "STRUCTURE"?

Recently, I had the opportunity to give a one-hour workshop titled "Demystifying Thai Cuisine." How do you demystify Thai cuisine, or any cuisine for that matter, in less than an hour!? So, I thought hard about how I could present practical, immediately usable information about Thai food, without resorting to overwhelming details. That was when I discovered the concept of "structure."

> *"Once you become familiar with the ingredients and structures of Thai dishes, you will be free from the boundaries of recipes and you will have the confidence to experiment and create your own Thai dishes."*

What do I mean by "the structure" of a dish? Let me give you an analogy. If you were to make a car, you'd need to have wheels, seats, an engine, a body, etc. Those make up the structure—the parts common to all cars regardless of what kind of car you are making. Within each of these structures, however, you can play around with the details as much as you'd like—you can customize the design, the choice of materials, the type of engine, and the list goes on.

In the same way, if you were to make a Thai curry, for example, there are a few components that you'd need to have in order for it to be a Thai curry, but you can then fine-tune the details however you wish: the vegetables, meat, herbs, liquid, seasoning, etc.

Here's the best part: once you become familiar with Thai ingredients and understand the structures of Thai dishes, Thai food will begin to look different to you. You will start seeing patterns across dishes. You will be able to identify the components of a new dish and you will be able to recreate it at home. You will look at Thai recipes with a new-found understanding of the role of each ingredient and the reasons behind the methods. Most excitingly, you will be free from the boundaries of recipes and you will have the confidence to experiment and create your own Thai dishes!

Cooking Thai food without recipes may sound impossible to some, especially if you're the type that likes to follow recipes to a tee. If this is how you feel, just remember what I said in *Getting Over the Fear of Ethnic Cuisine* (p.22). And, of course, it will take practice. After following enough recipes, especially if you make each recipe multiple times, what seems now like an intimidating, foreign cuisine will soon feel like it's within your comfort zone.

In The Pages Coming Up . . .

I've divided Thai dishes into categories and I will discuss the structures of the four major categories: curry, soup, salad, and stir-fry. These four types of dishes make up most of what we regularly eat at home, because they are relatively simple to prepare and do not require any special equipment. I will also go over the general procedures for each of these categories.

The role of steaming, grilling, and deep-frying will be touched upon briefly. These cooking techniques involve more elaborate setup and breakdown or require special equipment, so they are not used as frequently in a home setting.

Dips also deserve a mention because they are a major part of the Thai diet, even though they are essentially unknown outside of Thailand.

Finally, I will include an overview of Thai desserts to start familiarizing you with the common ingredients and cooking techniques used, even though it is a huge subject that could be an entire book in itself.

CURRY

Curry แกง

A curry in Thai is loosely translated as *gaeng*. I say "loosely translated," because what may be considered a *gaeng* in Thailand may not necessarily strike you as being a "curry." Curries are usually thought of in the Western world as being thick, rich, stew-like dishes that are full of spices. This is true of some Thai curries, but we also have curries that are thin, light, and brothy, which look more like a soup. Here's what it takes for a dish to be a classified as a *gaeng*.

The Structure of a Thai Curry

The Paste: Curries get their flavour from a paste of herbs and spices, i.e., a curry paste. This is what distinguishes a curry from most soups. A handful of Thai curries have become popular across the world—*massaman*, green, red, and yellow curries—but there are many more. In fact, there are infinite types of curries because you can create your own, which people do! There are many curry paste recipes for you to explore in *Part 2* of this book and also on my website. See also *Curry Paste*, p.51.

The Liquid: A curry can be water-based or coconut-milk-based. When making a water-based curry, I recommend using stock rather than plain water for the best flavour. Choose coconut milk if you're looking for a richer dish, although most of the time a coconut-milk-based curry also uses water or stock to balance out the consistency so as not to be unpalatably heavy. The amount of liquid is also adjustable; most curries have a lot of liquid, like a bowl of soup, but some others are *kluk klik*, which means saucy but not soupy. *Panang* curry is an example of a *kluk klik* curry.

The Nuggets: For lack of better terms, this is what I call all of the edible pieces in the curry: the meat, the vegetables, and the herbs. You have complete freedom here! There are some common combinations for each type of curry, and I will use those in my recipes, but there really are no rules, so use whatever your palate desires!

The Seasoning: The standard seasoning for a curry is fish sauce and a bit of sugar to balance out the saltiness. Some curries also have an element of acid from either lime juice or tamarind juice, with tamarind juice being the preferred choice for richer, heavier curries.

General Procedures for Making a Curry

Once you have decided on the curry paste, the liquid, the nuggets, and the seasoning, there are generally two methods of curry making: sauté-the-paste and no-sauté methods. I have provided the general procedures for each method so you can get the big picture, but the exact steps may vary depending on the nature of your ingredients. I recommend that you also study the instructions of the curry recipes in *Part 2* and try to identify repeating patterns and differences. Once you truly get this, you can make any Thai curry without a recipe!

Sauté-the-Paste Method: This method is used mostly with coconut-milk-based curries, but it can be used with water-based curries as well.

1. Sauté the curry paste, either in oil or in reduced and separated coconut milk (see *Separation of Coconut Milk*, p.52). This enhances the flavours of the herbs and spices. Keep your heat low since the curry paste can burn, and add a little of the liquid to deglaze if the paste is sticking to the pan. After 3–4 minutes, or as I like to say, until the whole house can smell it, add your liquid and stir to mix.

2. Bring the liquid to a boil to infuse the flavours of the paste into the liquid.

3. Add the seasoning, followed by the meat and vegetables. Time the adding of your meat and vegetables so that everything will finish cooking together.

4. Taste and make final adjustments to the seasoning.

5. Remove from the heat and stir in the finishing herbs.

No-Sauté Method: This method is usually used with simple curry pastes with fewer herbs and spices such as *gaeng som* (recipe p.111). It's also used mostly for water-based curries. Because there is no added fat, the resulting dish is light and "goes down easy," which is perfect when it is paired with fattier, richer dishes.

1. Bring the liquid to a boil, then add the curry paste and stir until the paste is dissolved. Simmer the curry for a few minutes to cook the herbs and infuse the flavours into the broth.

2. Add the seasoning, followed by the meat and vegetables. Time the adding of your meat and vegetables so that everything will finish cooking together.

3. Taste and make final adjustments to the seasoning.

4. Remove from the heat and stir in the finishing herbs.

Note: For both methods, if using lime juice, stir it in at the end because lime juice tastes best when uncooked.

What about browning meat? If you are familiar with making Western-style stews, you may be accustomed to searing the meats to develop colour and flavour before deglazing the pan with the liquid. This is not a step that is commonly done in Thai cooking, but it's certainly an option for you.

Curry paste being sautéed in separated coconut milk.

Curry Overview and Examples

Structure	Examples
Paste	• All types of curry pastes such as red, green, *panang*, etc.
Liquid	• Water • Stock • Coconut milk
Nuggets	• Meat, poultry, and seafood • Vegetables • Herbs
Seasoning	• Salty: Fish sauce, salt • Sour: Lime juice, tamarind juice • Sweet: Palm sugar, granulated sugar

SOUP

Soup ต้ม

Thai soups usually carry the prefix *tom* in their names, and you may recognize names such as *tom yum* or *tom ka*. In many ways a soup is similar to a curry. The main difference is that a soup usually uses an infusion of herbs and spices rather than a paste. Soups also tend to be lighter in both flavour and body.

Unlike in Western dining cultures, soups are served with all other dishes and are not meant to be a first course. In fact, the concept of "courses" in a meal doesn't exist in the Thai dining culture. Thai soups are always served with rice, generally with other dishes as part of a meal. You can pour the soup over rice, add some rice to your individual soup bowl, or eat the soup on its own, letting the broth wash down other dishes as you enjoy your meal.

Exceptions to the norm. Now that we have talked about what makes a soup and what makes a curry, there is an important point to mention: there are, of course, exceptions to these norms. An obvious example is something called *gaeng jeud* or *tom jeud*, which literally means "bland curry" or "bland soup." (The fact that it goes by two names is quite telling of its ambiguous identity.) It's a mild and comforting soup that uses pork stock as a base. One can flavour *gaeng jeud* by pounding cilantro roots, garlic, and white peppercorns into a paste, which would make it more of a curry according to my definition. But it's also common for people to simply let these herbs infuse, more like a soup. The point is that the prefixes *tom* and *gaeng* in the name are consistent most of the time, but not always. So, consider them a general rule of thumb, but don't get too hung up on it! See recipe on p. 129.

"In many ways a soup is similar to a curry. The main difference is that a soup usually uses an infusion of herbs and spices rather than a paste."

Coconut galangal soup with dried gourami (tom ka pla salid)

The Structure of a Thai Soup

The Infusion: By infusion, I simply mean letting the herbs and spices hang out in the simmering liquid to extract their flavours, without any intention to eat them afterwards. Sturdy herbs, discussed in Chapter 2, are commonly used as infusions. Less frequently, we use spices like cinnamon, star anise, and coriander seeds. Traditionally, we serve the soup with the infused herbs still in it, but Thai people commonly know that they are not meant to be eaten. This may not be obvious to your guests who are unfamiliar with Thai food, and they can be a hazard, so please let them know ahead of time or remove the herbs altogether.

The Liquid: Like curries, soups can either be water-based or coconut-milk-based. Again, I recommend using stock instead of plain water for water-based soups. Since soups in Thai cuisine are meant to be light (we don't do thick, creamy soups), coconut milk is never used as the only liquid in soups and is always diluted with water or stock.

The Nuggets: Exactly the same as in curries, the nuggets are the edible pieces such as meat, vegetables, and herbs. Go crazy and experiment with anything you like here!

The Seasoning: Fish sauce, lime juice, tamarind juice, and sugar are common seasoning for soups. Lime juice tends to be used more than tamarind juice because the freshness of the lime shows up well in light soups. If tamarind juice is used, it is often used in combination with lime juice.

General Procedures for Making a Soup

Again, these guidelines are just to give you an idea; the exact methods will depend on the nature of your ingredients.

1. Bring the liquid to a boil and add the infusions. Sturdy herbs only take a few minutes to infuse, but hard spices such as cinnamon and star anise take longer.

2. Add the seasoning, followed by the meat and vegetables. Time the adding of your meat and vegetables so that everything will finish cooking together.

3. Remove from the heat, add lime juice (if using), then taste and adjust the seasoning.

4. Stir in the finishing herbs.

Soup Overview and Examples

Structure	Examples
Infusion	• All sturdy herbs and spices
Liquid	• Water
	• Stock
	• Coconut milk
Nuggets	• Meat, poultry, and seafood
	• Vegetables
	• Herbs
Seasoning	• Salty: Fish sauce, salt, soy sauce
	• Sour: Lime juice, tamarind juice
	• Sweet: Palm sugar, granulated sugar

SALAD

Salad

There is no one word in the Thai language that would convey the same meaning as the English word "salad." So I am using the word "salad" to refer to dishes that are made by mixing together ingredients with a dressing. There are a few types of salads in Thai cuisine, namely *yum, pla, laab, nam tok,* and *tum.* In general, Thai salads are protein-heavy and don't involve many leafy salad greens like typical Western salads. Like our soups, our salads are not meant to be an appetizer—they are served with all other dishes.

> *"There is no one word in the Thai language that would convey the same meaning as the English word 'salad.'"*

The Structure of a Thai Salad

The Protein: Perhaps contrary to your intuition, protein is the star of Thai salads. Other components don't vary as greatly, but just about any protein imaginable is used to make Thai salads, including meats and seafood that are grilled, ground, blanched, fried, dried, "sausaged," and everything in between. We also use eggs and tofu in various forms. Occasionally, we make salads using noodles or mushrooms as the main ingredient instead of protein.

The Vegetables: As I mentioned, we don't normally use leafy salad greens. The vegetables are really there to serve as an element of freshness and crunch, so think crisp or juicy vegetables such as cucumber, onions, Chinese celery, tomatoes, and nuts (we're going to count nuts as a vegetable for now!). Occasionally, we serve green leaf lettuce alongside salads as an edible garnish.

The Herbs: Both sturdy herbs and finishing herbs can be used in salads, keeping in mind that fibrous herbs such as lemongrass should be finely chopped in order for them to be eaten comfortably. You could use any herbs you like, but common choices are green onion, cilantro, mint, sawtooth coriander, lemongrass, galangal, kaffir lime leaves, and shallots. Thai and holy basils are not commonly used in salads, but they certainly can be.

The Dressing: Unlike Western-style salads, Thai salads don't come with a plethora of dressings that can fill an entire supermarket aisle. In fact, most people make salad dressings from scratch because they are so wonderfully simple. Essentially all Thai salad dressings are variations of this basic formula: lime juice, fish sauce, sugar, and some type of chilies. I will discuss these variations in the following section about different types of Thai salads.

Previous page: Laab, a Northeastern salad of ground meat and mint

The Five Major Types of Thai Salads

There's not much to say about the methods for making a salad, except to mix everything together! So, I will take this opportunity to discuss what the five major types of Thai salads are.

1. *Yum* is the most loosely defined salad. You can *yum* just about any combination of anything, but the basic *yum* dressing always includes these four ingredients: lime juice, fish sauce, sugar, and fresh chilies. With this basic dressing, you can create endless kinds of *yum* by varying the other components and adjusting the ratio of sour, salty, sweet, and spicy to match your ingredients. To add a little more complexity, you can pound garlic and cilantro roots (or cilantro stems) into a paste and add it to the basic dressing. For a richer salad, we add chili paste (*nam prik pao*) and/ or coconut milk to the dressing. *Yum* features the refreshing acidity of lime juice as the main flavour, but it is almost always balanced by a hint of sweetness. Some common proteins for *yum* are grilled steak, blanched seafood, glass noodles, and fried eggs. Example: *Yum Kai Dao*, p. 134.

2. *Laab* is a Northeastern salad made with ground meat or ground seafood of any kind. *Laab* can involve many ingredients, but the must-haves are mint, cilantro, green onion, toasted rice powder, and shallots. Technically, sawtooth coriander is also a must-have, but since it is hard to find outside of Thailand, we can consider it optional. *Laab* dressing is simply lime juice, fish sauce, and chili flakes. While sugar rounds off the acid in a *yum*, there is no added sugar in a *laab*, so the nutty toasted rice powder fills this important balancing role. Example: *Laab Bped*, p. 144.

3. *Nam tok* is essentially the same as *laab* but with one major difference: the meat is grilled and then sliced thinly, rather than ground. *Nam tok* means "falling water" or "waterfall," and it refers to the dripping of the fat through the grill grates onto the fire. Example: *Nam Tok Neua*, p. 147.

4. *Pla* is our version of ceviche, where the acid from lime juice is used to cook some types of protein, specifically seafood and beef. *Pla* features plenty of thinly sliced lemongrass and a dressing similar to *yum*'s. It's an old cooking technique that is quickly disappearing, possibly due to fear of food-borne illnesses, and the word *pla* nowdays seems to refer simply to a *yum* that contains a lot of lemongrass. Example: *Pla Neua*, p. 140.

5. *Tum:* *Tum* means to pound using a mortar and pestle, and that is exactly how these salads are made. The poster child of *tum* is the world-famous *som tum* or green papaya salad. Even though green papaya is the most popular type, *tums* can be made using any ingredients you can imagine, from corn, cucumber, green apples, pickled crab, Thai eggplant, guava, carrot, pomelo, salted duck eggs, and even rice noodles. The dressing is typically made with garlic, fresh Thai chilies, fish sauce, lime juice, palm sugar, and tamarind juice. In the Northeast, it's common to add fermented fish paste (*pla ra*) to the dressing, making their style of *tum* saltier and with the funky smell that many love so much. Example: *Som Tum*, p. 150.

Salad Overview and Examples

Structure	Examples
Protein	• Ground/blanched/grilled/cured meats, seafood, eggs, etc. • Non-protein exceptions: mushrooms, noodles
Vegetables	• Non-leafy vegetables and nuts, e.g., tomatoes, Chinese celery, cucumber, onion, banana blossom, peanuts, etc.
Herbs	• All sturdy and delicate herbs
Dressing	• Fish sauce • Lime juice • Granulated sugar or palm sugar • Fresh chilies, chili flakes, or chili paste • Coconut milk

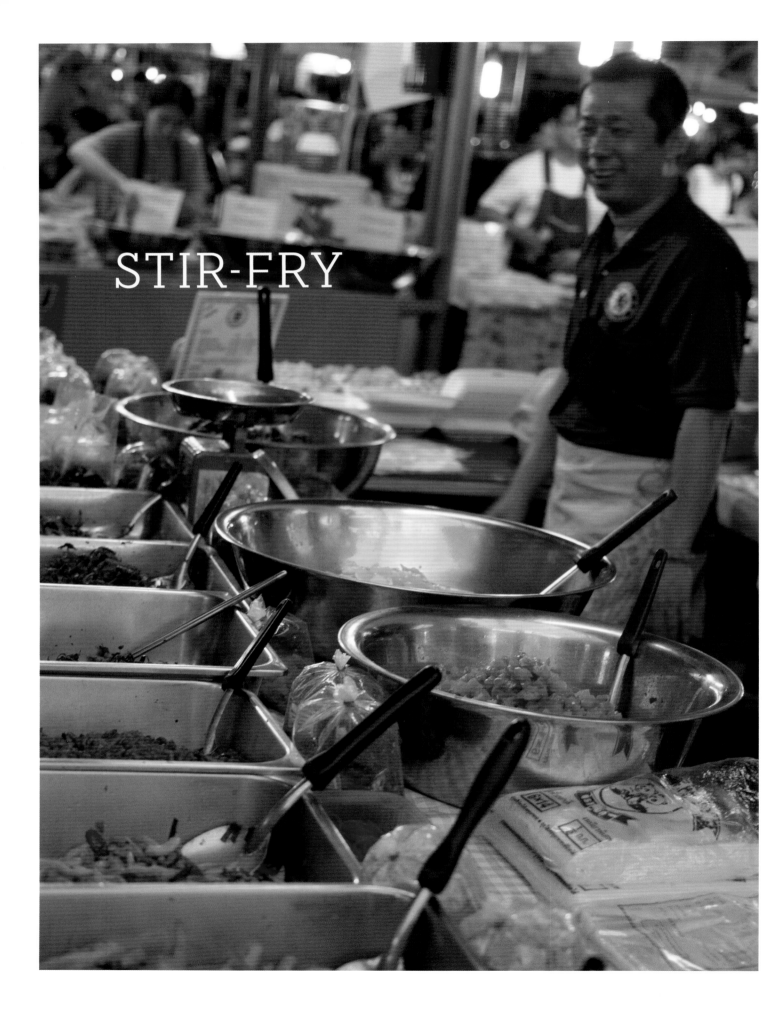

STIR-FRY

Stir-Fry ผัด

Pad means to stir-fry, and when we say *pad* we're also referring to all pan-fried noodles and fried rices. The technique of stir-frying in a wok was introduced to Thai people by the Chinese, so many Thai stir-fries will bear similarities to Chinese dishes both in flavour and ingredients. Over time, however, Thai people have applied this technique to dishes with Thai flavour profiles. So, when you look at stir-fries in Thailand today, you'll see two major styles: Chinese and Thai, and of course, there are hybrids of the two.

"The technique of stir-frying in a wok was introduced to Thai people by the Chinese, so many Thai stir-fries will bear similarities to Chinese dishes both in flavour and ingredients."

Chinese-style stir-fries use oyster sauce and the various types of soy-based seasonings discussed in Chapter 2, which were originally Chinese ingredients. They are light on the use of herbs, and the flavour tends to be primarily salty. Most dishes are not spicy in themselves, but many are served with a spicy condiment on the side (after all, it's for Thai people!). Example: *Pad See Ew*, p.158.

Thai-style stir-fries tend to be spicier and are much more heavy-handed with herbs such as lemongrass, kaffir lime leaves, Thai basil, etc. Curry pastes are also often used as a flavour base. Fish sauce, palm sugar, and tamarind are the main seasonings. The flavour profile is more of a mix between salty, sweet, and sour. Example: Red Curry Stir-Fry with Tilapia, p.166.

Hybrids often have a Chinese-style seasoning and flavour profile, but with added heat from chilies and added complexity from Thai herbs. Example: Holy Basil Chicken Fried Rice with Fried Egg, p.177.

The Structure of a Stir-Fry

The Aromatics: Aromatics include herbs and spices, which can be chopped or pounded into a paste. Any herbs or any curry pastes can be added to a stir-fry, so feel free to experiment! If using finishing herbs, remember to add them at the end to retain their fragrance and green colour.

The Nuggets: These are the bulk of the dish: meats, vegetables, eggs, rice, and noodles. It is common for people to visualize a stir-fry that contains both meat and vegetables, but many dishes contain only meat or only vegetables. Eggs are often scrambled into stir-fries. Since proteins are cut into bite-sized pieces, be careful not to cook them any longer than necessary because small pieces overcook quickly. Also, choose tender cuts of meat since you won't get a chance to slow-cook it until tender. Some ingredients are precooked or partially cooked before adding to the stir-fry, and this is done for different reasons depending on the nature of the ingredient. See also Tips for Making a Stir-Fry, p.82.

The Sauce: The sauce is made up of all seasoning ingredients and sometimes added liquid. All the salting agents discussed in Chapter 2 are available for you to play with. In some dishes, sugar is added for a distinct sweet flavour, but often it's just there to balance the salt and the sweetness is barely detectable. When acidity is desired in stir-fries, we use tamarind juice because it holds up through the intense heat better than lime juice. (See Tamarind Shrimp recipe on p. 168.) Water, stock, or coconut milk can be added if you want extra sauce to spoon over your rice.

Tips for Making a Stir-Fry

The procedure for a making a stir-fry varies greatly depending on the ingredients used, so I will simply give you some useful stir-frying tips.

1. Stir-frying goes very quickly once it starts, so make sure all the ingredients are ready to go and within arm's reach before you turn on the heat.

2. When using fragile ingredients, such as fish and tofu, deep-frying them ahead of time will firm them up and prevent crumbling.

3. For vegetables that take a long time to cook, such as big pieces of eggplant or broccoli, you can par-cook them beforehand by blanching or deep-frying.

4. Always start out by sautéing aromatics whose flavours benefit from cooking in high heat, such as garlic, chilies, and curry paste. These aromatics will also flavour the oil, which will help distribute flavours throughout the dish.

5. Time the adding of your ingredients so that they will finish cooking at the same time.

6. Always have some water or stock on hand to adjust the amount of sauce or to deglaze the pan if needed.

7. As always, toss in the finishing herbs at the very end to maintain their green colour and freshness.

Stir-Fry Overview and Examples

Structure	Examples
Aromatics	• Any herbs and spices • Curry pastes
Nuggets	• Meat, poultry, and seafood • Vegetables • Eggs • Rice • Noodles
Sauce	• Salty: all salting agents • Sweet: granulated or palm sugar • Sour: tamarind juice • Others: stock, coconut milk, chili paste *(nam prik pao)*, shrimp paste *(gapi)*

DESSERTS

Steamed coconut custard in mini kabocha squash, topped with threads of candied egg yolk

Desserts ของหวาน

When people think about Thai desserts, mango with sticky rice may come to mind, but little else. For some reason, Thai desserts haven't quite made it big overseas, even though Thai people eat desserts as often as any other nation, and there are just as many types of Thai desserts as there are French pastries. There is so much I could write about on this subject, but I will touch upon the key points here.

Desserts by Cooking Techniques

Baking is the most common method of making Western desserts, but in Thailand most people don't even have an oven. So, our desserts are almost never baked. Instead, they are steamed, boiled, stirred, candied, and fried. A handful of desserts are also grilled, although like most grilling in Thai cuisine, it's usually left to street vendors and restaurants.

The following is an overview of the five most common dessert cooking techniques. I have also provided a recipe for each of these techniques in *Part 2*.

Steamed นึ่ง

The steamer is to the Thai kitchen what ovens are to the Western kitchen. We steam batters, mixtures, custards, and doughs, which can be contained in cups or trays, or wrapped in banana leaves which infuse their subtle, foresty aroma into the dessert. For example, we make our version of banana cake by steaming the batter in banana leaf cups. The batter is made from mashed *namwa* bananas, coconut milk, coconut meat, and rice flour. This dessert is called *kanom gluay*, and it's what my mom always makes with the overripe fruit from our *namwa* banana tree. Steaming is also the most common method for making desserts containing sticky rice.

Boiled ต้ม

Thai desserts can be as simple as boiling fruits, beans, grains, or roots in a sweetened liquid. For example, bananas are boiled in sweetened coconut milk (*gluay buad chee*) and mung beans in simply sugar and water (*tua kiew tom namtaan*). This is in some ways similar to the French fruit compote.

Stirred กวน

By "stir" I mean stirring a batter constantly over heat to a desired consistency, much like how pastry cream is made. The cooked product is then shaped or put into a mold, and firms up as it cools. For example, one of my favourite dessert noodles, *sarim*, is made by stirring a mung bean starch batter on the stove until thickened. The cooked batter is then poured into a bucket with a perforated base and pressed so the noodles come out the bottom. They are served cold in a scented coconut soup with crushed ice—it's essentially a dessert noodle soup.

Candied เชื่อม

In the context of Thai desserts, candying is defined as cooking something in a concentrated syrup until it becomes saturated with sugar. The end product, however, isn't dried and crystallized like candied ginger. It is moist, tender, and often drenched in a thick, glossy syrup. We candy many different foods such as bananas, cassava, and even egg yolks!

Fried ทอด

Fried desserts can also be thought of as sweet snacks, and you can find them easily on the street and in open-air markets. They can take the form of battered-and-fried items, such as fried taro and fried bananas (recipe p.225), or some are fried doughs such as *kai nok grata*, which are like little beignets made from sweet potato!

Dessert Soup

I remember serving my non-Thai friend a bowl of *faktong gaeng buad* for dessert (recipe p.223). It took her a while to wrap her head around the concept of having soup for dessert (not to mention a squash soup!). It hadn't occured to me until then that Western desserts rarely, if ever, come in soup form. For us, warm or iced dessert soup is one of the most common types of sweets. You might think making a dessert soup requires boiling everything in a pot, but not always; for example, *kao niew turien* is a dessert soup made simply by pouring a coconut syrup over fresh durian and sticky rice—my dad's favourite!

Dessert Ingredients

A wonderful parallel can be drawn between Thai and Western dessert ingredients. This is because most desserts, regardless of ethnicity, can be deconstructed into a few basic components: starch, sugar, fat, liquid, flavouring, and add-ins. To make it easier for you to conceptualize, I have created a table on the following page comparing the differences between major Thai and Western dessert ingredients.

Namwa *bananas, the most frequently used fruit in Thai desserts*

Common Thai vs Western Dessert Ingredients

Components	Western	Thai
Starch Main structure of the dessert	• Wheat flour • Oats • Less frequently: cornstarch and other flours used in gluten-free baking	• Flours: rice flour, glutinous rice flour*, tapioca starch, mung bean starch • Sticky rice: white and black • Beans: black and mung beans • Root vegetables: cassava, sweet potato, taro • Kabocha squash • Less frequently: wheat flour, arrowroot starch, cornstarch
Sugar Sweetens and tenderizes	• White, granulated sugar • Brown sugar • Honey • Syrups: maple, corn, etc.	• Palm sugar • White, granulated sugar • Less frequently: brown sugar
Fat Tenderizes and moistens	• Dairy products: butter, cream, cream cheese, etc. • Vegetable oil	• Coconut milk • Vegetable oil
Liquid Binds, moistens, eggs give structure	• Dairy products: milk, cream, yogurt, etc. • Eggs (chicken) • Water	• Coconut milk • Eggs (duck and chicken) • Water
Flavouring	• Vanilla • Chocolate • Coffee • Fruit flavours • Mint	• Pandan leaves (see p.54) • Jasmine water • Aromatic candle smoke (*tien ob*)
Add-ins	• Nuts and seeds • Dried fruit • Chocolate chips • Fresh fruit	• Coconut meat • Beans (black and mung beans) • Nuts and seeds • Fresh fruit, e.g., *namwa* bananas, durians, jackfruits, mangoes

Glutinous rice flour is also known as sticky rice flour, and it is made from the same sticky rice that we use in cooking.

Of Desserts and Banana Trees

Growing up in Thailand, we didn't have muffin tins or cake pans . . . but we had banana trees. In elementary school, we learned how to use banana leaves to create different types of containers for classic Thai desserts.

Each banana leaf had to be harvested, cleaned, aired out, cut, and then made into little containers . . . one for each individual piece of dessert. Looking back, it seems laborious, but I remember enjoying it and didn't think it was work because it was all I knew—there was nothing to compare it to.

The lives of Thai people have long been bonded with the humble banana tree. Every part of the tree plays a role in our lives—the fruit, the flowers, the leaves, the stems, and even the trunk. If we don't eat it, then we make something out of it, be it functional, artistic, or recreational.

Today, when I sit down and make something out of banana leaves, I always feel a sense of gratitude for the banana tree. Thank you, banana tree, for always being supportive of the Thai way of living.

If you want to try making your own banana leaf cups, see the recipe for Tako, a layered coconut pudding, on p.218.

STEAMING, GRILLING, & DEEP-FRYING

Steamed buns with various fillings

Steaming, Grilling, & Deep-Frying

Since you probably don't use these cooking techniques frequently at home, I will touch upon them briefly so you get an idea of how they are used in Thai cuisine.

Steaming นึ่ง

As I mentioned previously, a steamer is to Thai cuisine what an oven is to Western cuisine. Steaming is our put-it-in-and-let-it-go kind of cooking, just like baking and roasting. We most often steam fish, shellfish, egg-based dishes, and desserts. It's a great cooking technique that maintains moisture in the food, which is why it is particularly great with fish and seafood, which easily become dry if overcooked.

Steaming Seafood: When steaming fresh seafood, the sauce is either steamed with the food or poured on the food after the cooking is complete. Steaming the sauce with the food allows the sauce to be absorbed, but this comes at a price. Water from condensation in the steamer and natural juices from the seafood collect on the plate, and while this liquid is often included as part of the sauce, one cannot control the amount collected. Adding the sauce from the beginning could cause the sauce to be too diluted if there is too much water. Adding the sauce after steaming allows the cook to pour off some water if there is too much. Some sauces, such as those that contain lime juice, also taste best when left uncooked.

Steaming Custards: A custard is simply a flavoured mixture of egg and liquid. The liquid could be stock, water, or coconut milk. Eggs, liquid, and flavourings are all combined before cooking. Sometimes pieces of protein or vegetables are added to the cup or bowl before pouring in the egg mixture, so they can be cooked right into the custard (just like pecan pie). Our most famous custard is *haw mok*, a red curry custard with fish steamed in banana leaf cups. Scan the QR code below for my *haw mok* recipe.

Haw mok

> *"A steamer is to Thai cuisine what an oven is to Western cuisine."*

Grilling ปิ้ง ย่าง

Grilling in Thailand is most commonly done on the street and in restaurants, but is not frequently done at home. In North America you can walk into any hardware store and buy a barbecue for your backyard or balcony, but in Thailand, they are pretty much non-existent. On the rare occasion that we grill something at home, we use what looks like a brick bucket filled with charcoal, with a metal rack placed on top.

Street grilling almost always uses charcoal as a heat source, which adds a unique smokiness not achievable with a gas grill. Many of our grilled products are skewered—pork, chicken, squid, bananas, and even a whole fish! Occasionally, you will also see grilled desserts, wrapped in natural materials such as banana leaves, palm leaves, or bamboo.

Deep-Frying ทอด

This is another common street food cooking technique, particularly for snack foods. Interestingly, I have noticed that deep-frying at home happens more frequently in Thailand than here. Perhaps this is because it's common for Thai homes to have an outdoor kitchen, which allows people to deep-fry without the house smelling like McDonald's for days!

Most people also own a wok, which makes deep-frying more convenient because the bowl shape allows less oil to be used, and its wide mouth gives you a large surface area to cook with. On the street you will often see vendors using massive woks for deep-frying for precisely this reason.

In addition to deep-frying the main ingredient of the dish, such as a whole fish or chicken wings, we also deep-fry many little things that are used as garnishes or as crispy components in another dish, such as dried chilies, holy basil leaves, garlic, shallots, and lemongrass. Also, because we don't have ovens, we often deep-fry nuts instead of roasting them.

Deep-frying is also used to pre-cook protein before incorporating it into a stir-fry. There are two main reasons for doing this: 1) Fragile proteins like fish and tofu crumble easily when tossed in a wok; when fried, however, they become firmer and crumble-resistant. 2) When certain meats and seafood are dredged in flour and fried, their surfaces become rough rather than smooth, which allows the sauce to adhere to them more easily. Tofu also develops this roughness when fried, but it doesn't need to be floured. See the recipe on p.193 for an example of this technique.

Rice crackers made by deep-frying dehydrated cooked sticky rice

Dips เครื่องจิ้ม

The One that Was Left Behind . . .

I feel that dips missed the boat when Thai food left Thailand to venture abroad, because rarely do I see dips on a Thai restaurant menu outside of Thailand. In some ways this is odd, because dips are as common in our diet as any other dish! In another way, it's completely understandable, because Thai dips have strong flavours that can be a bit of an acquired taste, which makes them "risky" food to offer to unfamiliar customers.

Dips are collectively known in Thai as *kreuang jim*. There are a few subcategories of dips, including *nam prik, lohn,* and *nam jim.*

Nam prik: Most types of *nam prik* are very spicy (after all, *prik* means chilies). *Nam prik* can be as simple as a bunch of raw ingredients pounded together in a mortar and pestle, such as *nam prik gapi* (recipe p.199), or they can involve cooking and more complex ingredients, such as *nam prik ong* (recipe p.200). We eat *nam prik* with rice, steamed and raw vegetables, and other proteins, such as boiled eggs, omelettes, fried fish, or crispy pork rind.

Not all *nam prik* are dips, however; some are actually dry and flaky, and have the added benefit of a longer shelf life. Dry *nam prik* is a spicy mix of chilies, herbs, and shredded, dried seafood, which is delicious when tossed in with some jasmine rice!

In many households, the family meal always includes a *nam prik* or it isn't considered to be complete. I have even heard that in the old days, Thai people used to plan other dishes in a meal to complement the *nam prik du jour!*

> *"I feel that dips missed the boat when Thai food left Thailand to venture abroad . . ."*

Lohn: Lohn is a category of creamy coconut-milk-based dips that are usually centred around a protein, such as ground pork and shrimp. Because there is protein and fresh coconut milk involved, *lohn* is always cooked. (Uncooked, fresh coconut milk spoils very quickly.) While *nam prik* is spicy with strong flavours that are primarily salty and sour, *lohn* is gentler with a well-rounded mix of sour, salty, and sweet. This is why I like to say that *lohn* is the dainty and delicate sister of *nam prik!* (For a *lohn* recipe, see p.204.)

Nam Jim: Unlike *nam prik* and *lohn, nam jim* are not stand-alone items; they are dipping sauces that complement other foods. For example, when we eat fried chicken, we often have it with *nam jim gai* (recipe p.211), or when we have grilled meats, *nam jim jeaw* is the perfect pairing (recipe p.209). The main difference is that *nam prik* and *lohn* are the star of the dish, while *nam jim* are supporting characters. So, you would ask, "What shall we eat with this *nam prik*?" but, "What *nam jim* shall we have with this dish?"

PART 2

Recipes

CURRIES
gaeng แกง

Thai coconut curries may be famous worldwide, but lighter,
water-based curries are no less common in Thailand.

COCONUT-MILK-BASED
Green Curry with Braised Beef Shank — *Gaeng Kiew Waan Neua*

Red Curry with Barbecued Duck & Pineapple — *Gaeng Ped Bped Yang*

Massaman Curry with Lamb Shoulder — *Gaeng Massaman Gae*

Pork Satay and Peanut Sauce — *Moo Sate*

Yellow Curry with Chicken & Potato — *Gaeng Garee*

WATER-BASED
Jungle Curry — *Gaeng Bpa*

Sour Curry with Thai Omelette — *Gaeng Som*

Green Curry with Braised Beef Shank

Gaeng Kiew Waan Neua

Serves: 4

Cooking Time: 2 hours + 30 minutes if making the curry paste

Special Tools: Heavy-duty mortar and pestle, or another device for making curry paste

Do-ahead Tips: Make the curry paste and braise the beef 1–2 days in advance. Or make the entire dish in advance, leaving the basil out until ready to serve.

1 lb	Boneless beef shank, bite-sized, 1/2-inch thick slices
2 cups	Coconut milk
1 recipe	Green curry paste (recipe follows) or 5 Tbsp store-bought
1 tsp	Salt
2 1/2–3 cups	Water
4	Kaffir lime leaves, torn into chunks
3 Tbsp	Palm sugar, finely chopped, packed
1–2 Tbsp	Fish sauce
2 cups	Bamboo shoots, julienned (see note)
1	Spur chili or 1/4 red bell pepper, julienned
3/4 cup	Thai basil leaves
For serving	Jasmine rice or rice vermicelli

Note: *Use pre-cooked bamboo shoots, which are available in cans or vacuum-packed plastic bags.*

Tip for Success: Remember that the rice will soften the curry's flavour when they are eaten together, so make sure the curry is strongly seasoned.

Gaeng = Curry; Kiew = Green; Waan = Sweet; Neua = Beef

Green curry gets its unique flavour from fiery green bird's eye chilies, which can also make it incredibly spicy. Any meat can be paired with any curry, but in Thailand certain combinations are more popular than others; for green curry, the usual pairings are beef, chicken, and, for some odd reason, fish cakes. I've chosen a tough cut of beef in this recipe to demonstrate how you can incorporate braising into your curry making, and it doesn't hurt that braising a tendon-rich beef shank yields a marvellously strong stock that further enriches the curry sauce.

. . . .

In a medium-sized pot, add the beef, 1/4 cup of the coconut milk, 1 Tbsp of the curry paste, and salt. Add enough of the water to completely cover the beef and bring to a simmer. Braise the beef, loosely covered, for 1 1/2–2 hours, or until the beef is fork tender. Add more water if needed to ensure that the beef stays submerged.

Remove the beef using a slotted spoon and set aside. Reserve 1 1/2 cups of the cooking liquid; if there isn't enough, add more water to make up the difference.

Reduce 3/4 cup of the coconut milk in a medium-sized pot over medium heat until very thick and the clear coconut oil starts to separate from the white portion, 10–15 minutes. (If this separation doesn't happen, just proceed with the recipe after reducing until thick—sometimes coconut milk is processed to prevent separation. See p.52 for more information.)

Add the curry paste to the reduced coconut milk and cook over medium-low heat for 3–4 minutes, stirring constantly, until the curry paste is very thick. Add the remaining 1 cup of coconut milk and stir to mix. Turn the heat up to medium-high and add the reserved beef cooking liquid, kaffir lime leaves, palm sugar, and 1 Tbsp of the fish sauce; bring to a boil.

When the curry boils, add the cooked beef and bamboo shoots; simmer for 3–4 minutes so they absorb the curry. Remove from the heat, taste, and adjust seasoning with the remaining fish sauce. Stir in the spur chilies and Thai basil.

Garnish the curry with the top of a Thai basil sprig and serve with jasmine rice. It's also common to pour green curry over rice vermicelli, pasta-style, for a one-dish meal.

(Continued)

Green Curry Paste

Toast the coriander seeds by adding them to a dry sauté pan and stirring constantly over medium-high heat until the seeds are aromatic and slightly darkened, about 4 minutes. Cool on a plate. Repeat with the cumin seeds.

Using a mortar and pestle, grind the toasted coriander seeds, toasted cumin seeds, and white peppercorns into a fine powder. Remove from the mortar and set aside.

Cut 8 of the green Thai chilies in half horizontally and, with a paring knife, scrape off and discard the seeds and pith, then finely chop along with the remaining chilies. *Note: The seeds and pith are removed from some of the chilies to tone down the heat.*

Add the chopped chilies and salt to a heavy-duty mortar and pestle; pound into a fine paste. If the mixture feels too wet at any point, add some of the ground spices to absorb the liquid.

Add the basil leaves; pound into a fine paste.

Add the lemongrass, galangal, kaffir lime zest, and cilantro roots; pound into a fine paste.

Add the shallots, garlic, and any remaining ground spices; pound into a fine paste.

Add the shrimp paste and pound to mix.

2 tsp	Coriander seeds
1 tsp	Cumin seeds
½ tsp	White peppercorns
15	Green Thai chilies (see note)
1 tsp	Salt
15	Thai basil leaves, finely julienned (see note)
3 Tbsp	Lemongrass, thinly sliced
1 Tbsp	Galangal, finely chopped
2 tsp	Kaffir lime zest, finely chopped
2 tsp	Cilantro roots or 2 Tbsp cilantro stems, finely chopped
3 Tbsp	Shallots, finely chopped
2 Tbsp	Garlic, finely chopped
1 tsp	Shrimp paste (*gapi*)

Note: The green colour comes primarily from the chilies, but to intensify the colour without the heat, we can add some green leaves. I'm using Thai basil because we have it for the curry anyway, but you can use other green leaves, such as spinach.

THE METHOD TO THE MADNESS

Why not just braise the beef in the curry sauce? If we simmered the beef in the curry, the vibrant green colour would start to fade and turn yellow from prolonged heat exposure. We work around this by braising the beef separately in a flavoured liquid, and since beef shank is full of tendons, the cooking liquid becomes a wonderfully rich beef stock that helps add body and flavour to our final product.

THE BREAKDOWN

The Paste	Green curry paste
The Liquid	Coconut milk and beef cooking liquid
The Nuggets	Beef shank, bamboo shoots, Thai basil, spur chili
The Seasoning	Fish sauce, salt, palm sugar
Flavour Profile	Spicy and salty, balanced with subtle sweetness. Creamy mouthfeel, but should not be thick or viscous.

Red Curry with Barbecued Duck & Pineapple
Gaeng Ped Bped Yang

Serves: 4

Cooking Time: 1 hour + 30 minutes if making the curry paste

Special Tools: Heavy-duty mortar and pestle, or another device for making curry paste

Do-ahead Tips: Make the duck stock and the curry paste in advance. You can also make the entire dish in advance, leaving the basil and tomatoes out until ready to serve.

1 whole	Chinese barbecued duck, uncut (see note)
As needed	Water
2 cups	Coconut milk
1 recipe	Red curry paste (recipe follows) or 5 Tbsp store-bought
3 Tbsp	Palm sugar, finely chopped, packed
2 Tbsp	Fish sauce
2 cups	Pineapple, fresh, bite-sized pieces
1 cup	Grape tomatoes or cherry tomatoes, whole
1 cup	Thai basil leaves
For serving	Jasmine rice

Note: When you buy barbecued duck, many vendors will cut the duck into small pieces by default. Ask them not to cut it so you can easily remove the bones. Note also that though the curry is gluten-free, barbecued ducks are often made with gluten-containing soy sauce.

Red curry

Gaeng = Curry; Ped = Spicy; Bped = Duck; Yang = Grilled or barbecued

For a while, my dad was fixated on perfecting this recipe, and I ended up getting involved in the project, so I owe this recipe to him. This curry is a great example of the weaving of Thai and Chinese culinary cultures. The quintessential Chinese barbecued duck is married to the Thai red curry, and the resulting dish just explodes with flavour. Barbecued duck is available in many Chinese restaurants and markets, but don't settle for any old duck! Buy the best duck you can find as the quality of the curry is tied to it. My dad's secret is making stock out of the duck bones and adding it back into the curry to tie the flavours of the duck and the sauce together. You can prep your own duck, but the flavour and texture of Chinese barbecued duck can't easily be replicated at home, so I like to leave this one to the experts.

....

Debone the duck and cut the meat and skin into bite-size pieces. Put the duck bones into a stock pot, cover with cold water, and bring to a simmer. Let simmer for 30–45 minutes, then discard the bones. Reserve 1½ cups of this stock; the rest of the stock can be used in other soups.

Reduce ¾ cup of the coconut milk in a medium-sized pot over medium heat until very thick and the clear coconut oil starts to separate from the white portion, 10–15 minutes. (If this separation doesn't happen, just proceed with the recipe after reducing until thick—sometimes coconut milk is processed to prevent separation. See p.52 for more information.)

Add the curry paste to the reduced coconut milk and cook over medium-low heat for 3–4 minutes, stirring constantly, until the curry paste is very thick. Add the remaining 1¼ cups of coconut milk and stir to mix. Turn the heat up to medium-high and add the reserved duck stock, 2 Tbsp of the palm sugar, and half of the fish sauce; bring to a boil.

When the curry boils, add the duck meat and pineapple; then simmer gently for 3–4 minutes so they absorb the curry (if you cannot fit all the duck meat into the pot, set the extra aside for later). While the curry simmers, pierce the grape tomatoes with the tip of a paring knife (if the tomatoes don't split naturally, this incision releases the built-up pressure so they won't explode in your mouth when you eat them!).

(Continued)

Taste and adjust the seasoning with the remaining palm sugar and fish sauce. Remove from the heat, then stir in the pierced grape tomatoes and Thai basil, letting the residual heat gently cook the tomatoes so they do not turn mushy.

Garnish the curry with the top of a Thai basil sprig and serve with jasmine rice.

....

Red Curry Paste

Grind the dry chilies into a powder using a spice/coffee grinder OR soak the chilies in water for at least an hour to soften. (See *Tips for Making Curry Paste in a Mortar and Pestle*, p.xvi)

If using dry, ground chilies:

In a heavy-duty mortar and pestle, add the salt, white peppercorns, lemongrass, galangal, cilantro roots and kaffir lime zest; pound into a fine paste.

Add the ground chilies and pound to mix.

Add the shallots and garlic; pound into a fine paste.

Add the shrimp paste and pound to mix.

If using soaked chilies:

Drain the chilies from the soaking water and dry off excess water with paper towel. Cut into small pieces.

In a heavy-duty mortar and pestle, add the chilies, salt, and white peppercorns; pound into a fine paste.

Add the lemongrass, galangal, cilantro roots and kaffir lime zest; pound into a fine paste.

Add the shallots and garlic; pound into a fine paste.

Add the shrimp paste and pound to mix.

....

THE DUCK AND THE FRUIT

There's something about duck and sweet-and-sour fruits that go brilliantly together. The French know it well, hence duck à l'orange. Apart from pineapple, try this curry with lychee or red grapes.

8	Large dried chilies, seeded
4	Small dried chilies, seeded (see note)
1 tsp	Salt
¼ tsp	White peppercorns
3 Tbsp	Lemongrass, thinly sliced
1 Tbsp	Galangal, finely chopped
2 tsp	Cilantro roots or 2 Tbsp cilantro stems, finely chopped
1 tsp	Kaffir lime zest, finely chopped
3 Tbsp	Shallots, finely chopped
2 Tbsp	Garlic, finely chopped
1 tsp	Shrimp paste (*gapi*)

Note: Large dried chilies are mild, while small dried chilies are quite spicy, so you can control the curry paste's spiciness by adding more or fewer of the small ones. Leave in the seeds of the small chilies for extra heat.

THE BREAKDOWN

The Paste	Red curry paste
The Liquid	Coconut milk and duck stock
The Nuggets	Duck, pineapple, grape tomatoes, Thai basil
The Seasoning	Fish sauce, palm sugar
Flavour Profile	Salty, followed by sweet, with bursts of acidity from the pineapple. Creamy mouthfeel but should not be thick or viscous.

Massaman Curry with Lamb Shoulder

Gaeng Massaman Gae

Serves: 4

Cooking Time: 2 hours + 30 minutes to make the curry paste

Special Tools: Heavy-duty mortar and pestle, or another device for making curry paste

Do-ahead Tips: Make the curry paste or make the entire dish in advance.

1½ lb	Lamb shoulder, 2-inch cubes
2½ cups	Coconut milk
1 recipe	Massaman curry paste (recipe follows) or 5–6 Tbsp store-bought
1 tsp	Salt
As needed	Water
3 Tbsp	Palm sugar, finely chopped, packed
1–2 Tbsp	Fish sauce
1–2 Tbsp	Tamarind juice
1	Bay leaf
1	Potato or sweet potato, large, cut into large chunks
1 cup	Onion, ½-inch-wide strips
¼ cup	Peanuts, roasted, plus extra for garnish
For serving	Jasmine rice or rice vermicelli

Tip for Success: Remember that the rice will soften the curry's flavour when they are eaten together, so make sure the curry is strongly seasoned.

Gaeng = Curry; Massaman = Name of curry, no other meaning in modern Thai language; Gae = Lamb

Massaman curry is special to me because it was the first coconut-based curry I learned how to make. This curry is not as soupy and spicy as most other Thai curries, but tends to be rich and stewy with fork-tender meat. *Massaman* with potato is more common nowadays, but before potato became widely available in Thailand, yellow-fleshed sweet potato was a classic ingredient. In 2011, CNNgo named this curry the most delicious food in the world, followed by Neapolitan pizza and chocolate—I was not surprised!

· ·

In a medium-sized pot, place the lamb, ½ cup of the coconut milk, 1 Tbsp of the curry paste, and salt. Add water to cover the lamb and bring to a simmer. Braise the lamb, loosely covered, for 1½ hours or until the meat is fork tender. Add more water if needed to ensure that the lamb stays submerged.

Remove the lamb using a slotted spoon and set aside. Reserve the cooking liquid. *Note: Cooking the lamb separately ensures a more vibrant colour in the end product.*

Reduce ¾ cup of the coconut milk in a medium-sized pot over medium heat until very thick and the clear coconut oil starts to separate from the white portion, 10–15 minutes. (If this separation doesn't happen, just proceed with the recipe after reducing until thick—sometimes coconut milk is processed to prevent separation. See p. 52 for more information.)

Add the remaining curry paste to the reduced coconut milk and cook over medium-low heat for 3–4 minutes, stirring constantly, until the curry paste is very thick. Add the remaining 1¼ cups of coconut milk, 2 Tbsp of the palm sugar, 1 Tbsp of the fish sauce, 1 Tbsp of the tamarind juice, and the bay leaf and stir to mix; bring to a boil.

Add the potato, onion, cooked lamb, and just enough of the reserved cooking liquid to almost cover the meat; simmer for 15 minutes or until the potato is done. Taste and adjust seasoning with the remaining palm sugar, fish sauce, and tamarind juice.

Stir in the peanuts and remove from the heat. Ladle into a bowl and sprinkle extra peanuts on top. Serve with jasmine rice.

WHAT HAPPENED TO MASSAMAN PORK?

In Thailand, you'll find *massaman* chicken, beef, lamb, and even goat. But you'll be hard pressed to find *massaman* pork despite the fact that Thai people consume pork more than any other meat. This is because *massaman* came from Thai Muslims who live primarily in the South. I never make it with pork out of respect for the curry's origin, but some people do, so feel free to try this with pork shoulder if you like!

THE BREAKDOWN

The Paste	Massaman curry paste
The Liquid	Coconut milk and lamb cooking liquid
The Nuggets	Lamb shoulder, potato or sweet potato, onion, peanuts
The Seasoning	Fish sauce, salt, palm sugar, tamarind juice
Flavour Profile	Salty and sweet, with a subtle tartness from the tamarind just to balance.

Massaman Curry Paste

Toast the coriander seeds by adding them to a dry sauté pan, stirring constantly over medium-high heat until the seeds are aromatic and slightly darkened, about 4 minutes. Cool on a plate. Repeat with the cumin seeds.

Grind the toasted coriander seeds, toasted cumin seeds, and white peppercorns into a fine powder; set aside.

Grind the dried chilies into a powder using a spice/coffee grinder OR soak the chilies in water for at least an hour to soften. (See *Tips for Making Curry Paste in a Mortar and Pestle*, p. xvi.)

If using dry, ground chilies:

In a heavy-duty mortar and pestle, add the salt, lemongrass, galangal, and cilantro roots; pound into a fine paste.

Add the ground chilies and all the ground spices; pound to mix.

Add the shallots and garlic; pound into a fine paste.

Add the shrimp paste and pound to mix.

If using soaked chilies:

Drain the chilies from their soaking water and dry off excess water with paper towel. Cut into small pieces.

Place the chilies and salt in a heavy-duty mortar and pestle; pound into a rough paste. Add the ground spices to help absorb the liquid from the chilies and continue pounding into a fine paste.

Add the lemongrass, galangal, and cilantro roots; pound into a fine paste.

Add the shallots and garlic; pound into a fine paste.

Add the shrimp paste and pound to mix.

1 tsp	Coriander seeds
1 tsp	Cumin seeds
¼ tsp	White peppercorns
10	Large dried chilies, seeded
1 tsp	Salt
3 Tbsp	Lemongrass, thinly sliced
2 Tbsp	Galangal, finely chopped
2 tsp	Cilantro roots, finely chopped
¾ tsp	Ground cinnamon
¼ tsp	Ground cloves
⅛ tsp	Ground nutmeg
¼ tsp	Ground cardamom
¼ cup	Shallots, finely chopped
2 Tbsp	Garlic, finely chopped
1 tsp	Shrimp paste (*gapi*)

Pork Satay and Peanut Sauce
Moo Sate

Moo = Pork; Sate = Satay

You are probably wondering why a recipe for grilled pork skewers is in the curry section. Thai curries can come in many different forms, and the dipping sauce for this famous street food is essentially a thick peanut curry that uses the same technique as other coconut milk-based curries. Peanut sauce has long been associated with Thai cuisine, and many people think it's a multipurpose sauce that we use to dress up many dishes. In reality, the only time we eat peanut sauce is with pork satay. Our peanut sauce is spicy and bursting with curry flavour, and has a gritty texture from ground peanuts. Oh, and why pork? Because it's essentially the only kind of satay we make in Thailand, but you can, of course, use chicken or beef instead.

Makes: About 25-30 small skewers
Cooking Time: 1 hour + 2 hours minimum to marinade
Special Tools: Food processor, mortar and pestle or another device for grinding spices
Do-ahead Tips: Make the peanut sauce and marinate the pork in advance.

MARINADE

1½ tsp	Coriander seeds, toasted
½ tsp	Cumin seeds, toasted
¼ tsp	White peppercorns
1 Tbsp	Lemongrass, chopped
1 tsp	Galangal, minced
½ tsp	Ground turmeric
⅛ tsp	Ground cinnamon
⅛ tsp	Ground cloves
2 tsp	Brown sugar
½ tsp	Salt
⅓ cup	Coconut milk
¼ cup	Water
½ Tbsp	White vinegar

PORK

1 lb	Pork chops, boneless, ¾-inch thick (see note)
30	6-inch bamboo skewers
¼ cup	Coconut milk for basting
4 slices	White bread, for serving

Note: If using chicken, both dark and white meat work well. If using beef, choose a tender cut.

For the pork and marinade:

Grind the coriander, cumin, and white peppercorns in a mortar and pestle until very fine. Add the lemongrass and galangal; pound until fine. Add the turmeric powder, cinnamon, cloves, brown sugar, salt, coconut milk, water, and vinegar; stir to mix well.

Cut the pork chops in half along the length of the fatty rind. Then slice each piece, along the short side, into ¼-inch thick slices.

Pour the marinade over the pork, massaging it in with your hands and making sure no pieces are stuck together. Cover and refrigerate overnight or at least 2 hours.

For the peanut sauce:

In a food processor or a mortar and pestle, grind the peanuts until mealy, being careful not to overprocess or they will turn into peanut butter. If using sesame seeds, grind them separately into a fine meal using a spice grinder or a mortar and pestle (a small amount of sesame seeds doesn't grind well in food processors).

In a small pot over medium heat, reduce ¼ cup of the coconut milk by about half. Add the curry paste and cook over medium-low heat, stirring constantly, for about 2 minutes until it is very thick. If it thickens too quickly, add a splash of coconut milk to help loosen it up.

Stir in the rest of the coconut milk, the ground peanuts, ground sesame seeds (if using), palm sugar, tamarind juice, and fish sauce. Simmer for a few more minutes until it has thickened into a dip consistency, stirring frequently to prevent the bottom from scorching.

Taste and adjust seasoning with more sugar, tamarind juice, and fish sauce as needed.

For the *ajaad*:

In a small pot, combine the vinegar, sugar, and salt; bring to a boil and cook just until the sugar is completely dissolved. Cool completely.

Place the cucumber, shallots, and chilies in a small serving bowl and keep covered and refrigerated until ready to serve.

To cook the satays:

Skewer the meat onto bamboo skewers, about three pieces to each skewer, making sure that there is at least one fatty piece on each skewer. Lay the skewers flat on a tray.

Preheat the grill to medium. Brush the top side of the skewers with coconut milk, then place on the grill, top side down. Brush the other side with coconut milk and cook for a minute or so just until halfway cooked. Flip the skewers and grill the other side just until done. These are thin skewers and should only take a couple of minutes.

When the pork is done, put the bread on the grill and toast.

When ready to serve: Finish the *ajaad* by pouring the cooled vinegar mixture over the vegetables. Cut each piece of toast into bite-sized squares. Serve the satay on a platter alongside the peanut sauce, *ajaad*, and toast. The toast can be dipped into the peanut sauce, and the *ajaad* can be eaten in between bites as a palate cleanser or together with the satay.

PEANUTS, NOT PEANUT BUTTER

When I was a kid, my dad went to America for work and returned with some American souvenirs, one of which was Skippy peanut butter. I was fascinated by it and thought it was such a cool invention! As much as we use peanuts in our cuisine, we never grind it so finely that it becomes peanut butter. Thai cuisine values a lot of textural variety in dishes, and nuts are an easy way to add one more layer of texture, like the grittiness in this satay sauce, so do not be tempted to use peanut butter!

PEANUT SAUCE

½ cup	Peanuts, roasted
2 Tbsp	White sesame seeds, toasted (or use another 2 Tbsp peanuts)
1¼ cups	Coconut milk
2 Tbsp	Red curry paste (see note)
2 Tbsp	Palm sugar, finely chopped, packed
2–3 Tbsp	Tamarind juice
1–2 tsp	Fish sauce

AJAAD (QUICK CUCUMBER PICKLE)

½ cup	White vinegar
¼ cup	Sugar, granulated
A pinch	Salt
½ cup	Cucumber, quartered lengthwise and thinly sliced
1 Tbsp	Shallots, thinly sliced
8–10 slices	Spur chilies or fresno chilies

THE BREAKDOWN

The Paste	Red curry paste
The Liquid	Coconut milk
The Nuggets	Ground peanuts and sesame seeds
The Seasoning	Fish sauce, palm sugar, tamarind juice
Flavour Profile	Salty and sweet with a little tartness to balance.

Note: Red curry paste is what I usually use, but you can customize the flavour of your peanut sauce by using panang or massaman curry pastes. I always use store-bought paste for this because it's already quite a time-consuming recipe.

Pork satay

Yellow Curry with Chicken & Potato
Gaeng Garee

Serves: 3-4
Cooking Time: 1 hour + 30 minutes to make the curry paste
Special Tools: Heavy-duty mortar and pestle, or another device for making curry paste
Do-ahead Tips: Make the entire dish in advance, adding the tomatoes when ready to serve.

1¾ cups	Coconut milk
1 recipe	Yellow curry paste (recipe follows) or 5-6 Tbsp store-bought
4-5	Chicken thighs, bone-in
1 cup	Water
1-2 Tbsp	Fish sauce
1½ Tbsp	Palm sugar, finely chopped, packed
2	Potatoes, medium, cut into chunks (see note)
½	Onion, medium, ½-inch strips
½ cup	Shallots, thinly sliced (optional)
1-2 Tbsp	Tamarind juice
1 cup	Cherry tomatoes (see note)
For serving	Jasmine rice

Note: You can use starchy or waxy potatoes depending on your preference; however, if using starchy potatoes, such as russet, be careful not to overcook them as they will quickly fall apart. Starchy potatoes should be peeled for this recipe, waxy can be used with their skin on.

Pierce cherry tomatoes with a knife to allow steam to escape and prevent them from exploding in your mouth when you eat them.

Gaeng = Curry; Garee = Has the same root as "curry"; in Thai language it refers to a mixture of Indian spices

Yellow curry is a great example of an Indian influence on Thai cuisine. Take a look at the curry paste and you'll find ingredients that are not often used in Thai food, but are very representative of Indian cuisine: curry powder, turmeric, and ginger. The richness and aroma of warm spices in yellow curry have a comfort-food effect on me, making it my go-to winter dish. Sweet, crispy, fried shallots are a classic garnish atop this curry, and while I don't always bother with them for a weeknight dinner, it's always worth the extra time when I have guests over.

Reduce ¾ cup of the coconut milk in a medium-sized pot over medium heat until very thick and clear coconut oil starts to separate from the white portion, 10-15 minutes. (If this separation doesn't happen, just proceed with the recipe after reducing until thick—sometimes coconut milk is processed to prevent separation. See p. 52 for more information.)

Add the curry paste to the reduced coconut milk and cook over medium-low heat for 3-4 minutes, stirring constantly, until the curry paste is very thick.

Add the chicken and toss to coat in the curry paste, then add the remaining 1 cup coconut milk and 1 cup water; stir to mix. Add 1 Tbsp of the fish sauce and 1 Tbsp of the palm sugar; simmer gently for 30 minutes.

Add the potatoes, onion, and more water as needed to keep the potatoes mostly submerged. Simmer for another 15 minutes or until the chicken is fork tender and the potatoes are fully cooked.

Meanwhile, spread the sliced shallots on a paper-towel-lined plate, sprinkle generously with salt, and let sit for 15 minutes. Press paper towel onto the shallots to dry off the water that the salt has drawn out. Heat 1 inch of vegetable oil in a pot over low heat to about 300°F, add the shallots, and stir constantly until they turn golden brown, keeping the heat low. Remove the shallots as soon as they are golden brown and the bubbling has subsided. Drain on paper towel.

When the curry is done, taste and adjust the seasoning with the remaining fish sauce and sugar and the tamarind juice. Turn off the heat, stir in the pierced tomatoes, and let the residual heat of the curry gently cook the tomatoes for a few minutes before serving.

To serve, sprinkle with fried shallots and serve with jasmine rice.

THE SECRET TO FRYING SHALLOTS

These crispy, fried shallots are highly addictive; however, there are a few tricks to making sure they are perfectly crisp and golden brown. Keeping the heat low is key—the bubbling should be gentle, which ensures that the moisture has time to completely evaporate. High heat will burn the shallots before they have a chance to crisp up. When the bubbling subsides, that's when you know they are close to being ready: bubbling is a sign that there is steam coming out of the food, and lack of steam means the moisture is gone and the food is crispy. P.S. You can buy jars of fried shallots at Asian grocery stores. They are fine in a pinch, but not half as good as homemade ones.

THE BREAKDOWN

The Paste	Yellow curry paste
The Liquid	Coconut milk and water
The Nuggets	Chicken, onion, potatoes, cherry tomatoes
The Seasoning	Fish sauce, sugar, tamarind juice
Flavour Profile	Salty and sweet, with a little tartness from the tamarind to balance.

Yellow Curry Paste

Toast the coriander seeds by adding them to a dry sauté pan and stirring constantly over medium-high heat until the seeds are aromatic and slightly darkened, about 4 minutes. Cool on a plate. Repeat with the cumin seeds.

Grind the coriander seeds, cumin seeds, and white peppercorns into a fine powder; set aside.

Grind the dry chilies into a powder using a spice/coffee grinder OR soak the chilies in water for at least an hour to soften. (See *Tips for Making Curry Paste in a Mortar and Pestle*, p. xvi.)

If using dry, ground chilies:

In a heavy-duty mortar and pestle, place the salt, lemongrass, galangal, and ginger; pound into a fine paste.

Add all of the dried spices and ground chilies; pound to mix.

Add the shallots and garlic; pound into a fine paste.

Add the shrimp paste and pound to mix.

If using soaked chilies:

Drain the chilies from their soaking water and dry off excess water with paper towel. Cut into small pieces. Add the chilies and salt to a heavy-duty mortar and pestle; pound into a rough paste. Add all the dry spices to help absorb the liquid from the chilies and continue pounding into a fine paste.

Add the lemongrass, galangal, and ginger; pound into a fine paste.

Add the shallots and garlic; pound into a fine paste.

Add the shrimp paste and pound to mix.

1½ tsp	Coriander seeds
¾ tsp	Cumin seeds
¼ tsp	White peppercorns
8–10	Large dried chilies, seeded
1 tsp	Salt
2 Tbsp	Lemongrass, finely chopped
1 Tbsp	Galangal, finely chopped
1 Tbsp	Ginger, finely chopped
¾ tsp	Ground turmeric
2 tsp	Curry powder
¼ cup	Shallots, finely chopped
2 Tbsp	Garlic, finely chopped
1 tsp	Shrimp paste (*gapi*)

Yellow curry   *Yellow curry paste*

Jungle Curry
Gaeng Bpa

Gaeng = Curry; Bpa = Jungle, forest

Truthfully, I don't know why it's called a jungle curry, but the abundance of herbs and vegetables makes this curry look kind of like a jungle in a bowl. The curry's complex herbaceous aroma is not only pleasant for the palate, it's also excellent for masking any gaminess or fishiness in the protein. This came in handy back when people cooked whatever wild animals they could hunt—perhaps the real reason for the curry's name! In a way, jungle curry paste is a combination of red and green curry pastes, a fantastic union of the fruity, smoky flavour of dried chilies and the grassy notes of fresh green chilies. Toasted rice powder is sometimes added to thicken the broth and add a toasty aroma.

....

Marinate your protein of choice with 2 tsp of the fish sauce; set aside for 20 minutes.

In a medium pot, add the vegetable oil and curry paste and cook over medium-low heat, stirring constantly with a rubber spatula until aromatic, 2–3 minutes.

Add the stock to the curry paste, stirring to dissolve the paste, and turn the heat up to medium-high; bring to a boil. Add the remaining fish sauce, sugar, and all the vegetables and herbs, except the basil. When the vegetables are almost done to your liking, add the meat and cook just until done. Remove from the heat, taste, and adjust the seasoning. *Remember that when the kaffir lime leaves are left in big pieces, they are not meant to be eaten.*

When ready to serve, stir in the holy basil and toasted rice powder, if using. Garnish with spur chili and serve with jasmine rice. If you wish to eat the young peppercorns for extra heat, pick the peppercorns from the stem and do not eat the stem.

Note: If using pork, chicken, or beef, choose a tender cut and slice into thin, bite-sized slices. If using fish, cut into big chunks. If using shrimp, peel and devein.

If using store-bought curry paste, use 4 Tbsp red curry paste plus 1–2 Tbsp green curry paste.

Baby corn, Thai eggplant, and pea eggplant are traditional but substitute other vegetables such as cauliflower, bamboo shoots, asparagus, carrots, peas, and kale.

(Continued)

Serves: 4
Cooking Time: 30 minutes + 30 minutes if making the curry paste
Special Tools: Heavy-duty mortar and pestle, or another device for making curry paste
Do-ahead Tips: Make the curry paste and the stock in advance.

---

12 oz	Protein of your choice (see note)
2 Tbsp + 2 tsp	Fish sauce
1 Tbsp	Vegetable oil
1 recipe	Gaeng bpa curry paste (recipe follows), or store-bought (see note)
2½ cups	Pork stock or chicken stock, unsalted (recipe p.232)
2 tsp	Palm sugar, finely chopped, packed
8	Long beans, 2-inch pieces
8 ears	Baby corn, fresh or canned, bite-sized pieces (see note)
4–6	Thai eggplants, small wedges (see note)
¼ cup	Pea eggplant (see note)
2 stems	Young peppercorns, fresh or brined, 2-inch pieces
¼ cup	Fingerroot (*grachai*), fresh or brined, thinly julienned
4	Kaffir lime leaves, torn into chunks
½ cup	Holy basil or regular basil leaves
1½ Tbsp	Toasted rice powder (recipe p.230, optional)
For garnish	Spur chili, sliced, or red bell pepper, julienned (optional)
For serving	Jasmine rice

Gaeng Bpa Curry Paste

Grind the dried chilies into a powder using a spice/coffee grinder OR soak the chilies in water for at least an hour to soften. (See *Tips for Making Curry Paste in a Mortar and Pestle*, p.xvi)

If using dry, ground chilies:

In a heavy-duty mortar and pestle, add the green chilies, salt, and white peppercorns; pound into a fine paste.

Add the lemongrass, galangal, fingerroot, kaffir lime zest, and cilantro roots; pound into a fine paste.

Add the ground chilies and pound to mix.

Add the shallots and garlic; pound into a fine paste.

Add the shrimp paste and pound to mix.

If using soaked chilies:

Drain the chilies from their soaking water and dry off excess water with paper towel. Cut into small pieces.

In a heavy-duty mortar and pestle, add both types of chilies, the salt, and white peppercorns; pound into a fine paste.

Add the lemongrass, galangal, fingerroot, kaffir lime zest and cilantro roots; pound into a fine paste.

Add the shallots and garlic; pound into a fine paste.

Add the shrimp paste and pound to mix.

....

TREASURE-HUNTING FOR HERBS

Although in Thailand we use fresh fingerroots, they are available brined in glass jars, either whole or julienned. I have seen the jars labelled as "Pickled Rhizome," "Rhizome in Brine," "Pickled Galingale," "Krachai," and "Grachai," and in Vietnamese, "Ngai Bun." Young peppercorns are also sold brined in glass jars, labelled as "Young Green Pepper" or "Pickled Young Pepper" (though they're not actually pickled!).

8	Large dried chilies, seeded
3–12	Green Thai chilies, seeded and finely chopped (see note)
1 tsp	Salt
¼ tsp	White peppercorns
2 Tbsp	Lemongrass, thinly sliced
1 Tbsp	Galangal, finely chopped
1 Tbsp	Fingerroot (*grachai*), finely chopped
1 tsp	Kaffir lime zest, finely chopped
1 tsp	Cilantro roots or 1 Tbsp cilantro stems, finely chopped
3 Tbsp	Shallots, finely chopped
1 Tbsp	Garlic, finely chopped
1 tsp	Shrimp paste (*gapi*)

Note: Since large dried chilies are mild, the level of spice is determined by the number of green chilies you add. Three will give you a gentle start, use 5–7 for medium, and 8 or more will cause some sweating! Fresh red Thai chilies can be used instead of green.

THE BREAKDOWN

The Paste	*Gaeng bpa* curry paste
The Liquid	Stock
The Nuggets	Protein of choice, baby corn, long beans, Thai eggplant, pea eggplant, young peppercorns, fingerroot, kaffir lime leaves, and holy basil
The Seasoning	Fish sauce and sugar
Flavour Profile	Spicy and salty. The sugar rounds off the sharp edges of the salt, but the curry should not taste sweet.

Sour Curry with Thai Omelette

Gaeng Som

Serves: 4

Serves: 4
Cooking Time: 30 minutes + 30 minutes if making the curry paste
Special Tools: Heavy-duty mortar and pestle, or another device for making curry paste
Do-ahead Tips: The stock, the curry paste, and the omelette can be made in advance. *Gaeng som* is well known for being tastier the next day, so consider making this dish the day before serving.

THAI-STYLE VEGETABLE OMELETTE

2	Eggs, large
1 tsp	Fish sauce
¾ cup	Sturdy vegetables, such as long beans, Chinese broccoli, or broccoli florets, finely chopped or julienned (see note)
As needed	Vegetable oil

Note: For the omelette shown in the picture, p. 112), I used climbing wattle or cha-om, which is traditional but can be hard to find, so you can use any other green, sturdy vegetables that don't give off a lot of liquid when cooked. You can also leave out the vegetables and make a plain omelette with 3 eggs.

Gaeng = Curry; Som = Sour (in food names), orange

Gaeng som is not a popular item in Thai restaurants overseas, so if you were wondering what kind of obscure things we eat at home, this is one. We eat *gaeng som* often in my family, because it's healthy and my mom loves sour food; the curry paste is also super easy to make. In fact, it's the first curry paste I remember making as a kid. The best part about *gaeng som* is the pieces of Thai omelette that soak up the broth like a sponge, then when you chew on them . . . whoosh . . . the spicy and sour broth bursts in your mouth! The omelette is technically optional, but trust me, you don't want to leave it out. *Gaeng som* is also unique in that it's one of the few Thai dishes that uses shredded fish meat as a broth thickener.

. . . .

FOR THE VEGETABLE OMELETTE:

Beat the eggs and fish sauce well with a fork; add the vegetables and mix well. Heat a wok or a small (8–10 inch) non-stick sauté pan over medium-high heat, with just enough oil to coat the bottom.

When the oil is hot, pour in the egg mixture, spread the vegetables out evenly with a fork, and turn the heat down to medium-low. Cook the omelette without stirring until the bottom side is golden brown and the omelette is firm enough to flip. Pay attention to the heat—if it's too hot, the omelette will burn before it sets.

Flip the omelette either by tossing the pan or using a wide spatula (don't worry if the omelette breaks), and brown the other side. When done, slide it onto paper towel to absorb excess oil. Cut the omelette into 1½-inch square pieces.

(Continued)

FOR THE CURRY:

Bring the stock to a simmer in a medium pot. Add the fish and poach just until cooked, then turn off the heat and transfer the fish to a mortar and pestle or a blender, leaving the stock in the pot.

Pound the fish in a mortar and pestle until completely shredded, or blend the fish with some of the stock, then add the fish back into the stock pot.

Add the curry paste to the stock and turn the heat on high, stirring to dissolve the curry paste. Add the fish sauce, tamarind juice, and sugar, then let the curry boil for 1 minute to cook the curry paste.

Add the cauliflower and cook for 1–2 minutes until about halfway done. Add the long beans and napa cabbage; cook for 1–2 more minutes or until done. Add the shrimp and cook just until done, 30–60 seconds depending on the size. Stir in the omelette and remove from the heat.

Taste and adjust the seasoning. The curry should lead with sour—if it is not sour enough, add lime juice to brighten it up.

Let the omelette absorb the curry for 5 minutes before serving. Serve with jasmine rice.

Tip for Success: Tasting your cooking is important, but particularly so when tamarind juice is a major seasoning, because each brand of tamarind juice varies significantly in acidity. If my gaeng som needs more acid in the end, I like to adjust it with lime juice because I like the sharp, citrus quality it adds, but you can also add more tamarind.

THE CURRY

3 cups	Chicken stock, unsalted (recipe p.232)
2 oz	White fish meat (see note)
1 recipe	Gaeng som curry paste (recipe follows) or 5 Tbsp store-bought (see note)
1½–2 Tbsp	Fish sauce
¼ cup	Tamarind juice
1½ Tbsp	Palm sugar, finely chopped, packed
¼ head	Cauliflower, small florets (see note)
10	Long beans, 2-inch pieces (see note)
4 cups	Napa cabbage, bite-size pieces (see note)
7 oz	Shrimp, peeled and deveined
1–2 Tbsp	Lime juice

Note: It's traditional to use snakehead fish (pla chon), but you can use any white, mild-flavoured fish such as barramundi, tilapia, or branzino.

In my experience, pre-made gaeng som curry paste is very hard to find outside of Thailand because it's not a popular curry.

Long beans, napa cabbage, and cauliflower are just three of the many vegetables often used in gaeng som. You can also try green papaya, daikon radish, and water spinach. There are no rules, so feel free to experiment.

(Continued)

Gaeng Som Curry Paste

10	Large dried chilies
3–5	Small dried chilies (see note)
1½ tsp	Salt
¼ tsp	White peppercorns
¼ cup	Shallots, finely chopped
2 Tbsp	Garlic, finely chopped
2 Tbsp	Fingerroot (grachai), fresh or brined, finely chopped
2 tsp	Shrimp paste (gapi)

Note: Large dried chilies are mild, while small dried chilies are quite spicy, so you can control the curry paste's spiciness by adding more or fewer of the small ones.

THE BREAKDOWN

The Paste	*Gaeng som curry paste*
The Liquid	Stock
The Nuggets	Omelette, vegetables, shrimp
The Seasoning	Tamarind, fish sauce, palm sugar
Flavour Profile	Sour should lead with just enough salt to balance. A hint of sweetness to round off the acidity.

Preheat the oven to 300°F. Lay both sets of chilies on a baking tray without overlapping and roast in the oven for 5–7 minutes until the chilies have darkened slightly. Let cool, then remove the seeds. Leave in the seeds of some or all of the small chilies for a spicier curry.

Grind the chilies into a powder using a spice/coffee grinder OR soak the chilies in water for at least an hour to soften. (See *Tips for Making Curry Paste in a Mortar and Pestle*, p.xvi.)

If using dry, ground chilies:

In a heavy-duty mortar and pestle, add the salt, white peppercorns, shallots, garlic, and fingerroot; pound into a rough paste.

Add the ground chilies; pound into a fine paste.

Add the shrimp paste and pound to mix.

If using soaked chilies:

Drain the chilies from their soaking water and dry off excess water with paper towel. Cut into small pieces.

Add the chilies and salt to a heavy-duty mortar and pestle; pound into a fine paste.

Add the shallots, garlic, and fingerroot; pound to a fine paste.

Add the shrimp paste and pound to mix.

THE INVISIBLE FISH

Yes, I know adding shredded fish to a curry is somewhat odd, but without the fish, this water-based curry would be thin and unsatisfying. The fish adds richness and body, allowing the broth to cling to the vegetables and rice. You can make the curry even thicker simply by adding more fish. Stick with white, mild-flavoured fish so it doesn't clash with the curry. I once wanted to use up the last can of tuna, so out of curiosity I made *gaeng som* with it . . . let's just say I won't be doing that again!

SOUPS

tom ต้ม

As discussed in *Part 1*, Thai soups can be coconut milk–based or water-based. Here are some examples of both types.

COCONUT-MILK-BASED

Coconut Galangal Chicken Soup — *Tom Ka Gai*

Lemongrass Soup with Shrimp & Young Coconut
— *Tom Yum Goong Nam Kon Maprao On*

WATER-BASED

Five-Spice Soup with Eggs & Pork Belly — *Kai Palo*

Northeastern Pork Rib Soup with Toasted Rice — *Tom Sap Gradook Moo*

Pork Meatball Soup with Egg Tofu – *Tom Jeud Tao Hao Moo Sub*

Coconut Galangal Chicken Soup
Tom Ka Gai

Tom = Boil, soup; Ka = Galangal; Gai = Chicken

I always loved the days my high school cafeteria had *tom ka gai* on the menu. There's something so comforting and satisfying about it—it's smooth, clean, and subtle . . . a wonderfully quiet break from other "louder" dishes. Although the name credits only one herb, this soup thrives on the trinity of lemongrass, kaffir lime leaves, and galangal. Chicken is the usual suspect, but I have made this soup with fresh clams and it was like the tasty Thai sister of New England clam chowder!

....

In a medium pot, add the chicken stock, chicken thighs, and salt; simmer gently for 15 minutes, loosely covered, until the chicken is fork tender.

Add the coconut milk, lemongrass, galangal, kaffir lime leaves, Thai chilies, 1½ Tbsp of the fish sauce, and palm sugar. Simmer for 3–5 minutes to infuse. *Note: The lemongrass, galangal, and kaffir lime leaves are traditionally left in the soup, but are not meant to be eaten. You can remove them after this step or inform your guests not to eat them.*

Add the mushrooms and cook for another 1–2 minutes to soften. Remove from the heat and stir in 2 Tbsp of the lime juice. Taste and adjust the seasoning with more fish sauce and/or lime juice if needed.

Garnish the soup with chopped cilantro and/or green onions. You can pour the soup over rice, add rice to the soup bowl, or enjoy the soup on its own. This soup is usually mildly spiced, but you can break up the chilies to release more heat.

NO CHICKEN STOCK? THERE IS A SHORTCUT!

You can make a quick-fix chicken stock without adding any extra cooking time. Use chicken drumettes instead of chicken thighs and cook them, in water and salt as per the instructions, along with some of the aromatics you normally use for stock. The bones in the chicken will turn the water into stock by the time the meat is tender. You can also buy bone-in thighs, debone them, then crack the bones and throw them in to simmer with the chicken.

Tom ka gai

Serves: 4
Cooking Time: 30 minutes
Do-ahead Tips: Make the stock and cook the chicken in advance.

2 cups	Chicken stock, unsalted (recipe p.232)
1 lb	Chicken thighs, boneless, skinless, bite-sized pieces
1 tsp	Salt
1½ cups	Coconut milk
1 stalk	Lemongrass, bottom half only, smashed and cut into 2-inch pieces
10 slices	Galangal, sliced into thin rounds
5	Kaffir lime leaves, torn into chunks
2–3	Thai chilies, crushed just until broken
1½–2 Tbsp	Fish sauce
1 tsp	Palm sugar, finely chopped, packed
5½ oz	Straw or oyster mushrooms, bite-sized pieces
2–2½ Tbsp	Lime juice
For garnish	Chopped cilantro and/or green onions
For serving	Jasmine rice (optional)

THE BREAKDOWN

The Infusion	Lemongrass, galangal, kaffir lime leaves
The Liquid	Chicken stock, coconut milk
The Nuggets	Chicken, mushrooms
The Seasoning	Fish sauce, salt, lime juice, palm sugar
Flavour Profile	Salty with a soft acidity; sweetness is very subtle.

Lemongrass Soup with Shrimp & Young Coconut
Tom Yum Goong Nam Kon Maprao On

Tom yum = A sour, lemongrass-infused soup; Goong = Shrimp; Nam kon = Thick broth; Maprao on = Young coconut

I almost didn't include a *tom yum* recipe in this book, but somehow it felt wrong to leave out such an iconic Thai dish. But the standard *tom yum* just wouldn't do . . . for this book, I wanted something more special. So, out of the plethora of variations on *tom yum*, here is the one that I think is the most interesting. Normally, *tom yum* is what we call a *nam sai* kind of soup, which means it has a clear broth. To turn it into the opposite, *nam kon* soup, I like to add coconut milk, although nowadays many people use evaporated milk instead. This recipe also uses young coconut water, which adds a fragrant sweetness that, along with the velvety coconut meat, rounds out the acidity of the lime. This, essentially, is the rich and unctuous sister of the regular *tom yum*.

....

Peel and devein the shrimp, reserving the heads and shells. Heat the oil in a medium pot over medium-high heat, then sauté the shrimp heads and shells until browned bits (called *sucs* in culinary French) have started to form at the bottom of the pot. Add the water, scraping the bottom of the pot to release the *sucs*. Simmer this stock gently for 20–30 minutes while you prep the other ingredients.

Open the young coconuts and measure out 1½ cups of coconut water—you can drink the rest. Scrape out the coconut meat with a spoon and cut into roughly 1- x 2-inch strips. If you have less than 1 cup, add canned coconut meat to make up the shortfall.

When the shrimp stock is done, strain and measure out 1¾ cups of stock and return it to the pot. If there isn't enough, add water to make up the shortfall; if you have too much, reduce it longer or reserve for another use. You may wish to reserve some shrimp heads for garnish.

(Continued)

Serves: 4
Cooking Time: 40 minutes
Do-ahead Tips: Make the shrimp stock in advance.

12 oz	Shrimp, shell-on, head-on if possible
1 Tbsp	Vegetable oil
2½ cups	Water
1½ cups	100% coconut water, pre-packaged or from 2 fresh young coconuts
1 cup	Young coconut meat, canned or from fresh young coconuts (see note)
¾ cup	Coconut milk
2 stalks	Lemongrass, bottom half only, smashed and cut into 2-inch pieces
5 slices	Galangal, sliced into thin rounds
4–5	Kaffir lime leaves, torn into chunks
3–4	Thai chilies, minced for more heat, crushed for less
3 Tbsp	Fish sauce
2–3 Tbsp	Thai chili paste (*nam prik pao*)
¼ cup	Lime juice
For garnish	Cilantro
For serving	Jasmine rice (optional)

Note: Fresh young coconuts sometimes have very little meat inside, so it's a good idea to also have canned coconut on hand. You can also use oyster mushrooms instead of coconut meat.

THE BREAKDOWN

The Infusion	Lemongrass, galangal, kaffir lime leaves
The Liquid	Shrimp stock, coconut water, coconut milk
The Nuggets	Shrimp, young coconut meat
The Seasoning	Fish sauce, lime juice, Thai chili paste
Flavour Profile	Sour, salty, then sweet, in that descending order.

Bring the stock to a boil over medium-high heat and then add the coconut water, coconut milk, lemongrass, galangal, kaffir lime leaves, and Thai chilies; simmer for 3–5 minutes to infuse. *Note: The lemongrass, galangal, and kaffir lime leaves are traditionally left in the soup, but are not meant to be eaten. You can remove them after this step or inform your guests not to eat them.*

In a small bowl, combine the fish sauce and Thai chili paste; stir to loosen the chili paste and pour into the soup. Add the shrimp and coconut meat; cook just until the shrimp is done.

Remove from the heat and stir in the lime juice. Taste and adjust the seasoning.

When ready to serve, garnish with cilantro and add a few shrimp heads for an extra wow-factor if you wish. You can pour the soup over rice, add rice to the soup bowl, or enjoy the soup on its own.

MY SHRIMP HAVE NO SHELLS!

Finding shell-on shrimp, let alone head-on, can be quite a challenge if you're looking for them at Western supermarkets. At most Asian markets, on the other hand, they are the norm. You can also look for them at farmers' markets or fish markets, which often sell live or fresh, unprocessed shrimp. If you really can't find shell-on shrimp, you can still make this dish using a good chicken stock instead of water (recipe p.232).

Tom yum goong

Five-Spice Soup with Eggs & Pork Belly
Kai Palo

Serves: 4
Cooking Time: 2 hours + a few hours for the eggs
to marinate in the soup before serving
Special Tools: Cheesecloth or muslin bag for
wrapping spices
Do-ahead Tips: Make the dish the day before
serving to let the eggs absorb more flavour.

1½ lb	Pork belly, 1- to 2-inch cubes; for a leaner option, use pork butt
1 tsp	Salt
2 Tbsp	Vegetable oil
¼ cup	Palm sugar, finely chopped, packed
5 cups	Pork stock or chicken stock, unsalted (recipe p.232)
2 Tbsp	Soy sauce
1¼ Tbsp	Black soy sauce
1 Tbsp	Seasoning sauce, such as Golden Mountain or Maggi
1 Tbsp	Oyster sauce
¼ tsp	White pepper, ground
8	Whole cloves
2	Whole star anise
2	Cinnamon sticks
1 tsp	Coriander seeds, toasted
½ tsp	Sichuan peppercorns, toasted
4 cloves	Garlic, crushed
2	Cilantro roots, crushed, or 10 cilantro stems
4–8	Eggs (1–2 per person; add more if serving more people)
12	Tofu puffs, 1½-inch cubes (see note)
For serving	Jasmine rice

Kai = Egg; Palo = Five-spice

This is a soup, but there is no *"tom"* in the name. What's going on? Well, there is, but it's hidden. The general term for this dish is *tom palo*, but since this version uses eggs, we just sub in *kai* (eggs) for convenience. The duck version of this soup, *bped palo*, is also very popular. Aromatic and robust in flavour, this soup is a bit too strong on its own, but is perfect when poured over rice. The lack of chilies makes this dish very kid-friendly, and in fact, this was one of my favourite dishes as a child.

....

Toss the pork belly in the salt. Heat the vegetable oil in a large, heavy-bottomed pot over medium-high heat. Sear the pork belly on four sides until they are browned, controlling the heat to make sure you don't burn the bits that are stuck to the pan (called *sucs* in culinary French). Do not crowd the pot; you may need to do this in batches. When finished, set the pork aside in a bowl. Pour off and discard excess oil from the pot, leaving just enough to cover the bottom. *Note: If you have burnt the* sucs, *start the next step with a fresh pot.*

Return the pot to medium heat and add the palm sugar; stir until the sugar melts and caramelizes into a dark brown colour. Pour the stock quickly into the pot (it will bubble aggressively) and then add the pork, soy sauce, black soy sauce, seasoning sauce, oyster sauce, and white pepper. Bring to a simmer, stirring occasionally. The sugar will be hard and will stick to the bottom at first, but it will slowly dissolve into the liquid.

Put the cloves, star anise, cinnamon, coriander seeds, and Sichuan peppercorns into a piece of cheesecloth and tie it into a bag. Add this spice bag, the garlic, and cilantro roots to the stock pot. Cover the pot and let the soup simmer on low heat for 1½–2 hours, until the pork is fork tender. If needed, add more water or stock to keep the pork mostly submerged.

(Continued)

While the soup cooks, make medium-boiled eggs. Choose a pot large enough that the eggs will not be crowded (cook in batches, if needed), then add water to at least 1 inch above the eggs. Bring the water to a full boil over high heat, then slowly lower the eggs into the water with a slotted spoon and boil for 8 minutes. Meanwhile, prepare a large bowl of cold water for cooling the eggs. When cooked, remove the eggs with a slotted spoon and place them in the water. Peel the eggs carefully as the yolks will still be soft. *Tip: Peeling eggs under running cold water will help loosen the shell.*

When the pork is tender, remove the spice bag and cilantro roots. Add the peeled boiled eggs and the tofu puffs; let simmer gently for 8 minutes. Remove from the heat, taste, and adjust the seasoning with more salt as needed.

If possible, let the soup sit for at least a few hours or overnight before serving to let the eggs further absorb the flavour. Garnish the soup with chopped cilantro and serve with jasmine rice.

HOW WOULD YOU LIKE YOUR EGGS DONE?

Most recipes for *kai palo* call for the boiled eggs to be cooked with the pork for an extended period of time (30 minutes to 1 hour), which yields rubbery egg-whites—indisputably frowned upon by Western chefs. However, for many Thai people, this is a desired characteristic because it's a sign that the spices and seasoning have thoroughly permeated the eggs, making them thoroughly flavourful. You may choose to use this method if you wish, but for this recipe, I have provided instructions for a middle-ground method: cook the eggs just until done, but let them sit in the soup for one day before serving so they can absorb the flavour without cooking.

Pork stock

Note: *Tofu puff is a type of fried tofu that's light and airy on the inside. It is especially adept at absorbing flavourful broth. It is available at Chinese grocery stores, but you can substitute any other type of fried tofu.*

THE BREAKDOWN

The Infusion	Spices, garlic, cilantro roots
The Liquid	Stock
The Nuggets	Pork belly, eggs, tofu
The Seasoning	Palm sugar, soy sauce, seasoning sauce, oyster sauce, black soy sauce, salt
Flavour Profile	Salty and sweet. Prominent aroma of the spices.

Northeastern Pork Rib Soup with Toasted Rice
Tom Sap Gradook Moo

Tom = Boil, soup; Sap = Delicious, in Northeastern dialect; Gradook moo = Pork ribs (literally, pork bones)

Tom sap is, in a way, the forgotten sister of the wildly popular *tom yum*. It uses the same trinity of herbs—lemongrass, galangal, and kaffir lime leaves—but adds three favourite ingredients of the Northeast: sawtooth coriander, toasted rice powder, and dried chilies. Being from the Northeast, *tom sap* has none of the sweetness that is typical of the Central Region's *tom yum*. The salt and acid are instead balanced by the nuttiness of the toasted rice powder and the natural sweetness of the pork stock.

....

Cut the shallots in half lengthwise, or in quarters if large. Grill them over medium heat or broil them on high in the oven, cut side up, until they are charred around the edges.

Grill the dried chilies over low heat until they have darkened slightly and developed a smoky aroma. Alternatively, broil them in the oven on low, about 8 inches away from the elements. The chilies will take less than a minute to toast and can burn quickly, so don't walk away!

Rinse the pork in cold water and add it to a medium-sized pot. Cover with the cold water, add the salt, and bring to a simmer. After 15 minutes of simmering, skim off the scum that has surfaced.

Add the cilantro roots, charred shallots, and toasted dried chilies; simmer gently for another 30 minutes or until the pork is fork tender.

Note: Sparerib tips are used often in Asian cuisine, and they're what butchers trim off a full sparerib in order to get the nicely rectangular St. Louis Style ribs you see on barbecues. At Chinese butchers, you can often find rib tips already cut into small pieces, or thin strips, which you can then separate into individual bones. You can also use boneless pork butt for this soup, but make sure you use a good pork stock (recipe p.232) instead of water.

(Continued)

Serves: 4
Cooking Time: 1 hour
Special Tools: Mortar and pestle, or another device for making toasted rice powder
Do-ahead Tips: Braise the pork in advance. Toast the rice a day in advance.

2–3 heads	Shallots
5–10	Small dried chilies
1 lb	Pork sparerib tips, 1½-inch pieces (see note)
4 cups	Water
1 tsp	Salt
2	Cilantro roots, crushed, or 6 cilantro stems
5–6	Kaffir lime leaves, torn into chunks
2 stalks	Lemongrass, bottom half only, smashed and cut into 2-inch pieces
8 slices	Galangal, sliced into thin rounds
1½–2 Tbsp	Fish sauce
4 oz	Oyster mushrooms or straw mushrooms, bite-sized pieces
3 Tbsp	Lime juice
4 leaves	Sawtooth coriander or ⅓ cup cilantro, chopped
1–2 Tbsp	Toasted rice powder (recipe p.230)

Toasted rice powder

The Infusion	Lemongrass, galangal, kaffir lime leaves, shallots, dried chilies
The Liquid	Pork stock, made from braising the ribs
The Nuggets	Pork ribs, mushrooms, shallots, sawtooth coriander, toasted rice powder
The Seasoning	Fish sauce, lime juice
Flavour Profile	Sour first, followed by salty, with natural sweetness from the pork stock.

Once the pork is tender, pick out the cilantro roots and add the kaffir lime leaves, lemongrass, galangal, and 1½ Tbsp of the fish sauce; simmer for 3-5 minutes to infuse. *Note: The lemongrass, galangal, and kaffir lime leaves are traditionally left in the soup, but are not meant to be eaten. You can remove them after this step or inform your guests not to eat them.*

Add the mushrooms and cook for another 1-2 minutes until tender. Remove from the heat and stir in the lime juice and sawtooth coriander or cilantro. Taste and adjust the seasoning with more fish sauce and/or lime juice if needed.

When ready to serve, stir in the toasted rice powder. You can pour the soup over rice, add rice to the soup bowl, or enjoy the soup on its own.

ALL THAT TOASTING . . .

It may seem tedious to have to char the shallots and toast the chilies, but the smoky flavour, along with the nuttiness of the toasted rice powder, adds robustness to an otherwise light soup. The toasted rice powder should be added just before serving, because it absorbs liquid and settles to the bottom quickly. It's also fun to set it out on the table for people to sprinkle onto their soup when they're ready to eat.

Pork Meatball Soup with Egg Tofu

Tom Jeud Tao Hoo Moo Sub

Serves: 4
Cooking Time: 15 minutes + 2 hours to make the stock
Do-ahead Tips: Make the stock in advance

4–5 cloves	Garlic, chopped
As needed	Vegetable oil
3½ cups	Pork stock (recipe p. 232)
4 cups	Napa cabbage, bite-sized pieces
2 tsp	Soy sauce
2 tsp	Fish sauce
¼ tsp	White pepper, ground
9 oz	Egg tofu, ½-inch slices (see note)
As needed	Salt
1	Green onion, chopped
⅓ cup	Cilantro, chopped

PORK MEATBALLS

9 oz	Ground pork
1 Tbsp	Soy sauce
1 tsp	Fish sauce
1 tsp	Sugar, granulated
¼ tsp	White pepper, ground

Note: *Egg tofu has a similar texture to soft tofu but is made from eggs and is yellower and saltier. It's available in Asian grocery stores where you would find regular tofu; it usually comes in a clear plastic tube. You can substitute regular soft tofu or use 1 oz glass noodles instead.*

Tom = Boil, soup; Jeud = Bland; Tao Hoo = Tofu; Moo Sub = Ground pork

As mentioned on p. 75, this "bland soup" can also be called *gaeng jeud* or "bland curry." It is so named not because it's bland, but to emphasize the fact that unlike other Thai soups, it's not full of herbs and bold seasoning. Instead, it has soothing, mild flavours that are great to sip for a break between strong, spicy bites of other dishes. The secret is to use good pork stock, fried garlic, and white pepper for some subtle heat. For lack of a better term, I use the word "meatballs," but we don't actually roll them into neat little spheres. Instead, we simply drop them by the spoonful directly into the soup, resulting in rustic-looking, irregular chunks of goodness! There is perhaps no other soup more homey than this. The simple, comforting dish is made regularly in almost every home, and it was certainly a regular at our family dinners.

....

In a small pot, place the garlic and just enough oil to almost cover it. Fry over low heat until all the pieces are golden; drain the garlic from the oil, reserving both. Be careful not to let the garlic over-brown or it will be bitter.

Mix all the meatball ingredients in a bowl and set aside.

In a medium pot, place the pork stock and bring it to a boil. Drop the ground pork mixture into the soup by the spoonful. Add the napa cabbage, soy sauce, fish sauce, and white pepper; simmer for a few minutes until the pork is done and the cabbage is tender. Add the egg tofu and cook for a minute longer to heat it through. Taste and add more salt as needed.

Remove from the heat and stir in the green onion and cilantro. Ladle into a bowl, drizzle some of the garlic oil over, and top with some fried garlic. Serve on its own or with jasmine rice.

> ***Tip for Success:*** *If you have extra garlic oil and fried garlic, save them to drizzle over any dish that could use some extra garlic flavour.*

(Continued)

The Infusion	Aromatics in the stock, white pepper, green onions, cilantro
The Liquid	Pork stock
The Nuggets	Meatballs, napa cabbage, egg tofu
The Seasoning	Soy sauce, fish sauce, salt
Flavour Profile	Subtle saltiness balanced by natural sweetness of the stock.

THE KEY TO SUCCESS

When I was young, I kept being unsatisfied by *tom jeud* I made, and I couldn't understand why. As it turned out, it was the stock. I did not yet know how to make a proper stock and I was using weak, rushed stock and sometimes even water. Because of its simplicity, the quality of your stock is critical, so don't compromise on it. To shortcut the process, I sometimes make the soup using small pieces of sparerib tips instead of meatballs—the bones are built-in, so I just start with water and stock aromatics. Remember, despite its name, this soup should not be bland!

SALADS

yum · pla · laab · nam tok · tum
ยำ พล่า ลาบ น้ำตก ตำ

These are the five major categories of Thai salads as discussed
in *Part 1*. Consider their differences and think about how
you might create your own Thai salad.

YUM

Fried Egg Salad — *Yum Kai Dao*

Spicy Seafood Salad — *Yum Talay*

PLA

Beef "Ceviche" with Lemongrass — *Pla Neua*

LAAB

Ground Duck Salad with Mint— *Laab Bped*

NAM TOK

Grilled Beef or Pork "Waterfall" Salad — *Nam Tok Moo/Neua*

TUM

Green Papaya Salad — *Som Tum*

Savoury Fruit Salad— *Tum Polamai*

Fried Egg Salad

Yum Kai Dao

Serves: 4 as an appetizer, 2 as an entrée
Cooking Time: 30 minutes
Special Tools: Mortar and pestle for making the dressing (optional)
Do-ahead Tips: Make the dressing in advance and store in the fridge.

THE DRESSING

1–2	Thai chilies
2 Tbsp	Palm sugar, finely chopped, packed
¼ cup	Lime juice
3 Tbsp	Fish sauce

THE SALAD

4	Eggs, room temperature
As needed	Vegetable oil for frying eggs
¼	Onion, julienned
2 stalks	Chinese celery or inner stalks of regular celery, leaves left whole, stalks cut into 1-inch pieces
½ cup	Grape tomatoes, halved
1–2	Green onions, chopped
⅓ cup	Cilantro, chopped
¼ cup	Roasted peanuts, lightly crushed

Yum = A type of Thai salad; Kai = Egg; Dao = Star; "Kai dao" refers to fried egg

This simple salad carries the true essence of a home-cooked Thai meal. In Thai, there are no words dedicated to describing how we want our fried eggs done—no over easy, no sunny side up—*kai dao* is an egg fried in oil, and the specifics are up to the cook. For this dish, however, the fried eggs normally have browned, crisp, bubbly whites, with moist-but-not-runny yolks. To achieve this, the eggs need a lot of hot oil to swim in, so in a way, this is a deep-fried-egg salad!

....

For the dressing, pound the Thai chilies into a paste in a mortar, then add the palm sugar and pound until the sugar is dissolved. Add the lime juice and fish sauce; mix the dressing by swirling the pestle around. If not using a mortar and pestle, you can finely mince the chilies and stir all the ingredients together in a small bowl until the sugar is dissolved.

For the fried eggs, in a wok or a small frying pan, add about ½ inch of oil. For best results, fry one egg at a time. Heat the oil until very hot but not smoking. Crack an egg into the centre of the pan, and turn the heat down to medium; the egg white should start bubbling excitedly right away. As the egg cooks, baste the top with the hot oil. Once the edges of the egg white are browned and crispy, and the yolk is no longer runny, remove and drain on paper towel. Repeat with the remaining eggs.

For the salad, cut the fried eggs into bite-sized pieces and add to a large salad bowl along with the onion, Chinese celery, grape tomatoes, green onions, and cilantro. Pour the dressing over and toss gently. Taste and adjust the seasoning.

Transfer onto a plate, sprinkle with the crushed peanuts, and serve on its own or with jasmine rice.

TIPS FOR SUCCESSFUL THAI-STYLE EGG FRYING

1. Test the oil for readiness by dropping a little bit of food scrap into the oil; it should bubble immediately and excitedly.

2. Bringing the eggs to room temperature before frying will allow the whites to spread wider, resulting in crispier edges. It is also better to use an older egg because the whites are less viscous and can spread more.

3. Cracking the eggs directly into the oil will keep the yolks in the centre and protect them from breaking. Pouring a pre-cracked egg from a bowl often sends the yolk to the edge.

4. The egg should be floating in oil while frying, but if it sticks to the bottom, let it cook for a minute before gently nudging it off the pan with a thin spatula.

5. The yolks shouldn't be runny for this dish because we are cutting the eggs up. I like the yolks to still be moist in the centre, but no longer liquid.

THE BREAKDOWN

The Protein	Fried eggs
The Vegetables	Onion, Chinese celery, grape tomatoes, peanuts
The Herbs	Cilantro, green onions
The Dressing	Fish sauce, lime juice, palm sugar, Thai chilies
Flavour Profile	Leads with sour, followed by salty, with a supportive sweet note.

Fried Egg Salad

Spicy Seafood Salad

Spicy Seafood Salad

Yum Talay

Serves: 4 as an appetizer, 2 as an entrée

Cooking Time: 30 minutes

Do-ahead Tips: Make the dressing without the clam juice in advance and store in the fridge.

THE DRESSING

1–3	Thai chilies, finely minced
3 cloves	Garlic, finely minced or grated
3 Tbsp	Lime juice
2 Tbsp	Fish sauce
2½ Tbsp	Thai chili paste (*nam prik pao*)

THE SALAD

1 lb	Live clams
As needed	Water
3 Tbsp	Lemongrass, thinly sliced into rounds
9 oz	Seafood mix of your choice: shrimp, squid, fish, scallops, etc.
½ cup	Thai basil leaves, chopped
¼ cup	Shallots, thinly julienned
½ cup	Grape tomatoes, halved
1–2	Green onions, chopped
¼ cup	Cilantro, chopped
For serving	Jasmine rice

Yum = A type of Thai salad; Talay = Ocean; in the context of food it refers to a mix of seafood

I wanted to include this recipe to show you how the basic *yum* dressing used in Fried Egg Salad (recipe p.134) can be turned into something different. I'm adding a large proportion of clams to this recipe, because the briny juice that clams release blends brilliantly with our *yum* dressing. Thai chili paste, or *nam prik pao*, enriches the otherwise light dressing, and its sweetness allows us to eliminate sugar altogether.

....

Make the dressing by stirring all the dressing ingredients together in a bowl; set aside.

Wash the clams in cold water and discard any that are broken or will not close their shells when tapped. If you are using wild clams, there may be sand inside the shells, but farm-raised clams usually don't have this problem. To get the clams to spit out sand, feel free to use your favourite method, but I like to soak them in cold water with salt for 30 minutes to an hour. After the clams have released the sand, rinse them again in cold water.

In a pot just big enough to hold the clams, add 1 inch of water and bring to a boil. Add the lemongrass and clams, then cover and cook for 1–2 minutes until the clams open. Remove from the heat and transfer the clams into a large mixing bowl, leaving the cooking water in the pot (it's fine if some of the lemongrass comes along with the clams). If some of the clams did not open, return them to the pot, cover, and cook them for another minute or so—some clams are just late bloomers! Discard any that still won't open after the second cooking.

Spoon out 3 Tbsp of the clam cooking liquid and add to the dressing; stir to mix and set aside.

Return the pot to the stove, bring the remaining cooking liquid to a boil, and blanch the seafood of your choice in this liquid, adding more water if needed. Add the cooked seafood to the clam bowl. Repeat with the remaining seafood (see *Tip for Success* below).

Toss the Thai basil and shallots with the seafood while it's still warm and let the heat wilt the shallots and infuse the basil's aroma. Pour the dressing over the seafood, then add the grape tomatoes, green onions, and cilantro; toss gently.

Serve in a shallow bowl on its own as an appetizer, or with jasmine rice.

IMPROVING ON TRADITION

Using the cooking liquid in the dressing isn't traditional, but I find that it bridges the flavour of the dressing together with that of the seafood, creating a more cohesive dish with a more intense ocean flavour. Adding a touch of lemongrass helps mellow out any fishiness from the seafood. Usually, the seafood for *yum talay* is blanched in plain water, but since we have this delicious briny clam juice, let's take advantage of it and bathe the other seafood in this wonderful liquid!

THE BREAKDOWN

The Protein	Seafood
The Vegetables	Grape tomatoes
The Herbs	Shallots, lemongrass, cilantro, green onions, Thai basil
The Dressing	Chilies, garlic, lime juice, fish sauce, Thai chili paste, clam juice
Flavour Profile	Sour and briny, with a distinct sweetness from the chili paste.

Tip for Success: If you are using fish in the salad, to prevent it from crumbling when tossed with the clams, toss it with some of the dressing separately and place it on the salad once plated.

If you are using scallops, you may choose to sear them on a skillet instead to get a brown crust.

Beef "Ceviche" with Lemongrass

Pla Neua

Pla = A type of Thai salad; Neua = Beef

Pla made with beef is a rare find. If a restaurant serves *pla* nowadays, it is most likely made with shrimp. In its original form, *pla* is made by cooking raw beef or shrimp with the acidity of lime juice, so this dish is like a magical cross between carpaccio and ceviche. In the era of food-borne illness outbreaks, people have slowly moved from raw towards medium-rare and even well-done proteins. I've decided to briefly sear the exterior of the steaks for food safety and added flavour. I'd also like to report that all my recipe taste-testers have had the same reaction to this dish after their first bite: "Wow."

Serves: 4 as an appetizer, 2 as an entrée
Cooking Time: 20 minutes
Special Tools: Mortar and pestle for making the dressing (optional)
Do-ahead Tips: Sear the beef and make the dressing in advance.

FOR THE SALAD

As needed	Vegetable oil
9 oz	Beef tenderloin or another tender cut of steak
3 Tbsp	Lime juice
2 inches	Lemongrass, bottom half only, thinly sliced
2 Tbsp	Shallots, thinly julienned
¼ cup	Mint leaves, chopped
2–3	Kaffir lime leaves, very thinly julienned
5 sprigs	Cilantro, leaves chopped, stems reserved for the dressing
2 Tbsp	Toasted pumpkin seeds or sunflower seeds (see note)
For garnish	Spur chili or red bell pepper, short juliennes
For garnish	Small mint leaves
For serving	Crisp lettuce leaves

Drizzle vegetable oil on the steak and rub to coat. In a sauté pan, heat a little vegetable oil over high heat until the oil is very hot. Place the steak down and sear for 20–30 seconds until well-browned, flip, and repeat on the other side. Sear the edges of the steak briefly by holding it up with tongs. Let rest for at least 5 minutes while you make the dressing.

For the dressing, pound together the garlic, Thai chilies, and cilantro stems using a mortar and pestle until there are no chunks. Add the palm sugar and pound to dissolve, then add the fish sauce and swirl the pestle to mix. *Note: Without a mortar and pestle, you can finely mince all the ingredients.*

Slice the beef into very thin, bite-sized strips and transfer to a small mixing bowl. Pour the lime juice over the beef and mix well; let sit for at least 5 minutes until the meat has cooked slightly.

Note: The toasted pumpkin seeds serve as an element of nuttiness and crunch; you can also use peanuts, cashews, macadamias, or pine nuts.

Pour the dressing over the beef and toss to mix. Add the lemongrass, shallots, mint, half the kaffir lime leaves, and half the cilantro; toss to mix. Taste and adjust the seasoning.

To serve, spread the beef in one layer on a large plate. Sprinkle with the pumpkin seeds, julienned peppers, small mint leaves, and the remaining kaffir lime leaves and cilantro. Serve with lettuce leaves, which you can use to wrap the beef. Serve on its own as an appetizer, or with jasmine rice as part of a meal.

PLA NEUA IN POETRY

I felt compelled to include *pla neua* in this book because of its romantic story. King Rama II was as much a poet as he was a gourmand. In the early 1800s, he composed several poems that sing the praises of many Thai dishes, with an intention to compliment his wife's culinary skills. *Pla neua* was one of the dishes mentioned in his most famous poem, giving it a unique historical and literary importance.

THE DRESSING

3–4 cloves	Garlic
1–3	Fresh Thai chilies
5	Cilantro stems, chopped
2 tsp	Palm sugar, finely chopped, packed
2 Tbsp	Fish sauce

THE BREAKDOWN

The Protein	Beef
The Vegetables	Pumpkin seeds, lettuce on the side
The Herbs	Lemongrass, kaffir lime leaves, mint, cilantro, shallots
The Dressing	Garlic, chilies, cilantro stems, fish sauce, palm sugar, lime juice
Flavour Profile	Leads with sour, followed by salty, and barely detectable sweetness.

Beef "Ceviche" with Lemongrass

Ground Duck Salad with Mint

Ground Duck Salad with Mint

Laab Bped

Serves: 4 as an appetizer, 2 as an entrée
Cooking Time: 50 minutes
Special Tools: Mortar and pestle, or another device for making toasted rice powder
Do-ahead Tips: Grind the duck and fry the skin in advance. Toast the rice a day in advance.

2	Duck breasts, about 9 oz each (see note)
¼ tsp	Salt
2 Tbsp	Water or chicken stock
¼ cup	Shallots, short juliennes
2 Tbsp	Lemongrass, thinly sliced into rounds (optional)
1½ Tbsp	Galangal, finely minced (optional)
2–3	Kaffir lime leaves, finely julienned (optional)
2 Tbsp	Fish sauce
3 Tbsp	Lime juice
To taste	Roasted chili flakes (recipe p.231) or regular chili flakes
½ cup	Mint, large leaves chopped, small leaves left whole
¼ cup	Cilantro, chopped
4–6 leaves	Sawtooth coriander or extra cilantro, chopped
1–2	Green onions, chopped
1–2 Tbsp	Toasted rice powder (recipe p.230)
For garnish	Small mint leaves (optional)
For serving	Sticky rice (recipe p.234) and fresh vegetables such as long beans, cucumber, or lettuce

Laab = A Northeastern salad made of ground meat; Bped = Duck

Using duck in *laab* sounds like the humble Northeastern dish's attempt to be gourmet, but that's far from its true origin. Rural villagers of the Northeast lead simple, agricultural lifestyles, raising farm animals in their backyard, ducks included. When *laab bped* is made in the countryside, it begins with slaughtering the duck. The entire duck is used—the meat, the skin, and everything inside. The bones are used to make a duck soup (like the *Tom Sap* on p.127) to pair with the salad. I like to fry the skin until crisp and sprinkle it on top for a crackly finish (it's better than crispy bacon!). *Laab bped* is now arguably the most popular *laab* in Thailand, but since Thai restaurants overseas rarely offer it, you're going to need a recipe!

....

Separate the duck skin from the meat and cut the skin crosswise into ¼-inch strips. Season the skin with salt, then add it to a small pot or sauté pan. Cook the skin over medium heat, stirring frequently, to render the fat. Once the fat has started pooling, turn the heat down to low, and keep frying until the skin is a deep-brown colour and the bubbling has stopped. The whole process should take about 8–10 minutes. Remove it with a slotted spoon and drain on paper towel. *Note: The stopping of bubbling indicates that there is no more water in the skin, which means it's crispy.*

To grind the duck meat, slice the duck meat thinly, then cut each slice into small pieces. Gather the duck pieces into a pile on a sturdy cutting board, and using a heavy knife or cleaver, mince the duck meat in a quick up-and-down, chop-chop-chop motion, changing the angle of the knife occasionally. Once you have chopped this side thoroughly, flip the duck meat over and repeat the mincing on the other side. To check completeness, grab a chunk of meat and pull it apart to see if there are still large pieces.

Note: I make ground duck meat the old-school way using a cleaver, and the instructions are provided here. You can ask the butcher to grind it for you, just remember to keep the skin separate and intact. You can also use duck legs and thighs; I use breasts simply because they are easier to process.

Add the 2 Tbsp of water or chicken stock to a small pot and bring to a boil over high heat. Add the ground duck meat and stir constantly until fully cooked. Remove from the heat.

To the duck pot, add the shallots, lemongrass, galangal, and kaffir lime leaves; stir to wilt and distribute the flavours. Stir in the fish sauce, lime juice, and chili flakes.

Before serving, toss in the ½ cup mint, cilantro, sawtooth coriander, green onions, and toasted rice powder. Taste and adjust the seasoning.

Serve the salad on a deep plate and sprinkle the crispy duck skin over top. Garnish with small mint leaves. Serve with sticky rice, which you can use to soak up the juices, and fresh vegetables, which serve as palate cleansers between bites. Serve warm or at room temperature.

GETTING BACK TO THE BASIC *LAAB*

It may look like the recipe has a long list of ingredients, but don't be discouraged: many of them are optional! For Thais, *laab* is supposed to simple and rustic—we don't sweat it if a couple of herbs are missing. I'd like *laab's* spirit of simplicity to also be in your kitchen; so, apart from the meat and the dressing, the must-have ingredients are shallots, toasted rice powder, mint, cilantro, and green onions. Sawtooth coriander is always used in Thailand, but adding extra cilantro also works. Galangal, lemongrass, and kaffir lime leaves are welcome additions for *laab* made with duck, beef, and fish, because they help soften gamey and fishy flavours.

THE BREAKDOWN

The Protein	Duck
The Vegetables	Served on the side, none in the dish
The Herbs	Shallots, lemongrass, galangal, kaffir lime leaves, mint, cilantro, sawtooth coriander, green onions
The Dressing	Fish sauce, lime juice, chili flakes, toasted rice powder
Flavour Profile	Leads with sour, followed by salty, balanced by the nuttiness of the toasted rice powder.

Toasted rice powder

Dressing It Up: For a less traditional but more elegant presentation, try pan-searing whole duck breasts. Score the skin and sear both sides until you get crispy skin and medium doneness. Then slice the duck thinly before tossing with the herbs and dressing—it'll be a meal to impress!.

Grilled Beef or Pork "Waterfall" Salad
Nam Tok Neua / Nam Tok Moo

Nam tok = Literally waterfall or falling water, a type of Northeastern Thai salad using grilled meat; Neua = Beef; Moo = Pork

This ingredient list might look uncannily familiar. This is because *nam tok* is essentially *laab* (recipe p.144) with the meat grilled rather than ground. This seemingly minor distinction, however, results in quite a different eating experience. "Waterfall" refers to the dripping (falling) of fat and meat juices (water) onto the charcoal while grilling. So, technically, the meat must be grilled in order to be called *nam tok*. On cold, rainy days, however, I do make exceptions for indoor pan-searing. *Nam tok* with beef is my personal favourite, but I also included an option for pork because it is very common in Thailand.

....

FOR THE BEEF:

Combine all the ingredients under option 1, except the beef, into a large zip-top bag. Close the bag and shake to mix the marinade. Put the steaks in the bag and close, squeezing out as much air as possible. Massage the steaks to ensure they are evenly coated in the marinade. Marinate in the fridge for at least 2 hours and up to 1 day.

Bring the steaks to room temperature 1 hour before grilling. Remove from the marinade and shake off any excess. Preheat the grill, then cook the steaks to the preferred doneness; I recommend medium for flank steak, about 3–4 minutes per side. Let the steaks rest for at least 5 minutes before cutting.

FOR THE PORK:

Remove any silver skin from the pork tenderloin and set side. Combine all the remaining ingredients under option 2, except the vegetable oil, in a large zip-top bag. Close the bag and shake to mix the marinade. Put the pork in the bag and close, squeezing out as much air as possible, and marinate in the fridge for at least 2 hours and up to 1 day.

Note: In Thailand, we often use the fatty "pork neck" or pork jowl butchered into a thin, grill-friendly, flank-steak-like piece. In North America, this cut is less available, so I've opted to use pork tenderloin. As the name suggests, it is tender, but it is also lean and dries out easily. I've added water to the marinade so it doubles as a brine for extra juiciness.

Serves: 6 as an appetizer, 3 as an entrée
Cooking Time: 30 minutes
Special Tools: Mortar and pestle, or another device for making toasted rice powder
Do-ahead Tips: Marinate the meat and toast the rice a day in advance.

OPTION 1: BEEF

2 cloves	Garlic, finely minced or grated
2 Tbsp	Soy sauce
1 Tbsp	Vegetable oil
2 tsp	Black soy sauce
2 tsp	Lime juice
2 tsp	Sugar, granulated
¼ tsp	Black pepper, ground
¼ tsp	White pepper, ground
1 lb	Flank steak, or another steak you prefer for grilling

OPTION 2: PORK

1 lb	Pork tenderloin (see note)
¾ cup	Water
3 Tbsp	Soy sauce
1 Tbsp	Black soy sauce
2 Tbsp	Sugar, granulated
3 cloves	Garlic, finely minced or grated
½ tsp	Salt
¼ tsp	Black pepper
¼ tsp	White pepper
As needed	Vegetable oil

(Continued)

SALAD

⅓ cup	Shallots, short juliennes
2–3	Green onions, chopped
1 cup	Mint, large leaves chopped, small leaves left whole
⅓ cup	Cilantro, chopped
¼ cup	Lemongrass, thinly sliced
8 leaves	Sawtooth coriander or extra cilantro, chopped (optional)
4 Tbsp	Lime juice
2–3 Tbsp	Fish sauce
2 Tbsp	Toasted rice powder (recipe p.230)
To taste	Roasted chili flakes (recipe p.231) or regular chili flakes
For garnish	Mint sprigs
For serving	Sticky rice (recipe p.234) and fresh vegetables such as long beans, cucumbers, or lettuce

THE BREAKDOWN

The Protein	Grilled beef or pork
The Vegetables	Fresh vegetables on the side
The Herbs	Shallots, mint, cilantro, green onions, lemongrass, sawtooth coriander
The Dressing	Fish sauce, lime juice, chili flakes, toasted rice powder
Flavour Profile	Leads with sour, followed by salty, balanced by the nuttiness of the toasted rice powder.

Nam tok

Bring the pork to room temperature 1 hour before grilling. Remove the pork from marinade, brush off any bits of garlic and pat dry. Coat the pork generously with vegetable oil and grill on medium heat, covered, turning the pork every 2 minutes. Cook until the internal temperature reaches 140°F, about 12-15 minutes. Let the pork rest for at least 10 minutes before cutting. The pork should still be slightly pink in the centre. *Note: If you're not grilling, you can brown the pork briefly on a skillet, then transfer to a 350°F oven for another 10-15 minutes to finish cooking.*

ASSEMBLING THE SALAD:

Slice the pork or beef, against the grain, into very thin, bite-sized slices and add to a large mixing bowl. Add all the salad ingredients and toss to mix. Taste and adjust the seasoning with more lime juice, fish sauce, and chili flakes as needed. *Note: Do not toss the salad with the dressing until ready to serve as the meat will continue to "cook" in the acid of the lime juice.*

Garnish the salad with a mint sprig and serve with sticky rice and fresh vegetables. You can use the sticky rice to soak up the juices, and munch on the vegetables for extra crunch and freshness. Serve warm or at room temperature.

TUNING IT UP

Nam tok is pretty much all meat, but that's why it's such a great candidate for some creative "tune-ups." I've sliced some sweet corn off the cob and thrown it into *nam tok neua*—a tremendous success that I recommend you try. Rounds of radishes add a beautiful pop of colour and a refreshing crunch that's perfect for a summer potluck. Come up with other ideas and share them with me; it may not be traditional, but it's a great culinary exercise and a lot of fun!

Green Papaya Salad

Som Tum

Som = Isaan dialect for "sour"; Tum = To pound something in a mortar and pestle

Perhaps no other Thai salad is better known than this crunchy, spicy Northeastern specialty. What makes this salad exciting is the way it is made: pounded in a large, light-duty mortar and pestle (see p. 85). So many Western-style salads are all about gently tossing delicate greens, so pounding a salad may seem unintuitive, but the pounding serves many purposes: it helps grind the garlic and chilies, it releases the juice from the tomatoes which is part of the dressing, it crushes the peanuts to help distribute them more evenly, and it bruises the long beans to allow the dressing to penetrate their firm flesh. If you don't have a mortar and pestle, not to worry, I've included an alternate method in the instructions.

....

In the mortar, pound the garlic and chilies into a paste. Add the palm sugar and pound until most of it is dissolved.

Add the peanuts, long beans, and dried shrimp, and pound to crush the peanuts and bruise the long beans, using a large spoon to flip the mixture occasionally.

Add the fish sauce, lime juice, and tamarind juice. Throw in the squeezed lime, skin and all, for added lime flavour. Mix with a large spoon.

Add the tomatoes and papaya, and mix using the "pound and flip" technique: using the pestle to pound 3–5 times, then with a large spoon, flipping the salad from bottom to top. Repeat a few more times until the salad looks thoroughly mixed. Taste and adjust the seasoning.

Serve at room temp or chilled. *Som tum* is often served with sticky rice and barbecued chicken.

Serves: 2
Cooking Time: 15 minutes
Special Tools: Light-duty, large mortar and pestle (optional)

THE SALAD

2–3 cloves	Garlic
1–3	Thai chilies, to taste
2 Tbsp	Palm sugar, finely chopped, packed
¼ cup	Roasted peanuts
5	Long beans, 1-inch pieces
1½ Tbsp	Dried shrimp, small, roughly chop if you have large ones
2 Tbsp	Fish sauce (see note)
2 Tbsp	Lime juice
1 Tbsp	Tamarind juice
2 cups	Green papaya, peeled and julienned (see note)
¾ cup	Grape tomatoes, halved

Note: If you are feeling adventurous, you can substitute 1 Tbsp of fish sauce with pla ra, or fermented fish paste. It is sold in a glass jar or bottle at some Asian grocers and is a muddy grey colour.

To julienne, you can use a julienne peeler or a knife. If you want to try the Thai julienning technique, scan the QR code for my papaya salad video.

Papaya salad

No Mortar & Pestle Method: In a large mixing bowl, combine the fish sauce, lime juice, tamarind juice, and finely grated palm sugar; stir until the sugar is mostly dissolved. Grate the garlic with a zester and finely mince the chilies; add to the bowl. Roughly chop the peanuts and add to the bowl. Bruise the long beans with any pestle-like object (a bottle or a rolling pin), then add to the bowl. Add the tomatoes and press down gently with a spoon to release some juice. Add the dried shrimp and papaya and toss everything together.

LEFTOVER GREEN PAPAYA?

So you've used half the papaya for your salad. What will you do with the rest of it? Green papaya is a lot more versatile than you might think. We often add it to sour curries (*gaeng som* p. 111) and it's delicious in stir-fries. Treat green papaya like you would a firm vegetable like carrot and broccoli, and let your imagination run wild!

The Protein	Dried shrimp
The Vegetables	Green papaya, long beans, grape tomatoes
The Herbs	Garlic, Thai chilies
The Dressing	Fish sauce, lime juice, tamarind juice, palm sugar
Flavour Profile	The flavour profile of papaya salad varies greatly from region to region, so feel free to adjust to your own preferences, but most commonly it leads with sour, followed by salty and sweet.

Savoury Fruit Salad
Tum Polamai

Tum = To pound something in a mortar and pestle; Polamai = Fruit

This was the cool new food trend when I was in high school. Papaya salad vendors were trying to diversify by experimenting with new ingredients, and as it turned out, using a mixture of fruit really spoke to diners' taste buds. Any fruit can be used, but in Thailand, there will always be apples because, to us, apples are an exotic, fancy fruit, which is part of the appeal of this dish! I have three tips for choosing the best fruit combination: choose fruits with a mix of colours, flavours, and textures; always include a crunchy fruit; and avoid anything that's overly sweet.

···

In the mortar, pound the garlic and chilies into a paste. Add the palm sugar and pound until it is mostly dissolved.

Add the dried shrimp, long beans, and peanuts; pound to crush the peanuts and bruise the long beans, using a large spoon to flip the mixture occasionally. Add the tomatoes and crush gently to release some juice.

Add the lime juice and fish sauce, throwing in the squeezed lime, skin and all, for added fragrance. Toss with a spoon until well combined.

Add the fruit and carrot, and toss everything together. If your mortar is too small you can transfer everything to a large mixing bowl. Taste and adjust seasoning.

Serve at room temperature or chilled.

Serves: 2
Cooking Time: 15 minutes
Special Tools: Light-duty, large mortar and pestle (optional)

THE SALAD

2 cloves	Garlic
1–3	Thai chilies, to taste
2 Tbsp	Palm sugar, finely chopped, packed
1 Tbsp	Dried shrimp, small, roughly chop if you have large ones
5	Long beans, 1-inch pieces
3 Tbsp	Roasted peanuts or cashews
¾ cups	Grape tomatoes, halved
3 Tbsp	Lime juice
2 Tbsp	Fish sauce
3 cups	Mix of fruit of your choice, bite-sized pieces (see note)
¼ cup	Shredded carrots

Note: Pick 4-5 types of fruit that have contrasting colours and textures. Some great choices are Granny Smith apples, grapes, pomelo, dragon fruit, kiwi, Asian pear, green mango, pineapple, and sweet corn (it's botanically a fruit!).

No Mortar & Pestle Method: In a large mixing bowl, place the palm sugar, fish sauce, and lime juice; stir until the sugar is mostly dissolved. Grate the garlic with a zester, finely mince the chilies, and add to the bowl. Roughly chop the peanuts and bruise the long beans with any pestle-like object (a bottle or a rolling pin); add to the bowl. Add the tomatoes and press down gently with a spoon to release some juice. Add the fruit and carrots and toss everything together.

The Protein	Dried shrimp
The Vegetables	Fruit, carrots, long beans, grape tomatoes, peanuts
The Herbs	Garlic, Thai chilies
The Dressing	Fish sauce, lime juice, palm sugar
Flavour Profile	Sweet and sour, with just enough saltiness to balance.

GREEN MANGO SALAD

Speaking of fruit salads, I've had several requests for green mango salad, but I decided to include this recipe instead because the right green mango for the job is hard to find for most of us living outside of Thailand. However, if you get hold of one, you can simply substitute it for all the fruits and vegetables in this recipe. Add some shallots, green onion, and cilantro and you're golden. Adjust the amount of lime juice according to how sour the mango is. For the record, the perfect mango salad needs a mango with no hint of yellow, a very firm crunch, and a sharp acidity. Serve with some crispy, deep-fried fish and it's a culinary pair like no other!

STIR-FRIES

pad ผัด

Stir-fries in Thailand can be divided into three different styles: Chinese, Thai, and a hybrid of the two. The following are examples of each style. Note the differences in the aromatics and seasonings.

CHINESE STYLE

Chicken Stir-Fry with Ginger & Mushrooms — *Gai Pad King*

Stir-Fried Rice Noodles with
Soy Sauce & Chinese Broccoli — *Pad See Ew*

Pineapple Fried Rice — *Kao Pad Sapparod*

Crispy Spring Rolls — *Paw Pia Tod*

THAI STYLE

Red Curry Stir-Fry with Tilapia — *Pad Ped Pla Nin*

Pad Thai

Tamarind Shrimp — *Goong Pad Makaam*

HYBRID

Eggplant Stir-Fry with Thai Basil — *Pad Makeua Yao*

Holy Basil Chicken Fried Rice with Fried Egg — *Kao Pad Gaprao Gai Kai Dao*

Cashew Chicken — *Gai Pad Med Mamuang Himapan*

Chicken Stir-Fry with Ginger & Mushrooms

Gai Pad King

Gai = Chicken; Pad = Stir-fry; King = Ginger

This is a great dish to introduce kids to Thai food because the flavours are a bit more mellow, and I always found the crunch of the black fungus so much fun to eat. Contrary to many people's impressions, ginger is not used often in Thai cuisine. This spicy herb has been integrated into a handful of Thai dishes through the influence of Chinese cuisine, making this a great example of a Chinese-style stir-fry.

....

Marinate the chicken in 1 Tbsp of the soy sauce for at least 20 minutes.

Soak the black fungus in hot water for 8-10 minutes (it will expand to 3-4 times its original size). Drain and cut it into bite-sized pieces, discarding the core, if any.

In a small bowl, combine the remaining 1 Tbsp of soy sauce, 3 Tbsp of the chicken stock, oyster sauce, fermented soybean paste, black soy sauce, sesame oil (if using), sugar, and white pepper; stir to mix well.

Heat the oil in a wok or sauté pan over high heat until hot. Add the garlic and cook, stirring constantly, until the garlic starts to brown. Add the marinated chicken and toss just until the chicken pieces no longer stick together, about 30 seconds. Add the sauce mixture and ginger, then keep stirring until the chicken is 80% done.

Add the black fungus, onion, and spur chili; stir until the chicken is done, adjusting the amount of sauce you want with some or all of the remaining stock. Remove from the heat and stir in the green onions. Taste and adjust the seasoning. Serve with jasmine rice.

Note: Black fungus, also known as cloud ear fungus, is a type of mushroom that often comes dried (top right of picture) and needs to be rehydrated before use. You can also use 4 oz of another type of fresh mushrooms.

STIR-FRIES AND WATER

Achieving an ideal amount of sauce in a stir-fry requires some on-the-fly judgment. On a high-BTU stove, you will likely lose more water from the high heat input, and therefore need to add more stock than someone with a gentler burner. Likewise, if your pan is small and crowded, you will trap more steam, have a lower pan temperature, and consequently need less added liquid. So it's important that you pay attention to the amount of sauce in the pan and adjust accordingly. Also, if you purposefully add more water to get extra sauce, you may need to increase the amount of seasoning to compensate for the dilution.

Serves: 3-4

Cooking Time: 10 minutes + at least 20 minutes to marinate chicken

Do-ahead Tips: Soak the mushrooms in advance. Marinate the chicken a day in advance.

1 lb	Chicken thighs or breasts, boneless, skinless, ½-inch thick slices
2 Tbsp	Soy sauce
¾ oz	Dried black fungus (see note)
¼-½ cup	Unsalted chicken stock (recipe p.232) or water
1½ Tbsp	Oyster sauce
1 Tbsp	Fermented soybean paste (*tao jiew*) or ½ Tbsp miso paste
1 tsp	Black soy sauce
½ tsp	Toasted sesame oil (optional)
1½ tsp	Sugar, granulated
¼ tsp	White pepper, ground
2 Tbsp	Vegetable oil
4-5 cloves	Garlic, chopped
3-inch section	Ginger, peeled and finely julienned
¼	Medium onion, julienned
1	Spur chili or ½ small red bell pepper, julienned
2-3	Green onions, 2-inch pieces, halve white part horizontally
For serving	Jasmine rice

THE BREAKDOWN

The Style	Chinese
The Aromatics	Ginger, garlic, green onions
The Nuggets	Chicken, onion, black fungus, spur chili
The Sauce	Soy sauce, oyster sauce, *tao jiew*, black soy sauce, sugar, white pepper, sesame oil, chicken stock
Flavour Profile	Salty with a hint of sweetness.

Stir-Fried Rice Noodles with Soy Sauce & Chinese Broccoli

Pad See Ew

Serves: 2
Cooking Time: 10 minutes + 15 minutes to marinate protein
Do-ahead Tips: Make extra sauce and keep in the fridge for future uses. Make *prik nam som* in advance.

This recipe is for 2 servings, but I recommend cooking one serving at a time for maximum heat and noodle charring, so you may want to separate the ingredients into two lots.

6 oz	Protein of choice (see note)
1 Tbsp	Soy sauce (omit if using seafood or tofu)
3 Tbsp	Vegetable oil
4 cloves	Garlic, chopped
2	Eggs
4–6 stalks	Chinese broccoli, stems thinly sliced on a bias, leaves chopped
1 lb	Fresh, wide rice noodles, also called *ho fun* noodles (see note)
4 tsp	Sugar, granulated
To taste	White pepper, ground
For serving	*Prik nam som* (recipe p.231) and roasted chili flakes (recipe p.231)

Note: If using beef, pork, or chicken, slice them into thin, bite-sized pieces. If using shrimp, peel and devein.

If you cannot find fresh rice noodles, watch my tutorial on how to make your own fresh rice noodles by scanning the QR code on the facing page.

Pad = Stir-fry; See ew = Soy sauce

At the basic level, this dish is just noodles and soy sauce, making it a great example of a Chinese-style stir-fry, because both of these ingredients are of Chinese origin. But the combination of the umami punch, the sweet-salty interplay, and the satisfying chew of fresh rice noodles makes *pad see ew* one of the most popular lunch items in Thailand, especially for people who don't like spicy food.

....

If using beef, pork, or chicken, marinate with soy sauce for 10–15 minutes.

Grease a small bowl generously with cooking oil, then add all the sauce ingredients to the bowl. *Note: Greasing the bowl helps the thick sauce slide out more easily.*

Heat the vegetable oil in a wok or a large sauté pan over medium-high heat. When hot, add the protein and cook just until done. Remove and set aside in a small bowl.

To the same pan, add more oil if needed, then add the garlic and sauté until it starts to turn golden brown. Add the eggs, break the yolks, let them set halfway, then scramble. Add the Chinese broccoli and toss to cook just until it turns bright green, about 10–15 seconds.

Add the noodles, sauce, and sugar. Turn the heat up to high and toss to coat the noodles evenly in the sauce. Once coated, spread the noodles out to cover the entire pan and let them sit without stirring for about 10 seconds, or until some of the noodles have developed a "toasted" or "charred" look. Flip the noodles and let them sit again to toast the other side.

Add the protein back into the pan and toss briefly just to mix. All the sauce should be completely absorbed when done, so if it still looks wet, cook it a bit longer.

Transfer onto a plate and sprinkle with white pepper (a lot of white pepper is good for this dish!). Serve with *prik nam som* and roasted chili flakes. To use *prik nam som*, sprinkle a little bit of the vinegar onto the noodles and mix well; you can also eat the chilies for extra spice and tartness. The acid of the vinegar will help brighten the dish.

Tip for Success: You can make a large batch of sauce ahead of time and store it in a jar in the fridge. Whenever you want to make pad see ew, use 2 Tbsp + 1 tsp per serving. This sauce is also great for fried rice or a vegetable stir-fry—very handy for dinner on a busy night!

SIZE DOES MATTER

Make sure you use a large enough wok or pan so the noodles have a lot of room to spread. Crowding the pan will trap steam, which will make the noodles wet and they won't get the nice toasted flavour.

THE SAUCE

2 Tbsp	Oyster sauce
1 Tbsp	Soy sauce
½ Tbsp	Fish sauce
½ Tbsp	Seasoning sauce, such as Golden Mountain or Maggi
2 tsp	Black soy sauce

THE BREAKDOWN

The Style	Chinese
The Aromatics	Garlic, white pepper
The Nuggets	Noodles, protein of choice, Chinese broccoli, egg
The Sauce	Oyster sauce, soy sauce, fish sauce, seasoning sauce, black soy sauce, sugar
Flavour Profile	Salty and sweet with a little acidity from the condiment.

Fresh rice noodles

Pineapple Fried Rice
Kao Pad Sapparod

Kao = Rice; Pad = Stir-fry; Sapparod = Pineapple

I have a soft spot for fried rice, and I usually eat too much of it in one sitting because I just find it so hard to stop, especially with pineapple fried rice. With all of its many ingredients, there is a lot going on—the nuttiness of the cashews, the sweet-tartness of the pineapple, and the fragrance of the curry powder. Choose any kind of curry powder that you like for this, there is no right or wrong. I actually started out with store-bought curry powder and doctored it up with the spices in my pantry until the smell of it really struck a chord with me. It's a great way to make your version unique!

....

Note: Leftover cold rice is perfect for fried rice, but if you need to make fresh rice, use a little less water than normal and, if possible, refrigerate before using.

This shrimp paste is not to be confused with fermented shrimp paste (gapi). This one is made from shrimp tomalley that has been cooked with some herbs and seasoning. It is orange, comes in a glass jar, and is usually labelled "shrimp paste with soybean oil."

Serves: 2
Cooking Time: 10 minutes
Do-ahead Tips: Cook the rice ahead of time, fluff to loosen the grains, and refrigerate.

2 Tbsp	Vegetable oil
8	Shrimp, medium size, leave 4 whole, and cut the rest into small pieces
1	Egg
1½ cups	Cooked jasmine rice (see note)
¼ cup	Onion, small dice
1 Tbsp	Soy sauce
1 tsp	Fish sauce
1 tsp	Shrimp paste (shrimp tomalley, optional, see note)
1 tsp	Curry powder
1 tsp	Sugar, granulated
⅛ tsp	Salt
¼ tsp	White pepper, ground
½ cup	Pineapple, fresh, small bite-sized pieces
⅓ cup	Cashews, roasted
½ cup	Tomatoes, seeds removed, ½-inch cubes
2	Green onions, chopped
For serving	Cucumber slices

In a wok or a large frying pan, heat 1 Tbsp of the vegetable oil until hot. Sear the four whole shrimp until done; remove and set aside. In the same pan, add the small pieces of shrimp and cook until done; remove and set aside.

Add more oil to the wok if needed, then add the egg and scramble it slightly. When the egg is halfway set, add the rice and onion; toss to mix. Add the soy sauce, fish sauce, shrimp paste (if using), curry powder, sugar, salt, and white pepper; toss until the rice grains are separated and evenly coated by the seasoning. If there are clumps of rice, press on them with the back of your spatula to break them apart.

Add the pineapple, cashews, and small pieces of shrimp; toss until the rice is dry and the pineapple is heated through. Turn off the heat and toss in the tomatoes and most of the green onions, reserving some for garnish.

Plate and top with the whole shrimp. Sprinkle over the reserved green onion for garnish. Serve with fresh cucumber slices to add freshness and crunchiness and balance out the richness of the fried rice.

FRESH OR CANNED?

Even though canned pineapple can be used for this recipe, I suggest using fresh. For a savoury application, I find canned pineapple to be too sweet. The tartness of fresh pineapple works well to balance the saltiness of the rice without making it too sweet.

THE BREAKDOWN

The Style	Chinese
The Aromatics	Onion, curry powder, white pepper, green onion
The Nuggets	Rice, shrimp, pineapple, tomato, cashews
The Sauce	Soy sauce, fish sauce, sugar, salt, shrimp paste
Flavour Profile	Salty balanced by the sweetness and tartness from the pineapple.

Crispy Spring Rolls
Paw Pia Tod

Paw Pia = Spring Rolls; Tod = Deep fried

Stir-frying in Thai cuisine is often used in combination with other cooking techniques. Fillings for things such as stuffed pastries, dumplings, and spring rolls are almost always made by stir-frying. The filling for these crispy spring rolls is basically stir-fried glass noodles, and it's so good that I've been known to just eat the filling and skip the wrapping altogether! If you do get to the wrapping, these rolls are perfectly complemented by the sweet chili dipping sauce on p. 211.

....

Soak the glass noodles in room-temperature water for 10 minutes. Drain, then cut them into short pieces, about 2-3 inches long, with scissors.

Remove the shiitake mushrooms from the soaking water and squeeze the mushrooms firmly to remove as much water as possible. Finely chop the mushrooms and set aside.

Mix the ground pork with 1 tsp of the soy sauce and set aside.

In a wok or large sauté pan, add a little vegetable oil, the garlic, black pepper, and white pepper; stir until the garlic turns slightly golden. Add the pork and cook until no longer clumpy and almost done. Add the shiitake mushrooms, noodles, cabbage, carrots, cilantro stems, sugar, salt, and the remaining 2 tsp soy sauce. Toss until the noodles are fully cooked and the cabbage is wilted, adding a splash of water if the noodles start sticking.

Remove from the heat, taste, and add more salt as needed. Put the filling into a bowl and let cool before wrapping.

To wrap: Place one spring roll wrapper on a clean surface with a corner pointing towards you. Place a heaping ¼ cup of filling on the wrapper slightly off centre and towards you, and spread the filling out into a log shape, about 5 inches long. Pull the corner closest to you over the filling and roll once, making the roll as tight as you can. Keeping the roll in place with one hand, fold the left and right corners inward with the other hand and keep rolling until the side corners are tucked under. Use your finger or a brush to brush the beaten egg along the edges of the remaining wrapper; continue rolling until the end.

Makes: 12–14 rolls
Cooking Time: 10 minutes to cook the filling + 20 minutes to fry
Do-ahead Tips: Make the filling in advance, or make the rolls and refrigerate for up to 2 days or freeze for up to a few months.

1½ oz	Glass noodles, dry
3–4	Shiitake mushrooms, soaked in water until soft (at least 1 hour)
4 oz	Ground pork
1 Tbsp	Soy sauce
As needed	Vegetable oil for frying
4 cloves	Garlic, minced
¼ tsp	Black pepper, ground
½ tsp	White pepper, ground
1½ cups	Cabbage, finely shredded
1 cup	Carrot, grated
6	Cilantro stems, finely chopped
1 Tbsp	Sugar
½ tsp	Salt
12–14	8-inch spring roll wrappers, thawed
1	Egg, beaten

Tip for Success: Thawed spring roll wrappers can be hard to separate from one another, so I like to peel them apart ahead of time so that when I wrap, they are loose and easy to use. Keep the wrappers covered under a damp kitchen towel when not using them to prevent them from drying out.

To fry: Heat 2–3 inches of oil in a pot to 350°F. Add the spring rolls and fry until golden brown, about 5 minutes.

Let cool slightly before serving. You can cut the spring rolls in half on a sharp bias for a nicer presentation. Serve with sweet chili dipping sauce (recipe p. 211).

CHANGING UP THE FILLING

One of the beauties of spring rolls is that they are like a blank canvas—feel free to exercise your cook's creativity and come up with your own filling. You can start by changing up the protein, or perhaps you want to add some Thai chili paste to the seasoning. Try a samosa-style filling using potato, chicken, and yellow curry paste, or you can even make dessert spring rolls with bananas, drizzled with sweetened condensed milk!

Spring rolls

The Style	Chinese
The Aromatics	Garlic, white pepper, black pepper, cilantro stems
The Nuggets	Glass noodles, cabbage, carrot, shiitake mushrooms, pork
The Sauce	Soy sauce, salt, sugar
Flavour Profile	Salty with just a hint of sweetness to balance.

*Stir-Fried Noodles with
Soy Sauce & Chinese Broccoli*

Red Curry Stir-Fry with Tilapia

Red Curry Stir-Fry with Tilapia

Pad Ped Pla Nin

Serves: 3

Cooking Time: 30 minutes + 30 minutes for making curry paste

Special Tools: Heavy-duty mortar and pestle, or another device for making curry paste

Do-ahead Tips: Make the curry paste in advance.

As needed	Vegetable oil for deep-frying
1¼ cups	Holy basil or Thai basil leaves (see note)
1 lb	Tilapia filet, skin optional, 1-inch cubes
1 cup	All-purpose flour or cornstarch
2 Tbsp	Vegetable oil
1 recipe	Red curry paste (recipe p. 101) or 4 Tbsp store-bought paste
½–1 cup	Chicken stock, unsalted (recipe p.232)
2 tsp	Fish sauce
2 Tbsp	Palm sugar, finely chopped, packed
⅓ cup	Fingerroot (*grachai*), brined or fresh, finely julienned
3 stems	Young peppercorns, brined or fresh, cut each stem in half (optional)
4-5	Kaffir lime leaves, finely julienned
1	Spur chili, sliced, or ¼ red bell pepper, julienned
For serving	Jasmine rice

Note: Some of the basil is used for deep-frying, so it's important that the leaves are extremely dry. If the leaves are wet, the oil will splatter aggressively, which can be dangerous. If you must wash the basil leaves, make sure they dry off completely before frying.

Pad = Stir-fry; Ped = Spicy; Pla Nin = Tilapia

If you're looking for an unabashed, unadulterated experience of Thai herbs and spices, this is it. This dish should not be saucy like most stir-fries are; the sauce should all end up coating the fish, which is why the flavour of the curry paste in this dish is so intense. Traditionally, this dish uses a type of catfish that is not available here in Canada, so I've chosen tilapia, a versatile fish that is used often in Thai cuisine.

....

For crispy basil: In a pot, heat 1 inch of vegetable oil over medium heat to 350°F and have a paper-towel-lined plate ready. Fry ½ cup of the dry basil leaves in small batches. The oil will bubble quite aggressively at first, so stand back after you drop in the leaves. When the bubbling has almost completely stopped, it means they are crispy (this will only take a few seconds). Remove the leaves with a wire skimmer and drain on the paper towel. Keep the oil for frying the fish.

Pat the fish dry with paper towel. Put the flour or cornstarch in a mixing bowl and toss the fish in it to coat. Shake off as much excess flour as possible by tossing the fish cubes in a sieve or a wire skimmer—there should be just a thin, translucent film of flour.

Using the same oil you used to fry the basil, bring it to 375°F over medium-high heat. Fry the fish until fully cooked, golden brown, and crispy, about 3 minutes. Drain on paper towel.

Heat 2 Tbsp of oil in a wok or a large sauté pan over medium heat, add the curry paste and cook until aromatic, about 1-2 minutes. Add ½ cup of chicken stock, fish sauce, and sugar; stir until the sugar is dissolved. Add fingerroot, young peppercorns, and kaffir lime leaves; stir for 30 seconds to infuse.

If the sauce has dried up, add some or all of the remaining stock so you have enough sauce to coat the fish. Add the fried fish and spur chili; toss gently to evenly coat all pieces. When the sauce is no longer pooling, turn the heat off and fold in the remaining fresh basil.

To serve, top the fish with crispy basil and serve with jasmine rice. For extra heat, diners can eat the young peppercorns by picking them off the stems and discard the stems.

CAN WE DO WITHOUT THE FRYING?

If you don't like to deep-fry because of health reasons, or simply because it's a messy, oil-wasteful affair, trust me, I empathize. The fish is deep-fried to create a rough surface that will allow the sauce to adhere well to the fish. It also makes the fish sturdy enough to withstand tossing without crumbling. You can still enjoy the essence of this dish without the frying by omitting the fried basil and choosing another type of protein that can withstand stir-frying—pork, beef, chicken, scallops, or shrimp all work well. The sauce won't coat the protein quite as well, but it'll still be delicious. Since raw protein will give off some liquid when cooked, you will need less stock.

THE BREAKDOWN

The Style	Thai
The Aromatic	Curry paste, kaffir lime leaves, young peppercorns, fingerroot, Thai or holy basil
The Nuggets	Fish, spur chili, crispy basil
The Sauce	Fish sauce, sugar, chicken stock
Flavour Profile	Salty and sweet.

Tamarind Shrimp

Goong Pad Makaam

Goong = Shrimp; Pad = Stir-Fry; Makaam = Tamarind

This dish is a great example of how the right balance of sweet, salty, and sour can be surprisingly delicious. Because the sauce is so simple, and because we're dealing with ingredients that differ from brand to brand, tasting and adjusting the sauce is key to your success. The crispy, fried shallots sprinkled on top are really the cherries on this sundae, so don't be tempted to skip them!

....

Spread the sliced shallots on a paper-towel-lined plate, sprinkle generously with salt, and let sit for 15 minutes. Press paper towel onto the shallots to dry off the water that the salt has drawn out.

Heat 1 inch of vegetable oil in a pot over low heat to about 300°F, add the shallots, and fry, stirring constantly, until they turn golden brown, keeping the heat low. Remove the shallots as soon as they are golden brown and the bubbling has subsided. Drain on paper towel. (See *The Secret to Frying Shallots*, p. 107.)

Pound the garlic, shallots, cilantro roots, and Thai chilies in a mortar and pestle into a rough paste. Alternatively, process them in a small food processor.

In a wok or a sauté pan, heat 2 Tbsp vegetable oil over medium-high heat. Add the shrimp and sear until browned. Flip and sear the other side. Turn off the heat, remove the shrimp from the pan, and set aside. It's okay if the shrimp are not fully cooked at this point.

Serves: 3
Cooking Time: 20 minutes
Special Tools: Mortar and pestle (optional)

¼ cup	Shallots, thinly sliced (for fried shallots)
A pinch	Salt
As needed	Vegetable oil for frying
3 cloves	Garlic
2	Shallots, small, chopped (for sauce)
2	Cilantro roots or 6 stems
1–2	Thai chilies
9 oz	Large shrimp
½ cup	Chicken stock or water
3 Tbsp	Palm sugar, finely chopped, packed
3 Tbsp	Tamarind juice
1½ Tbsp	Fish sauce
¼ cup	Mix of red and green chilies, sliced into rounds (e.g. spur chilies, jalapeños, or fresnos)
For garnish	Cilantro and fried dried chilies

If the oil looks brown, start the next step with a fresh wok. Over medium-low heat, sauté the herb paste in 2 Tbsp vegetable oil until aromatic. Add the chicken stock, palm sugar, tamarind juice, and fish sauce and stir until the sugar is dissolved. Let the sauce reduce until it is thick enough to coat the shrimp. Add the shrimp and toss to coat. If the shrimp are not fully cooked at this point, let them cook until done. Toss in the red and green chilies and remove from the heat.

Remove the shrimp, leaving the sauce behind, and set them aside in a bowl. Pour the sauce onto the serving plate, then arrange the shrimp neatly on top of the sauce. Top generously with the fried shallots, and garnish with the fried chilies and cilantro.

Serve as an appetizer or on its own with jasmine rice.

GO BIG OR GO SMALL

The larger the shrimp, the more elegant your dish will look. I like to use shrimp of at least 16–20 count, and larger if I can find them. The numbers denote the number of shrimp per pound, so the smaller the numbers, the larger the shrimp. Having said that, I sometimes use small, bite-sized shrimp to make little tamarind shrimp hors d'oeuvres: fry up some wonton chips or use tortilla chips, pipe on a little drop of Thai basil aioli, and top with the sauce-coated shrimp. Garnish with crispy fried shallots and cilantro leaves, and I promise your guests will be impressed!

THE BREAKDOWN

The Style	Thai
The Aromatic	Garlic, shallots, cilantro roots, Thai chilies
The Nuggets	Shrimp, fried shallots, red and green chilies
The Sauce	Palm sugar, fish sauce, tamarind juice, chicken stock
Flavour Profile	Lead with sweet and sour, backed by salt.

Tamarind Shrimp

Pad Thai

Serves: 2-3

Cooking Time: 15 minutes + 1 hour to soak noodles

Do-ahead Tips: Make the sauce in advance and store in fridge; soak the noodles in advance, drain, and store in fridge in a sealed container

THE SAUCE

3 Tbsp	Palm sugar, finely chopped, packed
3 Tbsp	Water
¼ cup	Tamarind juice (see note)
2 Tbsp	Fish sauce (see note)

THE REST

4 oz	Dry rice noodles, medium size (2½-3 mm)
4 oz piece	Pressed tofu, cut into small pieces, about ¾ cup (see note)
¼ cup	Sweet preserved daikon radish (chai po waan), finely chopped
3 cloves	Garlic, chopped
1	Shallot, chopped
1 Tbsp	Dried shrimp, rinsed and finely chopped
½-1 tsp or to taste	Chili flakes
2½ cups	Bean sprouts
1 cup	Garlic chives, 2-inch pieces
¼ cup	Roasted peanuts, chopped
2	Eggs
2-3 Tbsp	Vegetable oil
8-12	Shrimp, peeled and deveined
1	Lime

Pad = Stir-fry; Thai = Thai

Pad thai was created after the country had just changed its name from *Pratet Siam* to *Pratet Thai*. It seems ironic that the one dish whose name was honoured with "Thai"—a buzzword at the time—uses noodles, a Chinese ingredient. But that was the point: around the time of World War II, Chinese immigrants had made noodle dishes wildly popular among Thai people. The Prime Minister, known for his Thai patriotism, tried to fight the spread of Chinese culinary influence by creating a noodle dish that used Thai ingredients and flavours. This is why *pad thai* contains no ingredients common to other noodle dishes, such as soy sauce and oyster sauce.

. . . .

Soak the noodles in room-temperature water for about 1 hour, until the noodles turn white and are pliable.

Make the sauce by combining the palm sugar and water in a heat-proof bowl, and then microwaving for 30–45 seconds or until hot; stir to dissolve most of the sugar. Stir in the tamarind and fish sauce.

Organize your prep by combining the tofu, preserved radish, garlic, shallot, dried shrimp, and chili flakes in one bowl. In another bowl, combine the bean sprouts, garlic chives, and half of the peanuts. Crack your eggs into a small bowl, so you avoid having to fish egg shells out of a hot pan.

Heat 2 Tbsp of the oil in a wok or large sauté pan over medium-high heat until hot. Add the shrimp and let them cook, without moving, until they are halfway done. Flip the shrimp and cook the other side. Remove and set aside.

To the same wok, add everything in the tofu bowl. Cook, stirring constantly, until the garlic starts to turn golden brown, adding more oil if it seems dry.

Add the noodles and pour the sauce over the noodles; keep tossing until all the liquid is absorbed and the noodles are cooked. When the sauce is all absorbed, push the noodles over to one side and add the eggs into the empty space. Scramble the eggs slightly and swirl the pan to spread the eggs wide. Once the egg is 50% set, put the noodles on top of the egg and let it sit for 10–15 seconds to set the eggs.

Flip the noodles so the eggs are now on top; stir to break up the eggs. Add everything in the bean sprouts bowl and toss to incorporate into the noodles. Remove from the heat.

To serve, transfer the noodles onto a plate, making sure to distribute the tofu evenly, as it tends to slip off the noodles and stay in the wok. Arrange the shrimp on top of the noodles and sprinkle on the remaining peanuts. Serve immediately with a piece of lime. You can also serve extra bean sprouts, peanuts, chili flakes, and garlic chives on the side. If you can find fresh banana blossoms, they are also traditionally served with *pad thai.* Be sure to squeeze the lime over the noodles before you eat them!

> *Tip for Success: This ratio of liquid to noodles results in perfectly chewy noodles for me. But to be sure, taste the noodles to check their consistency after all the sauce has been absorbed; if they feel too chewy, add a splash of water and cook longer until dry.*

WHAT COLOUR IS IT?

I often get asked why some *pad thai* has a bright orange colour, while others are various shades of brown. In North America, some restaurants add tomato paste, ketchup, or paprika to enhance the colour or to make the flavour more familiar. Even though diners have become much more adventurous, the practice has stuck. In Thailand, where many varieties of *pad thai* exist, some are also orange, but these orange noodles are likely to come from shrimp tomalley or Thai chili sauce (scan QR code for *pad thai* variations).

Note: Each brand of tamarind juice varies greatly in acidity, so you may need to adjust this amount.

Fish sauce flavour is prominent in this dish, so it is important to use a good-quality, fresh bottle.

Pressed tofu (sometimes labelled as "bean curd") is almost as firm as cheddar cheese and can be tossed in the wok without breaking. You can also use extra-firm tofu, cut into small pieces, and then fried until golden brown, which will firm them up.

THE BREAKDOWN

The Style	Thai
The Aromatic	Garlic, shallots, chili flakes, garlic chives
The Nuggets	Noodles, shrimp, tofu, preserved radish, dried shrimp, eggs, bean sprouts, peanuts
The Sauce	Fish sauce, palm sugar, tamarind, water
Flavour Profile	A balance of sweet, sour, and salty

Pad thai   Pad thai variations

Pad Thai

Eggplant Stir-Fry with Thai Basil

Eggplant Stir-Fry with Thai Basil

Pad Makeua Yao

Serves: 3-4

Cooking Time: 25 minutes

Do-ahead Tips: Make the sauce in advance and store in the fridge.

As needed	Vegetable oil for deep-frying
14 oz	Chinese or Japanese eggplants, cut into 2-inch cylinders, then quartered horizontally (see note)
3-4 cloves	Garlic, chopped
2-5	Thai chilies, finely chopped
9 oz	Ground pork
1 Tbsp	Sugar, granulated
½ cup	Red bell pepper, julienned
1½ cups	Thai basil
For serving	Jasmine rice

Note: You want young eggplants for this dish because they can maintain a firmer texture when cooked. Choose small eggplants that are firm when squeezed and have tight-looking skin. When you cut open an eggplant, a sure sign of a young one is small, light-coloured seeds, or no visible seeds at all.

Pad = Stir-fry; Makeua yao = Long eggplant

I wasn't a vegetable-loving kid, but I loved this dish because the eggplant becomes so succulent with the sweet, basil-infused sauce that it no longer tastes like a vegetable! *Makeua yao* or "long eggplant" in Thailand looks like Chinese or Japanese eggplant, except it is a vibrant light green, rather than purple. For this recipe, the purple variety is a perfect substitute. To make this dish meat-free, leave out the ground pork or substitute crumbled firm tofu.

....

Add 1 inch of oil in a wok or pot and bring it to 350°F over medium-high heat. Add the eggplants, a small batch at a time, and fry for 20-30 seconds. Remove from the oil and drain on paper towel. *Note: We are just par-cooking the eggplants, so they should still be quite firm at this point. Do not fry them any longer than 30 seconds as they can absorb a lot of oil if they become too soft.*

Make the sauce by combining ¼ cup of the stock with all the other sauce ingredients in a small bowl.

Heat 1 Tbsp of oil in a wok or a large sauté pan over medium-high heat. Add the garlic and Thai chilies; stir until the garlic starts to brown. Add the ground pork and stir until the pork is broken apart and is about 60% done.

Add the sauce mixture and sugar, then stir to cook the pork to 90%—at this point the pork should be sitting in plenty of liquid; if it looks dry, add some or all of the remaining stock.

Add the eggplants and bell peppers; keep tossing until the eggplants are fully cooked but still hold their shape. Turn off the heat and fold in the Thai basil. Taste and adjust the seasoning.

To serve, transfer onto a deep plate, garnish with a sprig of Thai basil, and serve with jasmine rice.

TO FRY OR NOT TO FRY?

Admittedly, we usually don't fry the eggplants when making this at home. Having said that, our *pad makeua yao* also looks wilted and sad. Without frying, the skin turns a dull grey colour when cooked, and because the eggplants have to "boil" in the sauce until they're done, they can absorb a lot of water and become mushy if you're not careful. Briefly frying brightens and sets the skin colour, and the eggplants will be partially cooked before they even see water, making it easier to get that firm-but-cooked texture. If you're not concerned with pretty presentation or perfect texture, you can try adding the eggplants raw with a little extra stock, stirring frequently until done, adding more stock as needed.

Tip for Success: To test eggplant for doneness, press on a piece; it should give in to your pressure easily but bounce back. Cutting the eggplant too big will make this harder to achieve, as the outside will overcook before the inside is done. For eggplants larger than 2 inches in diameter, cut the cylinders into six pieces instead of four.

THE SAUCE

½ cup	Chicken stock, pork stock, or water
2 Tbsp	Fermented soybean paste *(tao jiew)* (see note)
1 Tbsp	Oyster sauce
2 tsp	Soy sauce
2 tsp	Fish sauce
¼ tsp	White pepper

Note: You can substitute 1 Tbsp of miso paste, loosened with some water to achieve a pourable consistency.

THE BREAKDOWN

The Style	Hybrid
The Aromatic	Garlic, Thai chilies, Thai basil, white pepper
The Nuggets	Eggplants, ground pork, bell peppers
The Sauce	Sugar, stock, *tao jiew*, oyster sauce, soy sauce, fish sauce
Flavour Profile	Salty followed by sweet. Ample Thai basil aroma.

Holy Basil Chicken Fried Rice with Fried Egg

Kao Pad Gaprao Gai Kai Dao

Kao = Rice; Pad = Stir-fry; Gaprao = Holy basil; Gai = Chicken;
Kai dao = Fried egg

The predecessor of this dish, *pad gaprao*, is a stir-fry of holy basil and ground meat served over rice and usually with a fried egg on top—unquestionably one of the most popular lunch items in Thailand. I discovered one day that some restaurants, instead of serving the rice beside the stir-fry, threw it all into a fine fried rice! I was hooked, and I'm pretty sure you will be, too. If you're tempted to skip the fried egg, please reconsider; I promise it'll be worth your time. You don't have to fry the egg Thai-style if you want to conserve some oil—a sunny-side-up or an over-easy egg will do.

....

Combine the ground chicken and 1 tsp of soy sauce in a bowl and mix thoroughly; let sit in the fridge while you prepare the other ingredients.

For the Thai-style fried eggs: In a wok or a small frying pan, add about ½ inch of oil. Heat over medium-high heat until very hot but not smoking. Crack an egg into the centre of the pan; the egg white should bubble excitedly right away. If you like a medium to well-done yolk, lower the heat so the white doesn't brown too quickly. As the egg cooks, baste the top of it with the hot oil. Once the edges of the egg white are browned and crispy, and the yolk done to your liking, remove and drain on paper towel. Repeat with the remaining egg. *Note: The egg should be floating on top of the oil; if parts of it stick to the pan, let it cook for a minute before gently nudging it off with a spatula.*

Grease a small bowl generously with cooking oil, then add all the sauce ingredients to the bowl. *Note: Greasing the bowl helps the thick sauce slide out more easily.*

(Continued)

Serves: 2
Cooking Time: 20 minutes
Do-ahead Tips: Pull the eggs from the fridge the night before so they come to room temperature, or soak them in warm tap water while you prep.

---

6 oz	Chicken, ground, or other ground meats
1 tsp	Soy sauce
As needed	Oil for frying eggs
2	Eggs, room temperature
2 Tbsp	Vegetable oil
2–3 cloves	Garlic, chopped
2–5	Thai chilies, finely chopped
5	Long beans, ½-inch pieces on a bias
⅓ cup	Onion, small diced
1	Spur chili or ¼ red bell pepper, short julienned
1½ cups	Cooked rice
1 tsp	Sugar, granulated
1 cup	Holy basil, Thai basil, or regular basil
Condiment	*Prik nam pla* (optional, recipe p.230)

THE SAUCE

1 Tbsp	Oyster sauce
2 tsp	Soy sauce
1 tsp	Fish sauce
1 tsp	Seasoning sauce, such as Golden Mountain or Maggi
1 tsp	Black soy sauce

THE BREAKDOWN

The Style	Hybrid
The Aromatic	Garlic, holy basil, Thai chilies
The Nuggets	Rice, long beans, onion, spur chili
The Sauce	Oyster sauce, soy sauce, fish sauce, seasoning sauce, black soy sauce, sugar
Flavour Profile	Salty and spicy, balanced by subtle sweetness.

Pineapple fried rice

Tip for Success: Mushy or clumpy fried rice is the most common fried-rice issue. Using cold rice helps, but the most important factor is that the rice is not cooked with too much water. Please refer to my Pineapple Fried Rice video for more tips on making good rice for fried rice (QR code above).

Heat the 2 Tbsp oil in a wok or a large sauté pan over medium-high heat. Add the garlic and Thai chilies; stir until the garlic starts to turn golden brown. Add the chicken and cook until it is 70% done. Add the long beans, onion, and spur chili; toss to mix well. Add the rice, followed by the sauce mixture and sugar. Toss until the rice is evenly coated in the sauce, pressing down on rice lumps to break them apart. When the sauce has been absorbed completely (the rice should look dry), turn off the heat and stir in the basil just until it is incorporated. Taste and adjust the seasoning.

Transfer onto a plate, top with one fried egg per portion, and serve with *prik nam pla* on the side. I like to use *prik nam pla* to season the egg, but it's also great on the rice if you feel it needs extra seasoning.

THIS LOOKS LIKE . . . DRUNKEN NOODLES?

Kao pad gaprao is essentially the rice version of the wildly popular *pad kee mao*, also known as "drunken noodles." They both use holy basil and similar sauces, and the only main differences are the vegetables and the egg. So, if you love one, you will certainly love the other.

Cashew Chicken
Gai Pad Med Mamuang Himapan

Gai = Chicken; Pad = Stir-fry; Med Mamuang Himapan = Cashew

Admittedly, I never ate much cashew chicken in Thailand, so when I moved to North America, I was quite surprised by how popular this dish is here! In Thailand, this isn't something you can find on the street like many other more rustic dishes in this book. It's considered a Thai-Chinese fusion, often served at sit-down restaurants because cashews are expensive. Its Chinese roots are evident in the use of toasted sesame oil, an ingredient not used in most Thai dishes, but the chili paste and fried dried chilies give this dish its Thai personality.

....

Mix the chicken and soy sauce together in a bowl and let marinate while you prep the other ingredients.

Mix all the sauce ingredients in a bowl; set aside.

In a wok or large sauté pan, add 2 Tbsp vegetable oil and heat over medium-high heat. When hot, sear the chicken on one side to obtain nice golden brown colour. Toss quickly and remove from the pan; set aside. The chicken should only be partially done at this stage.

To the same pan, add 1 Tbsp vegetable oil if the pan seems too dry, then add the garlic and onion; cook until the garlic starts to turn golden. Add the seared chicken, mushrooms, and spur chilies to the pan and toss quickly to mix.

Add the sauce mixture and sugar; keep stirring to finish cooking the chicken. At this point, you can add a splash of water or stock if it seems too dry.

When the chicken is done, turn off the heat and toss in the green onions and ½ cup of the cashews, reserving some for garnish.

Plate and top with fried dried chilies and the remaining cashews. Serve with jasmine rice.

Serves: 2–3
Cooking Time: 20 minutes
Do-ahead Tips: Make the sauce in advance.

1 lb	Chicken breasts, boneless, skinless, bite-size pieces
1 Tbsp	Soy sauce
3 Tbsp	Vegetable oil
3–4 cloves	Garlic, chopped
½	Onion, medium, ⅓-inch strips
1 cup	Straw or beech mushrooms
2	Spur chilies or ½ red bell pepper, julienned
1½ tsp	Sugar, granulated
¾ cup	Cashews, roasted
2	Green onions, green part only, cut into 2-inch pieces
5–7	Dried chilies, fried (optional)

THE SAUCE

1 heaping Tbsp	Thai chili paste (*nam prik pao*)
1 Tbsp	Oyster sauce
2 tsp	Soy sauce
1 tsp	Seasoning sauce, such as Golden Mountain or Maggi
1 tsp	Fish sauce
1 tsp	Toasted sesame oil

THE REAL CASHEW CHICKEN

I'll let you in on a secret: this is not quite the real deal. In most restaurants, the chicken is dredged in flour and deep-fried before being tossed in the wok. The flour provides a rough coating that allows the sauce to cling on to the chicken better—an option you're welcome to try if you feel up to it. I choose to pan-sear the chicken instead because I've found that the result is just as delicious, as well as healthier and faster, and the cleanup is much easier!

THE BREAKDOWN

The Style	Hybrid
The Aromatic	Garlic, green onion
The Nuggets	Chicken, mushrooms, onion, cashews, spur chilies, dried chilies
The Sauce	Oyster sauce, soy sauce, fish sauce, seasoning sauce, chili paste, sesame oil, sugar
Flavour Profile	Salty and a little sweet.

Cashew chicken

VEGETARIAN & VEGAN

mangsawirat มังสวิรัติ

CURRY

Panang Curry with Portobello Mushrooms & Eggplant
— *Panang Mangsawirat*

SOUP

Five-Spice Vegetable Stew — *Palo Jap Chai*

SALAD

Mixed Mushrooms & Mint Salad — *Laab Hed Ruam*

STIR-FRY

Red Curry Stir-Fry with Tofu & Long Beans — *Tao Hoo Pad Prik King*

How to Make Any Thai Recipes Vegetarian or Vegan

You will be hard-pressed to find traditional Thai dishes that are inherently vegetarian, because even if you took out the meat, our staple seasonings are heavily based on seafood—fish sauce, oyster sauce, and shrimp paste, among others. So, cooking truly vegetarian Thai food requires a little more than swapping out meat for tofu, but it's not complicated, and the results are delicious.

Coming up in this section are four vegetarian/vegan Thai recipes. I didn't include these just for the sake of giving you more recipes, but to demonstrate how you can take any Thai recipe and modify it to fit your dietary needs. I've included one recipe representing each category:
curry, soup, salad, and stir-fry.

After you have learned how these recipes differ from their non-vegetarian counterparts, you will be able to apply the same techniques and modifications to other recipes. To help you along in this process, for each recipe I've also included explanations on what I did to make that dish animal-product-free.

SEE ALSO:

How to Make an "Educated Substitution," p.60

Thai Food for People with Dietary Restrictions, p.61

Panang Curry with Portobello Mushroom & Eggplant

Panang Curry with Portobello Mushrooms & Eggplant

Panang Mangsawirat

Serves: 3

Cooking Time: 30 minutes + 30 minutes if making the curry paste

Special Tools: Heavy-duty mortar and pestle, or another device for making curry paste

Do-ahead Tips: Make the curry paste in advance. Finish the sauce 1-2 days in advance and store in the fridge.

As needed	Vegetable oil
9 oz	Chinese or Japanese eggplant, ½-inch pieces on a sharp bias
A pinch	Salt
7 oz	Portobello mushrooms
1¼–1½ cups	Coconut milk
1 recipe	Vegan panang curry paste (recipe follows), or 4 Tbsp store-bought paste
1 Tbsp	Palm sugar, finely chopped, packed
2–3 tsp	Soy sauce
4	Kaffir lime leaves, very thinly julienned
For garnish	2 Tbsp thick part of coconut milk (optional, see note)
For garnish	Spur chili or red bell pepper, julienned
For serving	Jasmine rice

Note: Panang is typically garnished with a drizzle of thick coconut milk—the fatty portion that naturally rises as coconut milk sits. Simply skim off the surface of refrigerated coconut milk with a spoon, or you can thicken coconut milk with rice flour using the recipe for Salted Coconut Sauce p.214).

Panang = Name of the curry, no other meaning in modern Thai language; Mangsawirat = Vegetarian and/or vegan

Most Thai curries have plenty of liquid for the nuggets to swim in, much like a soup. *Panang*, on the other hand, is what we call *kluk klik*, which describes a dish with just enough sauce to go around. Spaghetti Bolognese, for example, is *kluk klik*. It usually consists of thin slices of meat drenched in a thick, luscious sauce, which brings me to the other unique point of *panang*: it's all meat, no vegetables, making it the perfect example for "veganization." You can substitute whatever vegetables you like to roast in the oven (butternut squash or fennel perhaps?). If the weather permits, grilling the vegetables would be even better!

....

Preheat the oven to 375°F. Line a baking sheet with parchment paper and brush with vegetable oil. Lay the eggplant slices on the baking sheet and brush the top with more oil. Season with a pinch of salt and roast for 15-20 minutes, or until cooked through and tender.

Brush both sides of the portobello mushrooms with vegetable oil and sprinkle with a pinch of salt. Roast in the oven, stem side down, for 12-15 minutes, or until cooked through. *Note: Many of us have been told not to wash mushrooms. For what it's worth, I always rinse dirty mushrooms in cold water and have yet to encounter any problems.*

Make the curry sauce while the vegetables roast. In a small pot, reduce ½ cup of the coconut milk over medium heat until very thick and the clear coconut oil starts to separate from the white portion, about 10 minutes. (If this doesn't happen, just proceed with the recipe after reducing until thick. See p.52 for more information.)

Add the curry paste and cook over medium-low heat for 3-4 minutes, stirring constantly, until the curry paste is very thick. Add the palm sugar, 2 tsp of soy sauce, ¾ cup coconut milk, and 2 kaffir lime leaves; stir for another 2 minutes to let the flavours mingle. The sauce should be thick and luscious but still flow easily when poured. If needed, add more coconut milk to achieve the desired consistency.

Remove from the heat, taste, and add the remaining soy sauce if needed—remember that the sauce will later be mellowed out by the vegetables and rice, so it should taste quite strong on its own.

When the vegetables are done, cut the mushrooms into ½-inch slices. Pour the curry sauce onto a deep plate and arrange the mushrooms and eggplant on top of the sauce. Drizzle the thick coconut milk (if using) over the vegetables and garnish with the remaining kaffir lime leaves and spur chili. Serve with jasmine rice.

Vegan Panang Curry Paste

Grind the dry chilies into a powder using a spice/coffee grinder OR soak the chilies in water for at least an hour to soften. (See *Tips for Making Curry Paste in a Mortar and Pestle*, p.xvi.)

Toast the coriander seeds by adding the seeds to a small, dry pan and stirring constantly over medium-high heat until the seeds are aromatic and have darkened slightly, about 4 minutes. Remove from the heat and cool on a plate. Repeat with the cumin seeds.

Using a heavy-duty mortar and pestle or a spice/coffee grinder, grind the toasted coriander seeds, toasted cumin seeds, and white peppercorns into a fine powder. Remove and set aside.

Grind the roasted peanuts until fine; remove and set aside.

If using dry, ground chilies:

In a heavy-duty mortar and pestle, place the salt, lemongrass, galangal, kaffir lime zest, and cilantro roots; pound into a fine paste.

Add the ground dry spices, ground chilies, shallots, and garlic; pound into a fine paste.

Add the ground peanuts and pound to mix.

If using soaked chilies:

Drain the chilies and dry off excess water with paper towel. Cut into small pieces. Add the chilies and salt to a heavy-duty mortar and pestle; pound into a rough paste. Add the ground dry spices to help absorb the liquid from the chilies and continue pounding to a fine paste.

Add the lemongrass, galangal, kaffir lime zest, and cilantro roots; pound into a fine paste.

Add the shallots and garlic; pound into a fine paste.

Add the ground peanuts and pound to mix.

VEGAN TRANSFORMATION

Because *panang* is usually a meat-heavy dish, I chose meaty, savoury vegetables such as portobello mushrooms and eggplant. Roasting the vegetables intensifies their flavours, making them robust enough to stand up to the rich curry sauce. Fish sauce and shrimp paste in the curry paste would normally provide saltiness and umami, so I chose soy sauce as a substitute, as it is a source of both.

10	Large dried chilies, seeded
1½ tsp	Coriander seeds
¾ tsp	Cumin seeds
¼ tsp	White peppercorns
12	Peanuts, roasted; for nut allergies use 1½ Tbsp cooked mung beans
1 tsp	Salt
2 Tbsp	Lemongrass, finely chopped
1 Tbsp	Galangal, finely chopped
1 tsp	Kaffir lime zest, finely chopped
1 tsp	Cilantro roots, finely chopped, or 1 Tbsp cilantro stems, finely chopped
3 Tbsp	Shallots, finely chopped
1 Tbsp	Garlic, finely chopped

THE BREAKDOWN

The Paste	Vegan panang curry paste
The Liquid	Coconut milk
The Nuggets	Eggplant, portobello mushrooms
The Seasoning	Soy sauce, palm sugar
Flavour Profile	Salty backed by a little sweet.

Panang curry paste

Serves: 4

Cooking Time: 45 minutes

Special Tools: Cheesecloth or muslin bag for wrapping spices

Do-ahead Tips: Make the dish up to a few days in advance—it tastes better as it sits!

4–5	Dried shiitake mushrooms, soaked in hot water for 1 hour
2 whole	Star anise
2	Cinnamon sticks
8 whole	Cloves
1 tsp	Coriander seeds, toasted
½ tsp	Sichuan peppercorns, toasted
2 Tbsp	Vegetable oil
3 Tbsp	Palm sugar, finely chopped
5 cups	Water or vegetable stock, unsalted
4 cloves	Garlic, crushed
½	Large onion, diced
2	Cilantro roots or 6–8 stems
3 Tbsp	Soy sauce
2 Tbsp	Seasoning sauce, such as Golden Mountain or Maggi
1½ Tbsp	Black soy sauce
½ tsp	White pepper, ground
11 oz	Fried tofu, bite-sized pieces (see note)
6 oz	Carrots, bite-sized pieces
5 oz	Cabbage, bite-sized pieces
6 oz	Chinese broccoli or kale, bite-sized pieces
½–1 tsp	Salt
For serving	Jasmine rice

THE BREAKDOWN

The Infusion	Spices, onion, garlic, cilantro roots
The Liquid	Water or vegetable stock
The Nuggets	Vegetables, tofu
The Seasoning	Soy sauce, palm sugar, seasoning sauce, black soy sauce
Flavour Profile	Salty and a little sweet. Prominent aroma of spices.

Five-Spice Vegetable Stew
Palo Jap Chai

Palo = Five-spice; Jap chai = A mixed vegetable stew

This is a hybrid of two wonderful soups: *kai palo* (five-spice soup with pork belly and eggs (recipe p.123) and the ultimate comfort food called *jap chai*, a mixed vegetable stew that is wildly popular during the annual vegan festival (see p.62). *Jap chai* is the epitome of simple home cuisine, and my grandmother's go-to dish. In this recipe, I've woven together the five-spice flavour and the tender-braised vegetables. There are no rules about the choice of vegetables—daikon radish is normally used, but I'm not a fan so I conveniently left it out!

....

Remove the mushrooms from the soaking water and slice them thinly.

Wrap the star anise, cinnamon, cloves, coriander seeds, and Sichuan peppercorns in a piece of cheesecloth or muslin, and tie it into a bag.

Heat the vegetable oil and palm sugar in a large pot over medium heat and cook, stirring constantly, until the sugar melts and caramelizes. When the sugar turns dark brown, quickly add the water—the sugar will bubble aggressively. Add the mushrooms, spice bag, garlic, onion, cilantro roots, soy sauce, seasoning sauce, black soy sauce, and white pepper. Simmer the soup gently, covered, for 20–30 minutes.

Remove the spice bag and cilantro roots. Add the fried tofu and carrots; simmer for another 10 minutes or until the carrots are 80% done. Add the cabbage and Chinese broccoli and simmer for another 5 minutes, or until the vegetables are done to your liking.

Remove from the heat, taste, and adjust the seasoning with salt as needed. If it is too salty, just add a little more water to dilute.

Serve with jasmine rice. Because it's quite a strongly flavoured soup, we typically spoon the soup over rice.

Note: Most Chinese grocery stores sell pre-fried tofu cubes made specifically for soups and stews. You can also buy firm tofu and fry it yourself to add a nice chewy texture and a golden colour.

VEGAN TRANSFORMATION

The non-vegetarian version of *jap chai* is made with good pork stock, so trying to achieve the same richness without using pork stock is the biggest challenge here. Thankfully, both soy sauce and shiitake mushrooms add a lot of umami. The seasoning of the soup doesn't need much adjustment except for the elimination of oyster sauce, which can be substituted by more soy sauce and seasoning sauce. Your choice of vegetables will also affect the overall flavour of the dish, so choose wisely!

Serves: 4 as an appetizer, 2 as an entrée
Cooking Time: 30 minutes
Special Tools: Mortar and pestle, or another device for making toasted rice powder
Do-ahead Tips: Toast the rice 1 day in advance and store in an airtight container.

As needed	Vegetable oil
12 oz	Mushroom mix of your choice (see note)
A pinch	Salt
¼ cup	Shallots, short juliennes
2 Tbsp	Lemongrass, very thinly sliced
3 Tbsp	Lime juice
1–1½ Tbsp	Soy sauce
½ Tbsp	Seasoning sauce, such as Golden Mountain or Maggi
To taste	Roasted chili flakes (recipe p.231) or regular chili flakes
½ cup	Mint, large leaves chopped, small leaves left whole
¼ cup	Cilantro, chopped
1–2	Green onions, chopped
4 leaves	Sawtooth coriander or extra cilantro, chopped
1½ Tbsp	Toasted rice powder (recipe p.230)
For serving	Sticky rice (recipe p.234)
For serving	Fresh crisp lettuce leaves

Note: Some good mushroom choices: shimeji (beech), enoki, oyster, chanterelles, morels, and maitake. You can use crimini mushrooms, but keep in mind that they give off a lot of liquid and shrink significantly when cooked.

THE BREAKDOWN

The Protein	Mixed mushrooms as a protein substitute
The Vegetables	Lettuce served on the side
The Herbs	Shallots, lemongrass, mint, cilantro, green onion, sawtooth coriander
The Dressing	Lime juice, soy sauce, seasoning sauce, chili flakes, toasted rice powder
Flavour Profile	Lead with sour, followed by salty, balanced by the nuttiness of the toasted rice powder

Mixed Mushrooms & Mint Salad
Laab Hed Ruam

Laab = A type of Northeastern Thai salad; Hed = Mushroom; Ruam = Mix

I made this dish recently for a party and it was a hit, even with the self-proclaimed mushroom-hater. Savoury, herbaceous, and incredibly healthy . . . what's not to love? Feel free to use any types of your favourite mushrooms—the more varieties you use, the more beautiful this salad will look. Sautéing the mushrooms is quick and convenient, but if the weather permits, you can grill them for extra smokiness!

....

Heat a little oil in a wok or a large sauté pan over medium-high heat. Add one type of mushroom, season with a pinch of salt, and cook, stirring occasionally, until they are cooked and have browned slightly. Transfer to a large mixing bowl. Repeat with the remaining types of mushrooms and add them all to the mixing bowl.

If you notice a lot of liquid pooling at the bottom of the bowl, pour it off before adding the other ingredients. While the mushrooms are still warm, add the shallots and lemongrass; toss to mix. When ready to serve, add the lime juice, soy sauce, seasoning sauce, chili flakes, mint, cilantro, green onions, sawtooth coriander, and toasted rice powder; toss to mix. Taste and adjust seasoning.

Serve the salad with sticky rice, which you can use to soak up the juices. Also serve with some crisp lettuce leaves, which you can use to make little bite-sized wraps. Serve warm or at room temperature.

VEGAN TRANSFORMATION

Fish sauce is a major flavour component in all Thai salads, so any attempt to replace it will inevitably alter the flavour noticeably, but not necessarily for the worse—this salad is super tasty! Soy sauce is the best substitute, because not only does it still provide saltiness and umami, but it also maintains the volume of the dressing. Don't skimp on the toasted rice powder here, because without meat, the lime's acidity can feel a bit aggressive and the nuttiness of the toasted rice powder will be your only counterweight. You can also try making *laab* with crumbled tofu!

Red Curry Stir-Fry with Tofu & Long Beans

Tao Hoo Pad Prik King

Tao hoo = Tofu; Pad = Stir-fry; Prik = Chilies; King = Ginger (but there is no ginger in the recipe!)

Note to vegans, this dish contains a salted duck egg, but you can omit it and still have a tasty dish by adding a little extra soy sauce. The creamy salted egg yolk is incorporated into the sauce, adding a savoury richness that happens to work well as a shrimp paste substitute. The egg white, which has the consistency of a soft cheese, adds bursts of saltiness, much like crumbled feta cheese over a Greek salad. You may be tempted to skip frying the tofu, but it's quite important here, as frying creates a rough surface that allows the sauce to cling well, and it also prevents the tofu from crumbling in the wok.

· ·

To fry the tofu, add 1 inch of oil to a small or medium pot and bring to 350°F over medium-high heat. Pat the tofu dry with paper towel, then fry in small batches for 1–2 minutes, or until the exterior is golden brown and crispy. Drain on paper towel. *Note: Tofu pieces like to stick to each other when frying; if this happens, let them fry for 30–40 seconds to firm up before pulling them apart, and they should separate easily.*

Cut the salted duck egg in half right through the shell with a knife. Scoop out the yolk into a small bowl. Scoop out the egg white with a spoon and chop it into small chunks, keeping it separate from the yolk.

To a wok or a large sauté pan, add 2 Tbsp of oil, the curry paste, palm sugar, and soy sauce; stir over medium heat until the sugar is dissolved and the curry paste is aromatic. If the curry paste sticks to the pan, add a splash of water to loosen it. Once the sugar is dissolved, add the kaffir lime leaves and salted egg yolk, then mash the egg yolk until it's combined with the curry paste.

Add a splash of water to loosen the sauce into a pourable consistency. Turn the heat up to high, add the long beans, and toss to mix with the curry paste for 1 minute or until the beans are almost done to your liking. Add the fried tofu and salted egg white; toss until the tofu is evenly coated in the sauce and heated through. Taste and adjust the seasoning.

Transfer onto a plate and garnish with extra julienned kaffir lime leaves and spur chiles. Serve with jasmine rice.

Serves: 3–4
Cooking Time: 30 minutes + 30 minutes if making the curry paste
Special Tools: Heavy-duty mortar and pestle, or another device for making curry paste
Do-ahead Tips: Make the curry paste in advance.

As needed	Vegetable oil for deep-frying
11 oz	Extra-firm tofu, 1- x ½- x ½-inch pieces
1	Cooked salted duck egg (see note, omit if vegan)
1 recipe	Vegan red curry paste (recipe follows) or use 4 Tbsp store-bought paste
1½ Tbsp	Palm sugar, finely chopped, packed
2 tsp	Soy sauce
¼–½ cup	Water
5	Kaffir lime leaves, very thinly julienned, set some aside for garnish
20	Long beans, 1½-inch pieces
For garnish	Spur chili, thin rounds, or red bell pepper, julienned (optional)
For serving	Jasmine rice

Note: You can find salted duck eggs in most Chinese grocery stores; make sure the package says "cooked."

Vegan Red Curry Paste

8	Large dried chilies, seeded
2	Small dried chilies, seeded (see note)
1 tsp	Salt
¼ tsp	White peppercorns
2 Tbsp	Lemongrass, thinly sliced
1 Tbsp	Galangal, finely chopped
1 tsp	Kaffir lime zest, finely chopped
1 tsp	Cilantro roots or 1 Tbsp cilantro stems, finely chopped
3 Tbsp	Shallots, finely chopped
1 Tbsp	Garlic, finely chopped

Note: Large dried chilies are mild, while small dried chilies are quite spicy, so you can control the curry paste's spiciness by adding more or fewer of the small ones. Leave in the seeds of the small chilies for extra heat.

THE BREAKDOWN

The Style	Thai
The Aromatic	Vegetarian red curry paste, kaffir lime leaves
The Nuggets	Tofu, long beans, salted egg white
The Sauce	Soy sauce, palm sugar, salted egg yolk
Flavour Profile	Salty and a little sweet.

Grind the dry chilies into a powder using a spice/coffee grinder OR soak the chilies in water for at least an hour to soften. (See *Tips for Making Curry Paste in a Mortar and Pestle*, p.xvi.)

If using ground chilies:

In a heavy-duty mortar and pestle add the salt, white peppercorns, lemongrass, galangal, kaffir lime zest, and cilantro roots; pound into a fine paste.

Add the ground chilies; pound to mix.

Add the shallots and garlic; pound into a fine paste.

If using soaked chilies:

In a heavy-duty mortar and pestle, add the chilies, salt, and white peppercorns; pound into a fine paste.

Add the lemongrass, galangal, kaffir lime zest, and cilantro roots; pound into a fine paste.

Add the shallots and garlic; pound into a fine paste.

VEGETARIAN TRANSFORMATION

Pad prik king is a dish that is often turned vegetarian, because the intensity of the the curry paste makes the flavour resilient to ingredient changes. I replaced the fish sauce with soy sauce, as it's a source of both saltiness and umami, but with so much flavour from the curry paste, salt would've worked fine. The shrimp paste in the red curry paste is omitted, but the salted egg yolk provides a similar savoury richness. We also often use texturized vegetable protein (TVP), a soy-based meat substitute, instead of tofu, which I quite like for its fun, chewy texture.

DIPS &
DIPPING SAUCES
kreuang jim เครื่องจิ้ม

Dips and dipping sauces are an important part of a traditional Thai meal.
Read more about them on page 90.

NAM PRIK — UNCOOKED
Shrimp Paste Dip — *Nam Prik Gapi*

NAM PRIK — COOKED
Northern-Style Pork & Tomato Dip — *Nam Prik Ong*

LOHN
Coconut Shrimp Dip — *Lohn Goong*

NAM JIM
Dipping Sauce for Seafood — *Nam Jim Seafood*
Dipping Sauce for Barbecued Meats — *Nam Jim Jeaw*
Dipping Sauce for Chicken & Fried Foods — *Nam Jim Gai*

Shrimp Paste Dip
Nam Prik Gapi

Nam prik = A type of dip; Gapi = Fermented shrimp paste

The French have mother sauces, we have mother dips. *Nam prik gapi* is the basic uncooked *nam prik* upon which many other *nam priks* are built. It's the simplest dip that home cooks turn to when there's not much else in the pantry, since every ingredient needed is a staple in any Thai household. WARNING: This is not for the faint of heart. There is a reason why you will never find a Thai restaurant that offers *nam prik gapi* to a Western clientele—shrimp paste is pungent stuff, and this dip is certainly an acquired taste. Having said that, I encourage you to try it if only as a cultural experience, because no other dish can better represent the true essence of a simple Thai home-cooked meal.

....

Drain the dried shrimp and roughly chop into small pieces. Transfer them to a heavy-duty mortar and pestle and pound until they are shredded into fine, fluffy bits. *Tip: You can skip the soaking and grind the dried shrimp in a coffee/spice grinder.*

Add the garlic and Thai chilies to the dried shrimp and pound into a fine paste. Add the palm sugar and pound until the sugar is dissolved. Add the shrimp paste and pound to mix well.

Add 3 Tbsp of the lime juice, 1/2 Tbsp fish sauce, and 2 Tbsp water; swirl the pestle to mix. Taste and adjust the seasoning with the remaining lime juice, fish sauce, and water. It should lead with salt, follow with sour, and have just a hint of sweetness to balance. *Note: The consistency of the dip is a personal preference and can be thick or thin.*

Stir in the julienned red and green chilies, if using. Serve with jasmine rice and your "dippers" of choice (see ingredient list for options).

HOW TO EAT THIS DIP

This isn't like hummus or guacamole, so don't pile it on or eat it by the spoonful! Because it's very strong, treat it more like a hot sauce—a little goes a long way. Spoon a little over your rice, vegetables, or protein, and once you're committed, you can try tossing your rice in it, like many Thais like to do. Pan-fried *pla too*, or short mackerel (see photo), is a classic accompaniment to any shrimp-paste-based dip, but other fish will also pair well. My personal favourite combination is with a Thai-style vegetable omelette (recipe p.111).

Makes: About 1/2 cup
Cooking Time: 15 minutes
Special Tools: Mortar and pestle, or another device for grinding
Do-ahead Tips: Make the dip a day before serving.

2 Tbsp	Dried shrimp, soaked in hot water for 10–15 minutes
2–3 cloves	Garlic
2–6	Thai chilies, to taste
1½ Tbsp	Palm sugar, finely chopped, packed
2 Tbsp	Shrimp paste *(gapi)*
3–4 Tbsp	Lime juice
1/2–1 Tbsp	Fish sauce
2–3 Tbsp	Water
1/4 cup	Any red and green chili peppers, short julienned, e.g., bell peppers, jalapeños, fresnos (optional for extra colour)
For serving	Jasmine rice
	Vegetables, fresh, steamed or grilled
	Mackerel or another fish, pan-fried
	Thai-style vegetable omelette (recipe p.111)
	Boiled eggs

Tip for Success: If you're ready to "upgrade," you can start building upon this basic dip by choosing an "add-in." We often use sour fruits, such as sour green mango or tamarind, but sour green apple or pomelo will work. Also try adding protein, such as cooked fish or shrimp. Simply julienne or small-dice your add-in of choice and stir it in!

Northern-Style Pork and Tomato Dip
Nam Prik Ong

Makes: 1½ cups
Cooking Time: 45 minutes; if soaking dried chilies, allow 1 extra hour (see instructions)
Special Tools: Heavy-duty mortar and pestle, or another device for grinding
Do-ahead Tips: Make the dip up to a few days before serving.

2 oz	Shallots, cut in half lengthwise
6 cloves	Garlic, 3 cloves kept whole, 3 cloves finely chopped
6	Large dried chilies, seeded
2–5	Small dried chilies (see note)
½ tsp	Salt
2	Cilantro roots or 5–6 cilantro stems
3½ oz	Grape tomatoes, each cut into 4–6 pieces
7 oz	Ground pork
1 tsp	Shrimp paste *(gapi)*
1½ Tbsp	Vegetable oil
½ cup	Pork or chicken stock, unsalted (recipe p.232), or water
2–3 tsp	Fish sauce
2 tsp	Palm sugar, finely chopped, packed
1–2 tsp	Tamarind juice or lime juice
For garnish	Cilantro leaves (optional)
For serving	Fresh vegetables for dipping, such as carrots, cucumber, and cabbage
	Sticky rice or jasmine rice
	Crispy fried pork rind
	Plain rice crackers

Nam prik = A type of dip; Ong = No apparent meaning, but possibly comes from the word "om," meaning to stew for a long time, in the Northern dialect.

This iconic Northern dip is perhaps the best *nam prik* to get started with because it's not too far from Western flavours, unlike many other *nam prik*, which can be a bit of a shock to the palate. In fact, it is somewhat reminiscent of the Italian Bolognese sauce, but spiked with Thai herbs. It's usually a part of a bigger Thai meal, and a must-have during *kantoke*, the traditional Northern feast. I once served *nam prik ong* as an appetizer at a party alongside some rice crackers and veggies, and people were still raving about it the next day!

....

Grill or broil the shallots and whole garlic cloves until the edges are caramelized (this step is optional, but if you have time, it adds a nice flavour). Chop them into small pieces.

Grind the dried chilies into a powder using a spice/coffee grinder and transfer to a heavy-duty mortar and pestle OR soak the chilies in water for at least 1 hour until softened, cut into small chunks, then pound into a paste in the mortar and pestle.

To the chilies, add the salt, cilantro roots, grilled shallots, and grilled garlic; pound into a paste—this doesn't have to be as fine as curry paste, but there should be no big chunks. Add the grape tomatoes and crush them with the pestle to release all their juices. Add the ground pork and shrimp paste, and pound to mix thoroughly; if there's not enough room in the mortar, transfer to a large mixing bowl and knead the pork with the herb paste thoroughly.

Note: Control the heat of your dip by adding more or fewer of the small chilies.

Heat the oil in a small sauté pan or a wok over medium heat. Add the chopped garlic and stir until it turns golden brown. Add the pork mixture and cook, mashing the pork with a spatula to break up any lumps. When the pork is no longer clumping, add the stock, fish sauce, and sugar; stir constantly until the pork is fully cooked.

Simmer the pork on low heat, stirring frequently, for 5-7 minutes or until the mixture has reduced to very thick and the tomatoes have broken down completely.

Depending on the acidity of the tomatoes, you may or may not need to add tamarind juice. Taste the dip once it has reached the desired consistency, adjust the amount of fish sauce and sugar if needed, then if it still lacks sharpness, add a touch of tamarind juice or lime juice to brighten it up.

To serve, transfer into a small bowl, garnish with cilantro, and serve warm alongside your "dippers" of choice (see ingredient list for options). If serving with sticky rice, you can roll the sticky rice into a bite-sized ball and press your thumb into it to make a little crater to hold the dip! Rice crackers aren't traditionally served with this dip, but they're a convenient option that I think is delicious.

POUNDING THE PORK

Pounding the pork in the mortar and pestle may not be something you ever thought you would do. When meat is raw, it's easily penetrable by seasoning, so think of this as mechanically forcing flavours into the pork in its most vulnerable state. This allows the pork and the flavours from the herbs to coalesce quickly, without the need to cook it for a long time or letting it sit, like that better-the-next-day lasagna! Commercially ground pork can also be quite coarse, and the extra mashing grinds it down further, resulting in a finer dip consistency.

Northern-Style Pork and Tomato Dip

Coconut Shrimp Dip

Coconut Shrimp Dip

Lohn Goong

Makes: About 2 cups
Cooking Time: 20 minutes
Special Tools: Mortar and pestle or an electric grinder for shredding dried shrimp
Do-ahead Tips: Make the entire dip 1-2 days before serving.

1½ Tbsp	Dried shrimp, soaked in hot water for 10 minutes
7 oz	Shrimp, peeled and deveined
1 cup	Coconut milk
¼ cup	Shallots, thinly julienned
2.5 oz	Ground pork (see note)
1 Tbsp	Palm sugar, finely chopped
2-3 Tbsp	Tamarind juice
2 tsp	Fish sauce
½ tsp	Salt
1	Red spur chili or ¼ red bell pepper, short julienned
1	Green spur chili, jalapeño, or ¼ green bell pepper, short-julienned
To taste	Thai chilies, whole (optional)
For serving	Jasmine rice
	Vegetables, fresh, steamed, or grilled
For garnish	Cilantro leaves (optional)

Lohn = A type of cooked dip that uses coconut milk; Goong = Shrimp

If *nam prik* were the crude and crass brother, *lohn* would be the delicate and dainty sister. It's luscious and creamy with an unobtrusive flavour and mild spice. When I serve *lohn* to non-Thais, they often express surprise that it's a dip because it looks substantial enough to be a meal in itself, which isn't wrong. Its identity as a dip is in the fact that it's eaten with lots of fresh vegetables. *Lohn goong* is the basic *lohn*, the same way *nam prik gapi* is the basic *nam prik*. You can start playing around with the recipe by adding or substituting other proteins, such as crab, pork, fermented sausage (*naem*), fermented fish (*pla ra*), or even ham, which, believe it or not, has become common in Thailand.

....

Drain the dried shrimp and roughly chop into small pieces. Transfer them to a heavy-duty mortar and pestle and pound until they are shredded into fine, fluffy bits. *Tip: You can skip the soaking and grind the dried shrimp in a coffee/spice grinder.*

Set aside 2 oz of whole shrimp, and make ground shrimp with the remaining 5 oz. To grind the shrimp, first slice them into small pieces. Then, using a cleaver or a heavy chef's knife, mince them using a quick up-and-down chopping motion, changing the angle of the knife occasionally, until the shrimp resembles ground meat.

In a small pot, add the coconut milk, dried shrimp, and shallots; bring to a simmer over medium heat. Once simmering, add the ground shrimp and ground pork, stirring quickly to break apart any lumps. Once the meat is thoroughly mixed with the coconut milk, add the reserved whole shrimp, palm sugar, tamarind juice, fish sauce, and salt; stir until the shrimp and pork are fully cooked.

Note: A few whole shrimp are added to make the dip look more elegant, and it's a visual representation of what's in the bowl.

Stir in the red chili, green chili, and whole Thai chilies (if using). Remove from the heat, taste, and adjust the seasoning.

To serve, transfer the dip into a bowl and serve with jasmine rice and vegetables. You can use the vegetables to dip or simply spoon some of the dip over your rice and vegetables like a sauce. Thai chilies are added whole so that people can break them up on their own plates for extra heat.

NAM PRIK VS LOHN

Here are some major differences between *nam prik* and *lohn*, the two major types of Thai dips:

- Spice level: *Lohn* is mild or not spicy at all, while heat is arguably the whole point of *nam prik*.

- Cooking method: *Nam prik* can be cooked or uncooked, but *lohn* is always cooked.

- Main ingredient: *Lohn* always uses coconut milk as the base, but *nam prik* can be made with various main ingredients.

- Flavour: *Nam prik* has strong flavours that make it prominently salty and spicy, but *lohn* has a more balanced profile between salty, sweet, and sour.

Note: Ground pork is added for some extra fat and flavour. You can omit it and add more shrimp. For a luxurious occasion, substitute crabmeat by stirring it in at the end.

Dipping Sauce for Seafood
Nam Jim Seafood

Nam jim = Dipping sauce; Seafood = The borrowed English term we like to use in place of the more cumbersome Thai equivalent ahaan talay

The next time you splurge on fresh lobster, don't dip it in drawn butter . . . there IS a better way. When expensive seafood is at stake, Thai people never do without *nam jim seafood*. Garlicky, citrusy, spicy . . . it's everything the dungeness crab could ever ask for. When I went camping with friends who were diving for fresh abalone on the coast of Northern California, I made sure we packed *nam jim seafood* supplies, along with a mini mortar and pestle. I've even been tempted to smuggle it into North American seafood restaurants in a container!

. . . .

If using a blender, simply blend all the ingredients together until there are no more big chunks (it doesn't have to be smooth).

If using a mortar and pestle, pound the chilies and garlic together in a mortar and pestle until there are no more chunks. Add the palm sugar and pound until the sugar is dissolved. Add the cilantro stems and pound into a paste. Add the lime juice and fish sauce; stir to mix.

Taste and adjust the seasoning—the flavour should lead with sour, followed by salty, and the sweetness should be barely detectable, as the sugar serves only to round off the sharp edges of the salt and the acid.

MORE THAN JUST A DIPPING SAUCE

In case I haven't convinced you that this is the ultimate sauce for seafood, let me tell you how versatile it is! It also makes an incredible dressing for ceviche and a fantastic sauce for your next backyard barbecue. Whether you're grilling beef, pork, or chicken, the lightness and acidity of the sauce really brighten up the heaviness of grilled meats and gives them a whole new character!

Makes: About 1/3 cup
Cooking Time: 5 minutes
Special Tools: Mortar and pestle or a blender
Do-ahead Tips: You can make this 1–2 days in advance and store in the fridge, but for freshest flavour, make the dip the day it is served.

2–7	Thai chilies, to taste (see note)
4 cloves	Garlic
2 tsp	Palm sugar, finely chopped, packed
1 Tbsp	Cilantro stems, finely chopped
3 Tbsp	Lime juice
2 Tbsp	Fish sauce

Note: *If you want a red dip, use red Thai chilies; for a green dip, use green Thai chilies.*

Dipping Sauce for Barbecued Meats
Nam Jim Jeaw

Nam jim = Dipping sauce; Jeaw = Isaan dialect for dipping sauce

In the previous recipe, we covered your seafood dipping needs. Now let's tackle barbecue. Anything that is cooked on the grill, be it beef, chicken, pork, or even mushrooms, will benefit from a little dip in *nam jim jeaw*. I've even used it as an easy way to transform a boring dinner, like pan-seared chicken breast or fish, into something spicy and exciting! If you're looking for a Thai-style barbecue recipe to go with this dipping sauce, check out the two QR codes below.

....

Add the palm sugar to a small bowl and drizzle the hot water over it; mash the sugar into a paste. *Note: This step is just to help the chopped sugar dissolve more readily, so if you finely grated the sugar you may skip this step.*

Add the fish sauce, lime juice, and tamarind juice to the sugar; stir until the sugar is dissolved.

When ready to serve, stir in the shallots, chili flakes, green onion, cilantro, and toasted rice powder.

CUSTOMIZE IT

Green onion and cilantro are the two basic herbs we use in this dip, but you can also change it up. To stay true to the dip's *isaan* roots, try using herbs from that region: sawtooth coriander, mint, or even dill. (In Thailand, we call dill *Lao cilantro!*)

Makes: About ⅔ cup
Cooking Time: 15 minutes
Special Tools: Mortar and pestle, or another device for making toasted rice powder
Do-ahead Tips: The sauce can be made a few days in advance and stored in the fridge, but do not add the herbs and the toasted rice powder until serving time.

2 Tbsp	Palm sugar, finely chopped, packed (see note)
2 tsp	Hot water
3 Tbsp	Fish sauce
2 Tbsp	Lime juice
2 Tbsp	Tamarind juice
3 Tbsp	Shallots, thinly sliced, then chopped
To taste	Roasted chili flakes (recipe p.231) or regular chili flakes
3 Tbsp	Green onion, chopped
3 Tbsp	Cilantro, chopped
1½ Tbsp	Toasted rice powder (recipe p.230)

Note: Since the palm sugar will not be cooked, make sure there are no big chunks or it will not dissolve. You can also grate the sugar using a microplane zester or a fine grater, which will help it dissolve more easily.

Thai BBQ Chicken

Thai Grilled Steak

Dipping Sauce for Chicken & Fried Foods
Nam Jim Gai

Nam jim = Dipping sauce; Gai = Chicken

This is essentially the homemade recipe for the popular "Sweet Chili Sauce for Chicken" that is sold in glass bottles in many supermarkets worldwide. You might be surprised how easy it is to make a fresh batch at home without any additives! "For Chicken" is indeed how the sauce is often used, but it is also the go-to dipping sauce for deep-fried foods such as spring rolls (recipe p. 162) and fried chicken (see the QR code below). Deep-fried items are usually primarily salty, so the combination of sweet and sour perfectly completes the equation.

....

If using a blender, combine all the ingredients in the blender and blend until there are no big chunks (chili seeds are fine).

If using a mortar and pestle, pound the garlic, spur chilies, and Thai chilies into a fine paste, then stir in the sugar, salt, vinegar, and water.

Pour the mixture into a small pot and bring to a simmer over medium heat. Let simmer for about 5 minutes until the mixture has thickened and resembles a thin syrup. The mixture will thicken as it cools. If the cooled mixture is too thick, simply add more water. If it's not thick enough, reduce it down some more.

Store in the fridge in a tightly sealed container and reheat, if desired, when ready to serve. Stir in any or all of the optional add-in ingredients just before serving.

WHICH ADD-IN?

I gave you three choices for add-in ingredients and each one will contribute something a little different. If you want the dip to be richer, add the crushed peanuts. The cucumber helps keep things fresh and crunchy, which is great for heavier items. Finally, the shallot adds pungency, so if you like raw onions in your burger, you will probably enjoy it!

Makes: About ²/₃ cup
Cooking Time: 15 minutes
Special Tools: Mortar and pestle or blender
Do-ahead Tips: The sauce can be made in advance and kept in the fridge for a few months in a tightly sealed container.

3 cloves	Garlic
⅓ cup	Spur chilies or red bell pepper, seeds left in, finely chopped
1–3	Thai chilies, to taste
½ cup	Sugar, granulated
½ tsp	Salt
⅓ cup	Vinegar
3 Tbsp	Water
Add-ins for serving	Peanuts, finely chopped; cucumber, quartered and sliced; shallot, julienned

Thai Fried Chicken

DESSERTS
kong waan ของหวาน

As we saw in *Part 1*, Thai desserts can be divided into categories according to cooking techniques. Here are five dessert recipes representing each of the cooking techniques discussed.

STEAMED
Mango & Sticky Rice — *Kao Niew Mamuang*

STIRRED
Layered Coconut Pudding Cups — *Tako*

BOILED
Kabocha Squash Coconut Soup — *Faktong Gaeng Buad*

FRIED
Street-Style Fried Bananas — *Gluay Kag*

CANDIED
Candied Cassava — *Mun Cheuam*

Mango & Sticky Rice

Kao Niew Mamuang

Kao = Rice; Niew = Sticky; Mamuang = Mango

Even though desserts are a major part of our diet, few Thai desserts are known beyond our borders. Mango and sticky rice is the best-known dessert and for good reason: it tastes amazing. The unlikely pair of mango and rice combine flawlessly, with just the right amount of saltiness from the coconut sauce for balance. Over the years I have looked for, and failed to find, another fruit that can achieve the same harmony. I have included a bonus recipe for making purple sticky rice instead of the usual white rice—not only is it beautiful, it also has a unique flavour and a chewy texture, and is more nutritious. I once took the purple sticky rice to a party, and the host loved it so much that he snuck into the kitchen and ate all the leftover rice just on its own!

....

FOR THE COCONUT STICKY RICE:

If making white sticky rice: Wash the rice by covering it with cold water and swishing it around vigorously with your hands until the water is cloudy. Pour off the water and repeat 4-5 times, until the rinse water runs almost clear. Soak the rice in cold water for at least 4 hours or overnight. Drain the rice well, shaking off as much residual water as possible, then steam it according to the instructions on the next page.

If making purple sticky rice: Wash the white rice by covering it with cold water and swishing it around vigorously with your hands until the water is cloudy. Pour off the water and repeat 4-5 times, until the rinse water runs almost clear. Set aside in a medium-sized bowl.

Rinse the black rice once, then soak it in 2 cups of warm water until the water has turned purple, 10-20 minutes. *Note: We are making purple water, which we will use to dye the white rice, so the longer you soak, the darker the end product.*

After soaking, drain the rice, reserving the purple water. Pour the purple water over the washed white rice and soak for at least 4 hours or overnight. Cover the drained black rice with fresh cold water and also soak it for at least 4 hours or overnight.

Cook the black rice: Drain the soaked black rice, place it in a small pot, and cover with 2 cups of cold water. Bring to a boil over medium-high heat, then simmer for 7-9 minutes or until the rice is fully cooked. Drain well.

Mix the black and white rice: Drain the soaked white-turned-purple rice, shaking off as much residual water as possible. Fold the cooked black rice into the soaked white rice until well distributed (be gentle, the white rice is brittle after soaking).

Serves: 4-6

Cooking Time: 1½ hours + at least 4 hours for soaking rice

Special Tools: A steamer for steaming sticky rice

Do-ahead Tips: Soak the rice the night before. Make the salted coconut sauce and crispy mung beans in advance.

THE COMPONENTS

• Coconut sticky rice, white or purple (see recipe)

• Salted coconut sauce (see recipe)

• Crispy mung beans (see recipe)

• 2-3 Sweet, ripe mangoes, estimate 1 mango for 2 people

WHITE COCONUT STICKY RICE

1 cup	White glutinous rice (see note)
⅔ cup	Coconut milk
½ cup	Sugar, granulated
½ tsp	Salt

Note: White sticky rice can be labelled as "Thai Sweet Rice" or "Glutinous Rice." To ensure that it's the right product, check that it's a product of Thailand.

PURPLE COCONUT STICKY RICE

¾ cup	White glutinous rice
¼ cup	Black glutinous rice (see note)
½ cup	Coconut milk
½ cup	Sugar, granulated
½ tsp	Salt

Note: The black rice is actually a very dark purple.

To steam the rice: Preheat a steamer over high heat until the water boils vigorously. If using a rack-style steamer, line the perforated rack with muslin or lint-free cheesecloth and pour the rice into the middle of the rack, leaving space around the edges to allow steam to come up. Fold the edges of the cloth to cover the rice and steam for 20–25 minutes, or until the rice is fully cooked. You can also use a traditional bamboo cone steamer (see QR code).

While the rice steams, make a coconut syrup by combining the coconut milk, sugar, and salt in a small pot and stirring over medium heat just until the sugar is dissolved. Remove from the heat and cover the pot to keep warm.

When the rice is done, immediately transfer it to a bowl and quickly pour warm coconut syrup over it. Stir to mix well. Cover and let the rice absorb the syrup for 20 minutes. After 20 minutes, fold the bottom part of the rice up to the top with a rubber spatula, then cover and let sit for at least another 30 minutes before serving.

FOR THE CRISPY MUNG BEANS:

Rinse the beans twice in cold water, then add them to a small pot and add 2 cups of cold water. Over medium heat, bring the water to a gentle boil. As soon as the water boils, remove from the heat and cover the pot; let sit for 10 minutes. Drain and rinse the beans in cold water, then let them dry off on paper towel.

In a lightly greased sauté pan, toast the beans over medium-high heat, stirring frequently. (Stir gently in the beginning, as they will be soft.) When they are dry and crunchy, and have turned a light golden brown, they are done, about 7–8 minutes. Cool on a plate and store in an airtight container until ready to use.

FOR THE SALTED COCONUT SAUCE:

In a bowl, stir the rice flour and water together until completely dissolved, then stir in the coconut milk and salt. Pour the mixture into a small pot and cook over medium-high heat, stirring constantly, just until it boils. Remove from the heat.

To serve, place a portion of sticky rice on a plate, drizzle with salted coconut sauce, sprinkle with crispy mung beans, and serve beside freshly cut mango. The rice should be served at room temperature or slightly warmed. To reheat refrigerated sticky rice, spray it with a little water and microwave until hot and soft. Serve warm.

THE PROBLEM WITH PURPLE RICE

More commonly, to make purple rice, the white and black rice are simply soaked and steamed together. However, this leaves the white rice perfectly cooked and the black too hard, because black rice takes much longer to cook. Most people accept that this is the way purple rice is, but I didn't want to settle. So, I developed this method of extracting the purple water and using it to soak and dye the white rice, while keeping them separate so that we can cook the black rice properly. Trust me, it'll be worth the few extra steps!

SALTED COCONUT SAUCE

1–1½ tsp	Rice flour (see note)
1 Tbsp	Water
½ cup	Coconut milk
¼ tsp	Salt

Note: Some coconut milks are thicker than others, use only 1 tsp of rice flour if your coconut milk looks thick already.

CRISPY MUNG BEANS

2 Tbsp	Shelled, split mung beans
2 cups	Water

Mango & sticky rice

How to use a bamboo cone steamer

Mango & Sticky Rice

Layered Coconut Pudding Cups

Layered Coconut Pudding Cups

Tako

Makes: 20 small cups

Cooking Time: 1 hour if making option 1, 30 minutes if making option 2, plus 1 hour if making banana-leaf cups

Do-ahead Tips: The dessert can be made 1 day before serving. Cut the banana leaves into rounds a day before using and refrigerate, wrapped in plastic wrap.

BASE OPTION 1: TAPIOCA PUDDING

2	Pandan leaves (36 inches total)
2½ cups	Water
½ cup	Small tapioca pearls
¾ cup	Sugar, granulated
⅓ cup	Corn kernels, cooked (see note)

BASE OPTION 2: MUNG BEAN PUDDING

2	Pandan leaves (36 inches total)
2½ cups	Water
⅓ cup	Mung bean starch (see note)
2 Tbsp	Tapioca starch
¾ cup	Corn kernels, cooked (see note)
¾ cup	Sugar, granulated

CREAMY COCONUT "FROSTING"

¼ cup	Rice flour
½ cup	Water
1½ cups	Coconut milk
¼ cup	Sugar, granulated
¾ tsp	Salt

Tako = Name of this dessert, no other meaning in modern Thai language

Served in dainty little banana leaf cups, these are to us what petit fours are to the French. *Tako* comprises two layers. The top is always a salty-sweet, creamy coconut "frosting." The base varies depending on the preference and creativity of the cook, but it's always some type of a sweet pudding. I have given you two choices for the base, truthfully because I couldn't decide which one I preferred! Option 1 uses tapioca pearls; it takes longer and is more difficult to perfect, but it has a fun texture and I love how the pearls look like sparkly little jewels when you dig in. Option 2 is much quicker and easier, but it calls for mung bean starch, which can be quite elusive. They are both equally delicious, so you really can't go wrong.

....

You will need little cups for this dessert. To make traditional banana leaf cups, see p. 220. You can also use shot glasses or mini aluminum tart pans, or make one big tray rather than individual pieces. Make sure the cups are lined up and ready to go before you start cooking!

OPTION 1: FOR THE TAPIOCA PUDDING:

Make pandan juice by cutting the leaves into small chunks and blending in a blender with ½ cup of the water until smooth. Strain the juice through a fine mesh strainer, pressing out as much liquid as possible; discard the fibres.

In a medium pot, bring the remaining 2 cups of water to a full boil over high heat. Add the tapioca pearls and stir constantly with a rubber spatula until the water comes back to a boil. Turn down the heat to medium-low and cook, scraping the bottom constantly, for about 18 minutes until the mixture is very thick and sticky. If it has become very thick before 15 minutes, add 1–2 Tbsp of water, and keep cooking until thick. The mixture should be thick enough that you can momentarily see the bottom of the pot when stirring.

Stir in the sugar and pandan juice, then turn the heat up to medium-high to bring the mixture back to a boil. Keep stirring for another 8–10 minutes. The tapioca is ready when the mixture is very thick once again, and the white dots in the middle of the pearls are very small, but still visible.

Stir in the corn, or your substitute of choice, then immediately spoon into the prepared cups until each is about half-full. The heat of the pudding will activate the banana leaves' aroma.

OPTION 2: FOR THE MUNG BEAN PUDDING:

Make pandan juice by cutting the leaves into chunks and blending in a blender with ½ cup of the water until smooth. Strain the juice through a fine mesh strainer, pressing out as much liquid as possible; discard the fibres.

In medium bowl, whisk together the remaining 2 cups of water, mung bean starch, and tapioca starch until there are no more lumps. Pour into a medium pot through a strainer, then stir in the pandan juice and sugar.

Cook over medium heat, stirring and scraping the bottom constantly with a rubber spatula, until the mixture is very thick and looks translucent; this takes only a few minutes. You will first see little chunks as the mixture heats up, but just seconds after, the whole pot will thicken.

Stir in the corn, or your substitute of choice, then immediately spoon the pudding into the prepared cups so they are about half-full. The heat of the pudding will activate the banana leaves' aroma.

FOR CREAMY COCONUT "FROSTING":

Make sure the cups have a base layer in them before you start.

Combine the rice flour and water in a bowl and stir until there are no more lumps; stir in the coconut milk, sugar, and salt. Pour into a small pot through a strainer to catch any lumps.

Cook over medium heat, stirring and scraping the bottom constantly with a rubber spatula, just until it starts to bubble. It should look like thin yogurt.

Remove from the heat and immediately spoon the mixture over the base layer, filling each cup just slightly below the rim. The mixture will look too thin at this point, but it will set as it cools. Work as fast as possible, because the frosting thickens quickly, and you don't want to have lumpy-looking frosting!

Let cool to room temperature, or slightly warm, to allow the frosting to set. Garnish each *tako* with small, pesticide-free edible flowers, crispy mung beans (recipe p.215), or any other garnish you prefer. *Tako* will last one full day at room temperature; cover and refrigerate for longer storage. If it's refrigerated, you can serve it cold or let it come to room temperature first.

BALANCING SALTY AND SWEET

Like many Thai desserts, the balance between salty and sweet is key to *tako's* deliciousness. When tasted by itself, the frosting should be about as salty as it is sweet, but when combined with the singularly sweet pudding, it's at its happy place. This happy place, however, may be a personal preference. If you are not used to salty desserts, you may find that you prefer slightly less salt. It might take you a couple of tries to fine-tune, but that's part of the fun!

(Continued)

Note: Instead of corn, try water chestnuts or taro; make sure they are fully cooked before adding.

I have seen mung bean starch sold in paper-wrapped blocks labelled "Tepung Hun Kwe" (from Indonesia) and in plastic bags labelled as "Green Bean Amylum" (from China). It is white with a fine texture; do not use "mung bean flour" or "green bean flour," which is pale yellow.

Tip for Success: *The frosting sets quickly, so if you want a perfectly smooth surface, don't top off an already filled cup—the second round of frosting won't blend in seamlessly.*

How to Make Banana Leaf Cups

SUPPLIES:

1. 1 package banana leaves, available frozen at Asian grocery stores

2. A few damp kitchen towels

3. A pair of scissors

4. A sharp chef's knife

5. A small stapler and staples OR 1-inch wooden picks with a pointy end (you can cut the pointy ends off of toothpicks)

6. A 3½-inch round object for using as a pattern, such as a jar lid or a cardboard cut-out. It's okay to go slightly bigger, but don't go any smaller or the cups will be hard to fold.

METHOD:

1. The goal is to cut out as many 3½-inch circles from the banana leaves as possible. First, tear the leaves into roughly 4-inch wide strips along their natural lines. You may need to use scissors to snip off the last little bit attached to the leaf's centre rib. Tear off or trim off any parts that are broken or have blemishes.

2. Wipe the strips of banana leaves clean on both sides using a damp kitchen towel; they can be quite dirty, so you may need a few towels.

3. Stack the strips into one pile. Since they will be of different lengths, line all of them up along one of the short edges.

4. With a sharp knife, chop the stack into two, making sure that each stack is bigger than your round pattern; if the leaves are not long enough to make two stacks, just leave them as one stack.

5. Put your round pattern on top of each stack, pressing firmly, then use the knife to chop along the edges of the pattern, trimming any excess until you have a round stack.

6. To fold the cups, put two banana-leaf rounds together, shiny sides out, and place their natural lines perpendicular to each other. This will prevent leakage, because if the leaves crack, they will crack along these lines. *Tip: The pieces will have different thicknesses, and two thick pieces are difficult to fold, so make sure you pair a thick piece with a thin one.*

7. Follow the picture instructions on the next page to fold the cups. Staples are what most people use as fasteners in Thailand nowadays, but if you feel uneasy about using staples, you can go old-school and use little wooden picks to "pin" the folds. If using wooden picks, it's easier to make three folds instead of four, but make sure the folds are equidistant from each other, or else the cup won't stand up properly.

Kabocha Squash Coconut Soup
Faktong Gaeng Buad

Faktong = Kabocha squash; Gaeng buad = Suffix for items cooked by boiling or simmering in sweetened coconut milk

I often feel that Thai desserts are either a weekend project or a snap. This one is definitely a snap. Rest assured, however, that it is as delicious as it is simple, particularly if you are a squash fan. There is a whole category of Thai desserts that simply involves boiling or simmering an ingredient—fruits, grains, beans, or root vegetables—in a light syrup. If this syrup happens to be made of coconut milk rather than water, such as this one, we call the cooking technique *buad*.

....

Wash and dry the squash thoroughly. Cut it in half vertically and scoop out the seeds with a spoon, scraping off as much of the fibrous bits as possible. If the skin has blemishes, slice them off; otherwise, leave the skin on. Cut one half into ¾-inch wedges, then cut each wedge into small, bite-sized pieces, about ½-inch thick. Make sure the pieces are about the same size so they finish cooking at the same time. Save leftover squash for another recipe (see QR code below).

In a pot large enough to hold the squash, combine the water, coconut milk, sugar, salt, and pandan leaf, if using; stir over medium-high heat until the coconut milk is simmering and the sugar is mostly dissolved. Add the squash and turn the heat down to medium. Cook the squash at a gentle simmer until it is done but still firm, about 5-8 minutes, depending on the size of the pieces.

To determine doneness, insert a fork into the squash. It should go through with slight resistance. Remove from the heat and let the squash sit in the pot, covered, for another 10 minutes; the residual heat will keep the squash cooking a little bit more. Test for doneness again after 10 minutes. The squash should have no resistance when pierced with a fork.

This dish is best served warm, but it's also fine at room temperature. If possible, let the squash sit in the syrup for a few hours before serving to allow more flavour to be absorbed.

DID YOU SAY . . . LEAVE THE SKIN ON?

Yes, kabocha squash skin becomes soft and perfectly edible when cooked. It's more attractive with the skin on—the dark green contrasts with the bright orange flesh, not to mention it's more nutritious and less work! If you're wondering what to do with any leftover squash, check out my video for a quick and healthy stir-fry of kabocha squash and Thai basil (see QR code).

Serves: 4-5
Cooking Time: 20 minutes
Do-ahead Tips: Cut the squash in advance and store in the fridge. The entire dish can be made in advance and reheated at serving time.

---

14 oz	Kabocha squash, bite-size pieces, see instructions
½ cup	Water
1¼ cup	Coconut milk
½ cup	Palm sugar, finely chopped, packed
½ tsp	Salt
½	Pandan leaf (9 inches, optional)

Tip for Success: It's easy to forget about a simmering pot, so if you discover that you have overcooked the squash, immediately drain it from the syrup to cool it down and stop it from further cooking. Recombine once cooled.

Kabocha squash
stir-fry

Street-Style Fried Bananas

Gluay Kag

Gluay = Banana; Kag = People of South Asian descent; legend has it that they introduced to us the idea of frying bananas

Thai restaurants overseas often serve some sort of battered-and-fried bananas with ice cream, which is delicious, but it's not actually a Thai dish . . . not in that particular form. The idea of frying bananas comes from this street snack. It's not so much a dessert as it is a mildly sweet snack, perfect for a 3 o' clock refuel or even breakfast. Most *gluay kag* vendors also sell fried sweet potato and taro using the same batter, so you can certainly add those to your mix.

. . . .

Toast the sesame seeds in a dry sauté pan over medium heat, stirring constantly until golden brown, about 5 minutes. Let cool on a plate.

In a medium-sized mixing bowl, whisk together the toasted sesame seeds, rice flour, sugar, salt, and baking powder until well combined. Add the shredded coconut and mix well. Add the water and stir until combined—the batter should be thinner than pancake batter but slightly thicker than crepe batter.

Peel and cut the bananas lengthwise into 1/4-inch-thick pieces. If using plantains, peel and cut them into 3 sections, then slice each section horizontally into 1/4-inch-thick pieces.

Add about 1 1/2 inches of oil to a pot and heat to about 325°F. Dip the bananas into the batter and fry for about 5 minutes, until they are a deep pretzel-brown colour. Maintain the frying temperature below 350°F. When done, drain on paper towel or a rack. *Note: Based on your first batch, you can decide if you want a thicker or thinner coating by adding more flour or water. If you have leftover batter, drizzle it into the oil and fry it up into crispy, munchy bits. Many vendors add this extra fried batter into their customers' bags!*

Let cool just until the coating becomes crisp, then serve immediately.

OF TEMPERATURE AND CRISPINESS

Note that we're frying at a slightly lower than normal temperature, because this allows you to fry the bananas for longer, allowing the batter enough time to dry out and become crispy. The right temperature should take you about 4–5 minutes to achieve the desired deep-brown colour. Some people fry them at a lower temperature for even longer to dry out the bananas; this prolongs the crispiness because there is less moisture around to soften the coating. This is a fine method if you need to make these a few hours before serving, but the bananas won't be as plump and moist.

Makes: 24 pieces
Cooking Time: 30 minutes
Do-ahead Tips: Mix the dry ingredients for the batter in advance and add the wet ingredients when ready to fry. Peel and cut the bananas several hours in advance and keep them tightly wrapped in the fridge.

1 1/2 Tbsp	White sesame seeds
3/4 cup	Rice flour
1/4 cup	Granulated sugar
1/2 tsp	Salt
1/2 tsp	Baking powder
1/3 cup	Shredded coconut, unsweetened, fresh, frozen, or dried (see note)
1/3 cup	Water
6	*Namwa* bananas or 2 sweet plantains, (see note)
As needed	Oil for frying

Note: If using dried shredded coconut, let it rehydrate in 2 Tbsp of hot water for 10–15 minutes before using.

Namwa bananas are traditionally used because they hold their shape well when cooked—choose ones with just a tiny trace of green left on the skin. Sweet plantains, available at Latin American/Caribbean grocers, also work wonderfully—choose ones whose skins have turned at least 60% black so they will be sweet. Regular bananas aren't an option as they turn mushy when fried for a long time.

Candied Cassava
Mun Sumpalung Cheuam

Mun sumpalung = Cassava; Cheuam = Cooking something in a thick sugar syrup

If you're not familiar with Thai sweets, it might be hard to wrap your head around having a candied root vegetable for dessert, but trust me, it's worth a try! Root vegetables, squashes, and beans are a common part of the Thai dessert pantry. The starchy cassava slowly cooks in a syrup, and almost magically, it turns into a fudgey, chewy delight. The salted coconut sauce tames the sweetness and adds a creamy element, bringing our dessert to a nice balance. We also use this cooking technique for some types of bananas and sweet potatoes.

....

Peel and cut the cassava into 3-inch sections (halve large ones horizontally). For frozen cassava, use it whole directly from frozen and cut it later.

Bring the water to a boil in a heavy-bottomed pot just big enough to hold the cassava; boil the cassava for 10 minutes. If using frozen cassava, remove from the pot after boiling, cut into 3-inch pieces, and add it back to the pot. *Note: If the frozen cassava is large, you might need to boil it in a larger pot with enough water to cover; but after cutting, transfer it into a just-big-enough pot along with 3 cups of the cooking water for the next step.*

Add the sugar to the pot, bring to a boil, then simmer on low heat for 1½–2 hours, turning the cassava every 20–30 minutes. It is done when the syrup is thick and the cassava is mostly translucent (some parts may remain opaque). If the syrup dries up too quickly, add a little water. *Note: Some cassava will have hard parts that won't soften with cooking; this is okay, I just eat around it!*

Meanwhile, make the salted coconut sauce: In a bowl, stir the rice flour and water together until completely dissolved, then stir in the coconut milk and salt. Pour the mixture into a small pot and cook over medium-high heat, stirring constantly, just until it boils. Remove from the heat.

Remove the cassava, leaving the syrup in the pot. Stir some water into the syrup to achieve a thin syrup consistency and drizzle over the cassava to moisten.

To serve, drizzle the cassava with the salted coconut sauce. Serve at room temperature or warm.

DID YOU KNOW?

Cassava is the root from which tapioca starch and tapioca pearls (and the bubbles in bubble tea) are made. So, when you are finished with the candying, you will notice that the syrup looks gooey as if it has been thickened by tapioca starch . . . because it has!

Serves: 6
Cooking Time: 2 hours
Do-ahead Tips: The dish can be made a few days in advance and stored in the fridge; store the coconut sauce separately.

CANDIED CASSAVA

1 lb	Cassava (also called yuca and manioc), fresh or frozen (see note)
3⅓ cups	Water
2 cups	Sugar, granulated

Note: Good cassava roots should be completely white inside. When buying cassava, it can be hard to tell if the inside is in good condition. For this reason, I prefer using frozen cassava, which yields identical results for this dish.

SALTED COCONUT SAUCE

1–1½ tsp	Rice flour (see note)
1 Tbsp	Water
½ cup	Coconut milk
¼ + ⅛ tsp	Salt

Note: Some coconut milks are thicker than others, use only 1 tsp of rice flour if your coconut milk looks thick already.

PART 3

Basic Recipes

Toasted Rice Powder
Kao Kua

Cooking Time: 10 minutes
Special Tools: A mortar and pestle or an electric grinder

Uncooked sticky rice or jasmine rice

Amount as called for in the recipe; if the recipe calls for 1 Tbsp of toasted rice powder, use 1 Tbsp of rice.

Kao = Rice; Kua = Dry-toasting in a pan

I sometimes call this "magic powder" because of the drastic difference it can make to a dish. A Northeastern ingredient, toasted rice powder is traditionally made from sticky rice, a staple grain of the Northeast, but jasmine rice will also work. The nutty, toasty aroma is used to balance dishes that are primarily salty and sour.

In a small sauté pan, add the rice and toast over medium-high heat, moving the grains constantly, until they turn a deep golden-brown colour, about 5 minutes. If you are toasting a lot of rice, it will take longer. Let cool on a plate.

When ready to use, grind into a powder using a mortar and pestle or an electric grinder. If not using immediately, do not grind the rice and store in an airtight container at room temperature. I recommend making only as much as you need, as the fragrance fades over time.

Fish Sauce & Chilies Condiment
Prik Nam Pla

Cooking Time: 3 minutes
Do-ahead Tips: The condiment will last for several weeks in the fridge.

3 Tbsp	Fish sauce
3–5	Thai chilies, chopped
2 tsp	Lime juice
1 clove	Garlic, chopped (optional)
1 Tbsp	Shallots, thinly sliced (optional)

Prik = Chilies; Nam pla = Fish sauce

This is our equivalent of the table-side salt and pepper. If anything feels like it needs extra seasoning, *prik nam pla* is the condiment of choice.

Combine all the ingredients in a small glass jar—plastic tends to absorb the fish sauce smell. Store in the fridge. While it won't spoil for several weeks, the chilies and added herbs will eventually look dodgy, so don't make too much at once.

Pickled Chilies Condiment
Prik Nam Som

Prik = Chilies; Nam som = Short for nam som sai choo, *which means vinegar*

This tangy condiment is perfect for rich, salty dishes that don't already have an acidic element, such as *pad see ew* (recipe p.158) and most noodle soups.

Slice chilies into rounds and add to a glass jar—it's up to you how much you want to make, but I like to make just 1–2 chilies each time so I use it up quickly. Add vinegar to completely submerge the chilies and let sit for at least 20 minutes before using. You can sprinkle just the vinegar over your dish or eat the chilies, too. Alternatively, you can blend the chilies and vinegar together into a thin pesto-like consistency. If blending, you can char the chilies for added smokiness and/or add some garlic.

Store in a sealed container, and it should last for months in the fridge.

Cooking Time: 3 minutes
Do-ahead Tips: The condiment will last for several months in the fridge

Spur chilies, jalapeños, serranos, fresnos, or another kind of medium-to-mild chili

White vinegar

See instructions for amounts

Roasted Chili Flakes
Prik Pon

Prik = Chilies; Pon = Ground

This is our all-purpose heat booster and it can also be added to any dish that needs a little (or a lot of) extra spice! Roasting the chilies develops a smokey aroma that is unique to this condiment. Traditionally we dry-roast the chilies in a wok like toasting spices, but when making just a small amount, the oven provides more even heat.

Preheat the oven to 300°F. Rinse the chilies quickly in cold water to get rid of dirt or mold dust. Don't expose the chilies to water for more than a few seconds or they will absorb too much water and won't crisp up readily. Dry them off as much as possible with a tea towel.

Lay the chilies and lime leaves on a baking tray without overlapping and roast in the oven for 5–7 minutes, rotating the pan halfway through, until the chilies are smokey and crisp, and have darkened slightly. The lime leaves should also be dry and crisp by this point. Let cool completely.

Grind the chilies and the lime leaves to a powder. If using a mortar and pestle, cover your mouth and nose with a cloth when grinding to avoid inhaling chili dust. If using an electric grinder, let the dust settle before opening the grinder.

To store: Chili flakes can grow mold over time, so I freeze most of this and keep just a small amount at room temperature in a well-sealed container.

Makes: ¼ cup
Cooking Time: 20 minutes
Do-ahead Tips: A mortar and pestle or an electric grinder

1 cup	Small dried chilies
2–3	Kaffir lime leaves (optional, see note)

Note: I like to toast and grind a few kaffir lime leaves along with the chilies to enhance the aroma.

Thai-Style Stock
Nam Stock

Makes: 6–8 cups
Cooking Time: 1½–2 hours
Special Tools: A large stock pot
Do-ahead Tips: Make the stock in advance and freeze for future use.

2 lbs	Chicken bones or pork bones (see note)
15 cups	Water
1	Medium onion, large dice (see note)
5 cloves	Garlic, crushed
2	Cilantro roots, crushed or 8 cilantro stems
1 stalk	Lemongrass, top half only, smashed and cut into 2-inch pieces
½ tsp	White peppercorns, lightly crushed

Note: Pork bones are available at Chinese butchers and grocery stores.

Daikon radish is often used in Thailand instead of onions.

Nam = Water; also refers to anything in liquid form; Stock = Stock . . . yes, we use the same word

In *Part 1*, I discussed the importance of using stock instead of water as a liquid base for soups, curries, and even stir-fry sauces. But on a busy weeknight when you're just trying to feed whining children (or spouse), making stock just seems like an obstacle you really don't have time to tackle. I suggest you make a big batch of stock on a weekend and freeze it in small portions that are easy to grab and use. Your weeknight self will thank you. Also, don't worry about having all the vegetables and aromatics; if all you've got is bones and water, make it anyway!

Rinse the bones with cold water and put them in a large stock pot. If there is a large amount of fat on the chicken bones, trim it off. Cover the bones with cold water and bring to a simmer over high heat. Once the stock is simmering, turn down the heat to low to maintain the simmer.

After 45 minutes of simmering, skim off any foam or impurities that have floated to the top.

Add the onion, garlic, cilantro roots, lemongrass, and white peppercorns. If making chicken stock, let simmer for at least another 30 minutes. If making pork stock, let simmer for at least 1 more hour.

When finished, strain, and the stock is now ready for use.

Storage tips: I like to freeze stock in zip-top freezer bags. Don't overfill the bags so they are quick to thaw, and also because stock expands when frozen and can rupture the bag. Lay the bags flat when freezing so they freeze into flat, space-efficient discs.

Cooking the Perfect Rice (Without a rice cooker)
Kao Suay

Kao = Rice; Suay = Literally beautiful, and when used with rice it refers to plain white rice

Rice cookers are so common in Thai homes that many people, my childhood self included, never learn how to make rice without one. In fact, it didn't occur to me that rice COULD be made without a rice cooker until I went to New Zealand as a teen. My homestay mother made rice in the microwave! How revolutionary! I later learned that a rice cooker is nothing but a pot that knows when to turn itself off, and as long as you manage to heat the rice and the water together in SOMETHING, you will get cooked rice. Here are some frequently asked questions about cooking rice.

How much rice should I cook?
Jasmine rice has a raw-to-cooked ratio of about 1 to 3. For a Thai meal where rice is the star, I usually estimate ½ cup of uncooked rice per person (1½ cups cooked) and I know that I won't run out even with a hungry crowd to feed. You can always make a little extra to be sure.

To rinse or not to rinse?
In Thailand, we always rinse, and it's not because the rice is dirty. When you add water to rice and swish it around, you will notice that the water turns cloudy. That is the excess starch from the rice, which acts like glue and makes the rice grains more sticky when cooked. By rinsing the rice, you remove this starch so the rice grains will separate from each other beautifully. It's worth noting that sometimes the opposite is desired. When making a risotto, for example, the excess starch is what helps create the luscious creaminess.

How much water?
Unfortunately, I can only give you an estimate, as different types of rice don't necessarily absorb the same amount of water.

When I work with a new brand of jasmine rice, I always start with the ratio of 1 part rice to 1¼ parts water. I then adjust the amount of water based on the result of the first round. If you're using new-crop rice, or you're making rice for fried rice, start with a ratio of 1:1. For more information on new-crop rice, see page 54.

Most importantly, use cold water. Never cook with hot tap water because it absorbs unpleasant flavours and odours from the pipes it sits in.

Avoiding the burnt bottom.
We've all done it, me included. To avoid a layer of burnt rice at the bottom, keep your heat as low as possible when the rice is simmering to buy yourself more time between "done" and "burnt."

METHOD

Add the rice to a heavy-bottomed pot and add plenty of cold water. Swish the rice around with your hands until the water turns cloudy; pour off most of the water. Add fresh water and rinse again; this time drain off as much water as possible.

Add the required amount of cold water to the rice (see above), cover the pot, and bring to a simmer over medium heat.

Once it is simmering, turn the heat down to low and let it simmer very gently until all the liquid has been absorbed, 15–20 minutes. To check if all the liquid has been absorbed, insert a rubber spatula against the side of the pot all the way to the bottom, then slightly push the rice aside to see if there is still liquid on the bottom.

Turn off the heat and let it sit for 15 minutes before serving. The bottom of the pot may be dry but there may be moisture remaining between the rice grains; this rest time allows any moisture to be fully absorbed into the rice.

Cooking Perfect Sticky Rice
Kao Niew

Kao = Rice; Niew = Sticky

The satisfying chew of sticky rice is so addictive that I usually end up eating way too much of it. Thai sticky rice is so sticky that the best way to eat it is with your fingers, and it's a perfect vehicle for sopping up sauce. Thai sticky rice is often labelled as "Glutinous White Rice" or "Thai Sweet Rice." Look for opaque, thin grains that are slightly shorter than jasmine rice, and check that the package says it's a product of Thailand. *Note: Since sticky rice is much denser than other rice, I estimate about ⅓ cup of uncooked sticky rice per person, plus a little extra for insurance.*

SOAK-AND-STEAM METHOD:

Add sticky rice to a large bowl and cover with plenty of cold water. Swish the rice around with your hands until the water turns cloudy. Pour off the rinse water and repeat two more times. Let the rice soak for at least 4 hours or overnight.

Drain the rice; be gentle when handling it, as the grains are brittle once soaked. If using a steamer rack, line the perforated rack with a piece of muslin or lint-free cheesecloth. Pour the rice onto the cloth and fold in the edges to cover it. Do not cover the entire rack; leave some space on the sides so steam can come up. Steam the rice over rapidly boiling water for 20–25 minutes.

> **Tip for Success:** *Sticky rice is best served when fresh and hot, but if circumstances won't allow, here's a handy trick that will keep your sticky rice soft even after it has cooled: after soaking, steep the rice in just boiled water for 10 minutes, then drain and steam as per the instructions for 15 minutes.*

You can also use a bamboo cone steamer, made specifically for steaming sticky rice. *For instructions on how to use this fun tool, scan the QR code below.*

Serve the rice while hot. To reheat sticky rice, spray it with some water and microwave, loosely covered, until hot.

NO-SOAK METHOD:

I never plan my dinners unless I am recipe-testing or cooking for guests—I open the fridge 30 minutes before dinner time, and whatever's in there is going to have to work. So, I was ecstatic to discover that I can still have decent sticky rice even if I don't plan, and therefore soak the rice, ahead of time. The soak-and-steam method yields a slightly chewier texture, but this method is plenty good in an emergency!

Add sticky rice to a bowl and cover with plenty of cold water. Swish the rice around with your hands until the water turns cloudy. Pour off the rinse water and repeat 3–4 more times until the water runs almost clear. Drain the rice very well and transfer it into a heatproof bowl.

Add water to the rice at the ratio of 1 part rice to ⅔ part water. Steam the rice bowl in a steamer over rapidly boiling water for 25–30 minutes. You can also use a wire steamer rack set inside a big pot with a lid. Turn the heat off and let the rice sit in the steamer for 10 minutes before serving.

How to use a bamboo cone steamer

No-soak method

Acknowledgements

THANK YOU.

To fans of Hot Thai Kitchen all over the world, thank you for the support and encouragement that made this book come to life. Dave, thank you for making the photoshoots fun; your photos are as beautiful as you are kind. Big hugs to T.J., I could not have asked for more beautiful pottery for this book. Byron & Alana, only true friends let friends raid their kitchen in search of props, thank you. Jesse, you are a winning agent and a wonderful friend. Robert, thank you for believing in this book and for being a delight to work with. Zoe, your passion for this book and your sweetness make me a very lucky author. Adam, I don't tell you enough how grateful I am for your part in this journey. Craig, thank you for your sacrifices and for always believing in me. P'Art, I owe you for those long, tiring trips to the market, but your photos truly made this book shine. P'Erd, I will never forget that without you, none of this would have ever happened. Mom and Dad, thank you for your never-ending love and support, no matter what I do. Grandma, the way you showed your love through your cooking made me who I am today.

Index

Pork Satay and Peanut Sauce, 104–5
Red Curry Paste, 101
Vegan Panang Curry Paste, 187
Vegan Red Curry Paste, 194
Yellow Curry Paste, 107
garlic, 30–31, *31*
ginger
about, 34
Chicken Stir-Fry with, & Mushrooms, 156, *157*
Yellow Curry Paste, 107
glass noodles, 56
about, 57
Crispy Spring Rolls, 162–63
gluten intolerance, and Thai food, 62
glutinous rice. *See* sticky rice
grachai. See fingerroot
grains, measuring tips for, xv
grapes
Savoury Fruit Salad, 152–53, *153*
green bean amylum. *See* mung bean starch
Green Curry Paste, 98
Green Curry with Braised Beef Shank, *96*, 97–98
Green Mango Salad, *7*, 153
green onions, *38*, 39
Green Papaya Salad, 150–51
Grilled Beef or Pork "Waterfall" Salad, *146*, 147–48
grilled dishes, as part of balanced Thai meal, *8*, 9
grilling, as cooking technique, 89
Ground Duck Salad with Mint, *143*, 144–45

herbs. *See also* finishing herbs; sturdy herbs; *and other individual types*
chopping tips for curry pastes, xvi
measuring tips for, xv
in Northeast Region, 15
as part of balanced Thai meal, *8*, 9
in Thai salads, 78
holy basil, *38*. *See also* Thai basil
about, 39
freezing, tips for, 41
Chicken Fried Rice with Fried Egg, *176*, 177–78
Jungle Curry, *108*, 109–10
Red Curry Stir-Fry with Tilapia, *165*, 166–67

imperial to metric conversions, xvi
ingredients, Thai, 26–62. *See also* acids; finishing herbs; salting agents; spices; sturdy herbs; sweeteners; *and individual ingredients*
buying, tips for, 59
categories of, 26

substitutions for, 55, 60 (*see also* dietary restrictions, and Thai food)
vs Western, in desserts, 86
insects, in Northeast Region cooking, 15, *21*

jalapeños
Coconut Shrimp Dip, 203, 204–5
Pickled Chilies Condiment (*Prik Nam Som*), 231
Tamarind Shrimp, 168–69
Japanese eggplants
choosing young, tips for, 174
Eggplant Stir-Fry with Thai Basil, *173*, 174–75
Panang Curry with Portobello Mushrooms & Eggplant, *185*, 186–87
jasmine rice. *See also* rice
about, 8, 54
in Central Region, 19
cooking tips for, 233
Pineapple Fried Rice, 160–61
Toasted Rice Powder, 230
Jungle Curry, *108*, 109–10

Kabocha Squash Coconut Soup, *222*, 223
kaffir lime leaves, 30. *See also* kaffir limes
about, 30
Beef "Ceviche" with Lemongrass, 140–41, *142*
Coconut Galangal Chicken Soup, 118, *119*
Green Curry with Braised Beef Shank, *96*, 97–98
Jungle Curry, *108*, 109–10
Lemongrass Soup with Shrimp & Young Coconut, *120*, 121–22
Northeastern Pork Rib Soup with Toasted Rice, *126*, 127–28
Panang Curry with Portobello Mushrooms & Eggplant, *185*, 186–87
Red Curry Stir-Fry with Tilapia, *165*, 166–67
Red Curry Stir-Fry with Tofu & Long Beans, *192*, 193–94
kaffir limes. *See also* kaffir lime leaves
about, 30
Gaeng Bpa Curry Paste, 110
Green Curry Paste, 98
Red Curry Paste, 101
Vegan Panang Curry Paste, 187
Vegan Red Curry Paste, 194
kale
Five-Spice Vegetable Stew, 188, *189*
kantoke (North Region dining tradition), 17
kiwi
Savoury Fruit Salad, 152–53, *153*
krachai. See fingerroot